2.50

Democracy and Catholicism
will give you

a balanced and precise analysis of
Catholic beliefs which have social and
political implications.
an interpretation of the American
Democratic tradition in terms of decision-
making processes.
a systematic and incisive critique of
American Liberal beliefs and principles.

CURRIN V. SHIELDS
has had extensive political experience in
the California Democratic Party, and has
written for magazines and radio. He has
taught political science at Boston University,
the Universities of New Hampshire and
Wisconsin, and Yale as well as at UCLA.

McGRAW-HILL PAPERBACKS
ON CONTEMPORARY DILEMMAS

Prices subject to change without notice.

Democracy
and
Catholicism
in
America
Currin V. Shields

McGraw-Hill Book Company, Inc.
New York   Toronto   London

This book is dedicated to my mother
HARRIET SWANSON SHIELDS

PREFACE

Every week thousands of civic-minded Americans get together for meetings in their local communities. Typical of such meetings are those held by the Westside Civic Improvement League which meets the first Monday of every month at the Westside Elementary School.

What distinguishes the members of the League is their desire to improve the community in which they live and raise their families. They always have a zoning problem on the agenda, what with the planning commission set on industrializing the Westside and the city council so ready to hear the call of business. A few years ago, their main project was the Youth Center: playing fields, tennis courts, a swimming pool, picnic shelter, club rooms—the works. The dedication ceremony for the Center was last spring. Now the League's project is a community hospital. To promote a better community—that is the League's cause.

What does not distinguish the League's membership is agreement about a number of rather serious matters. They have fixed beliefs about religious, economic, social, and political questions, or at least they seem to be fixed. Certainly the members differ in their beliefs. Take the officers, for example. The president is Mr. Cooper. He calls himself a "liberal Republican"; one of his prized possessions is a personal letter from President Eisenhower. He's a member of the Izaak Walton League, Kiwanis, the Masons, and a dozen other organizations. His wife teaches Sunday school at the Methodist Church. Mr. Adams is the vice-president, only his name really isn't Adams; his father was a Polish refugee who decided Adams was a good American name and a name with eleven consonants was not. Mr. Adams is a business agent for a building-trades union. He's a member of the Knights of Columbus and the Democratic County Committee. He even voted for Truman in 1948. Mr. Stein, the League's secretary, is a school teacher and active in the PTA. Aside from the fact that he's the local leader of the American Civil Liberties Union and reads the *Nation,* he seems like a decent sort of fellow, for a teacher. His wife is a pillar in Hadassah. The League's treasurer is a supervisor for the telephone company and past president of the Chamber of Commerce. Mr. Thompson has never taken much interest in politics, and he leaves the family's religion in the care of his wife. She's a member of the Ladies Guild of the Episcopal Church and was a founder of the Republican Women's Club, which was organized to support Senator Taft's presidential ambitions. Since he became treasurer of the League, Mr. Thompson hasn't spent as much time at the country club, but he still manages to roar with the Lions every week.

None of the members of the Westside Civic Improvement League has ever heard of the doctrine of subsidiarity, except Mr. Adams who once attended a Catholic Labor Institute. Except for Mr. Stein, who read John C. Calhoun's *Disquisition on Government* while in college, they all assume that the doctrine of concurrent majorities must have something to do with parental supervision of teenage dating. Perhaps this is all to the good. At least they are not bothered about the Trinity, original sin, judicial review, or gerrymandering when it comes to furthering the League's cause. They proceed undisturbed to promote a better Westside Community.

You have never before heard about the Westside Civic Improvement League. For that matter, neither have I. But the chances are that you have attended, as I have, many meetings of similar organizations. You are no doubt a member of several yourself, perhaps an officer and mainstay in one. In this country there are many thousands of organizations like the League. Most Americans are members of one or two of them, maybe a local chapter of the PTA, the women's auxiliary of a church, a political committee, a labor-union local, an adult-education forum, a fish and game club, a bowling league, a youth council, a chamber of commerce, a fraternal order, a professional association, a veterans group, or the like. Such organizations abound in every American community.

This book is written for people who are members of organizations like the Westside Civic Improvement League. It is written for Americans who are members of community groups devoted to common causes. If you have had experiences as a member of such organizations, this book will, I hope, make some sense to you. For as a member of such organizations, you have probably participated in group decision-making. This book is in part about a kind of group decision-making familiar to most Americans—a kind of group decision-making process called Democracy.

It is also about religion, or at least one religion—Catholicism. This religion is embraced by many of our fellow Americans, like Mr. Adams, the League vice-president.

Most of us have some notions about Catholicism and about Democracy, and perhaps some very definite ideas about the relations between them. Unfortunately, many ideas we Americans express about Catholicism and Democracy are not well founded. This is unfortunate because misunderstandings about religion and politics serve no useful purpose and can do much harm. They can disturb our personal relations with friends and family. They can acerbate the social relations we must have with business associates in the course of our daily work. They can disrupt our relations with neighbors and the other members of the community in which we live. Such misunderstandings can upset our personal and social lives, and worse.

It is my hope that this book will set straight the thinking of some thoughtful Americans at least about the relation between Catholicism and Democracy.

Currin V. Shields

ACKNOWLEDGMENTS

It is customary in a case such as this for an author to inform his reader about his accomplices before the literary fact. As is so often the case, I cannot here adequately acknowledge my indebtedness to others. The contributions of those who played some role in the protracted process by which my puzzlement about Catholicism and Democracy was converted into this printed volume you now hold in your hands are too numerous to enumerate. For example, I cannot properly acknowledge my debt to those accommodating librarians at Loyola University of Los Angeles, or to those stimulating students at the University of California at Los Angeles, in my undergraduate seminars on contemporary political ideologies and in my graduate seminars on problems of Democratic theory.

But a few contributions, without which this book could not have been written, I must not allow to go unmentioned:

I am deeply indebted to Dean Gerard F. Yates, S.J., of Georgetown University, whose critical evaluation of an unpublished monograph I wrote on Catholic political and social doctrines—from which part of this study was derived—was invaluable; to Professor Edgar A. Jones, of the School of Law, University of California at Los Angeles, who read the final draft of the manuscript and suggested worthwhile changes in my presentation; to Miss Judith Hoffberg, a student at the University of California, who assisted me in library research; to my cousins, Mrs. Lillian Brown, of Carmel, California, who typed the manuscript, and Mrs. Myrtle Neil, of Felton, California, who generously provided me with an opportunity to work undisturbed on the manuscript at a stage when such effort was imperative.

I owe a special debt to a friend and colleague and former student whose offers of assistance and criticism at each step in the preparation of the manuscript were gratefully received and deeply appreciated—Mr. Carlo Valentino, now of the Department of Government, St. Louis University.

Most of all, I am indebted to my mother, Mrs. Harriet Swanson Shields, of Pacific Grove, California. She read the manuscript in full, offered helpful criticisms, and assisted me in reading proofs. But much more than that, in many ways, large and small, throughout the period of three years I devoted mainly to this book, she gave me the support and encouragement which every author needs. In expression of my appreciation, this book is dedicated to her.

CONTENTS

Chapter One

THE CONTEMPORARY ISSUE

I.

The issue of Catholicism and Democracy is often raised by people in this country but seldom resolved to anyone's satisfaction. Why the issue is seldom resolved is a rather complicated question, but I attempt in this book an answer to it. Why the issue is raised is much easier to explain.

The Church of Rome is the most venerable institution in Western civilization. For more than a thousand years the Roman Church was Christianity's only enduring institution. In the religious struggles of the Reformation, Christendom was dismembered, but the Mother Church emerged from the ordeal to thrive and expand. It survived the migrations of peoples from continent to continent, the radical changes in the ways of producing and distributing goods symbolized by the Industrial Revolution. It survived the plagues, the famines, the land reforms, the leveling of social classes. It survived the mechanical inventions and scientific discoveries, the civil wars and revolutions, the world upheavals in which millions of persons perished. These shattering human experiences which have wrought our modern age meant destruction for other ancient institutions entrenched in Western civilization. But not for the Church of Rome.

Today Catholicism is still a most vital religious movement. The Church claims a membership of more than 400 million persons throughout the world. In many countries Catholicism remains the dominant religious faith; it is the national religion in Italy, France, and other European countries, and in most Latin-American countries. In the United States, traditionally a Protestant nation, almost one-third the members of Christian sects are Roman Catholics. More Americans belong to the Catholic Church than to the two largest Protestant denominations (Baptist and Methodist) combined. And the number of Roman Catholic communicants continues to increase in this country as elsewhere in the world.

But Catholicism is not just a world-wide religious movement with millions of faithful believers. It is also a Church, a worldly institution with great political and social significance in modern life. The Catholic Church owns much land and many buildings; operates numerous schools, hospitals, orphanages, and other welfare agencies; sponsors youth organizations, labor and service groups, with huge memberships. The Catholic Church has an officialdom spread throughout the entire globe. Prominent roles as leaders in national and world affairs are played by its communicants, lay and ecclesiastical. Some are religionists by profession, but many are scientists, artists, businessmen, labor leaders, scholars, teachers, engineers—and statesmen. By any standard, Catholicism is a major social and political force in our world today.

Another virile movement, also a significant social and political force of our times, is as young as the Roman Church is old. Democracy has no Church: no bishops, no cathedrals, no Vatican. But it too has a creed, though not a religious one: Democracy's beliefs are about life on this earth. These beliefs have captured the hearts and minds of peoples throughout the world. Democracy's champions, too, play prominent roles in the affairs of our day. Democracy, like Catholicism, pervades the daily lives of many millions of men and women, especially in this country.

The issue of the relation between these two great twentieth-century movements is grave and vital. It bears directly on the lives of Catholics and of members of Protestant sects who share with the Catholics many religious tenets. It bears directly, too, on the lives of Democrats who work alongside communicants of the Catholic Church. For those American Catholics like Mr. Adams, who cherish Democracy, whose daily lives are suffused by both Catholicism and Democracy, the issue is most critical.

In recent years this issue has been much debated, and bitterly so. It is lamentable that most of the literature has been the handiwork of writers who were either ardently "pro-Catholic" or ardently "anti-Catholic." These writings have merely compounded the confusion over the issue.

It is my intention in this book neither to praise nor to condemn the Catholic Church or its teachings. I am not a Catholic, but neither am I "anti-Catholic."

However, this book is written from a definite bias: from the bias of one who calls himself an American Democrat. By a Democrat I do not mean a person who belongs to a certain political party. I mean a person who accepts certain beliefs and practices certain principles. Throughout this book I shall present and advocate the Democratic case as I understand it. But my main purpose is to make clear what the actual relation is between those Democratic beliefs and principles which I subscribe to and the teachings of the Church of Rome. That is my mission in this book.

2.

Neither Catholics nor Democrats set the stage for the current controversy over Catholicism and Democracy. It was set by Liberals. The distinctive modern creed and movement known as Liberalism has indeed played a strategic role in the controversy. Later I shall discuss in detail the Democratic and the Catholic

3

traditions. But we can understand them better in relation to the creed and movement both the Catholic and the Democrat reject. So what is Liberalism?

To understand any political movement we must appreciate what its partisans oppose as well as what they favor. Such movements are generated out of protest, from discontent with things as they are. Their creeds are first stated as critiques of a *status quo* which is denounced and repudiated. The creeds are first propounded as alternatives to what already exists. Liberalism is not an exceptional political movement.

Liberalism was historically offered by its partisans as an alternative more desirable to modern man than Catholicism, a product of medieval culture. Since the birth of the movement, the Liberal has looked on the Catholic as an enemy of progress, and the Catholic has regarded the Liberal as a wrongheaded heretic. The traditional hostility still exists today.

The split between Liberalism and Democracy has been just as sharp, though much less attention has been paid to it. Recent writers, especially English-speaking writers, have unfortunately tended to confuse the Liberal with the Democratic movement. There is no more excuse to confuse Liberalism and Democracy than there is to confuse Liberalism and Catholicism. It is true that Democracy emerged out of a modern culture and that the Democrat does share certain beliefs with the Liberal. For example, both accept a principle of popular sovereignty. But in his political views the Liberal is by no means Democratic and the Democrat does not accept the distinctive Liberal teachings. In fact the Democratic movement in this country arose in reaction against Liberal beliefs and practices about the exercise of authority. Democracy has been promoted by its partisans as an alternative more desirable to Americans than Liberalism. It is in the historic evolution of Liberalism and Democracy in America where the contrast between the two movements has been most sharply drawn.

But we must begin the story of modern Liberalism with an account of the system the Liberal movement arose to challenge and eventually destroyed.

4

Today we are all familiar with a form of political organization called the "nation state." We are familiar with it because for several centuries Americans, Englishmen, Frenchmen, and others have lived in societies so organized politically. But this form of political organization is peculiar to modern times. Ancient Greeks lived in small communities called a "city-state," or *polis*. Romans were citizens of an imperial regime. If we had lived during the Middle Ages, we could not even have comprehended the notion of a nation state. There was no such form of political organization in the medieval scheme of things. A medieval man was of course subject to authority, as we are today. Rather he was subject to authorities, since authority was nowhere concentrated then as it is today in the modern state. Authority over his religious life was exercised by numerous ecclesiastical officials—priests, friars, bishops, cardinals, canons, and the like. Authority over his political life was exercised by numerous feudal rulers, such as barons, dukes, knights, princes, counts, and kings. Not only did the medieval man owe allegiance to two separate sets of rulers, one ecclesiastical and one secular. He also owed allegiance to many different Church and feudal rulers, since each medieval ruler possessed some authority, as set by canon law and feudal contract, yet none possessed very much.

But this pluralistic scheme was gradually abandoned during the era which gave birth to the modern age. The motley medieval rulers had what ambitious kings needed to forge large, independent, self-sufficient kingdoms. Feudal nobles and Church officials controlled land tenure, collected tax revenues, commanded military resources, regulated trade and manufacture, and conducted legal proceedings in the canon law and civil courts. Eventually a few powerful noble families extended, by marriages, military exploits, and alliances, their dominion at the expense of weaker rulers. Ancient medieval institutions were displaced, as the authority customarily exercised by petty nobles and ecclesiasts passed into the hands of royal officials in the service of a powerful monarch. A few strong kings, the hereditary heads of royal families, took away from the many feudal rulers their civil and ecclesiastical authority. Thus the modern nation state was created. Indeed in its original meaning the term "state" meant simply the private estate of the ruling dynasty, the property of the monarch.

When dynastic kings acquired "sovereign" authority, the "universal community" of the Holy Roman Empire was of course broken apart. Dynastic rulers declared their independence from the Emperor and the Pope. The one universal empire gave way to a number of dynastic regimes, with each king claiming full authority over civil affairs within the national territory. The one universal church gave way to a number of national churches. The Church of Rome lost the predominant influence it enjoyed in medieval times, since the church of the realm, whether Protestant or Catholic, was made a department of state; church officials were absorbed into a royal bureaucracy subservient to the civil ruler. The "sovereign monarch" became the actual if not the titular head of the state church and claimed complete authority over all political and religious affairs within the kingdom.

Dynastic rule was impacted on a social and economic scheme barely removed from the Middle Ages. If you had lived during this period, you would have been born into a family of social rank. Ranks in society were "ordered," as custom prescribed, rigidly structured as a pyramid of classes from the serfs to the nobility. Your status and your legal rights and duties as well would have depended on the position of your family in the social hierarchy. The nobles owned the land, which was the basis of wealth and power. The serfs were bound by law to work the land for the benefit of the noble families. A few "freemen" of the towns were neither serfs nor nobles; they were guild craftsmen and merchants. If you had been a member of this "middle class," your life too would have been stringently controlled, and not for your own good. The dynastic state managed the production and distribution of commodities for the benefit of the privileged elite.

This dynastic mercantilist system was shaken by radical changes in European life which came with the opening of the overseas colonies, the expansion of international trade, the development of printing, the growth of religious nonconformism. The "commercial revolution" resulted in a new kind of wealth and in the new middle class playing a more prominent role in national life. Through mercantile enterprise, members of the middle class acquired impressive monetary wealth. They also achieved impressive secular learning and patronized the worldly arts and sciences. The wealth and talent they displayed set them apart from the "lower orders," yet they still were not privileged members of society. They enjoyed scant social prestige or political influence; both were a monopoly of the landed nobility who received their privileges, as their wealth, from birth. This system of privilege, encased in custom, was prescribed by the law of the land and sanctioned by the church of the realm. The dynastic state, then, imposed an elaborate scheme of controls over religious, political, social, and economic life, enforcing gross inequalities among members of different social classes, regardless of individual merit.

It was out of this situation, where dynastic rule was used to secure the status of a privileged few at the expense of the growing middle class, that the Liberal movement came. The movement was in protest against the discriminatory controls which blighted middle-class lives. What the Liberals demanded was an end to state interference in the affairs of individuals— freedom from those religious, political, social, and economic restraints designed to benefit a small noble class. The achievement of Liberalism and the eventual destruction of dynasticism meant the emancipation of the middle class.

3.

During the period when Dynasticism was on the decline and Liberalism was on the rise in Europe, North America's Atlan-

7

tic seaboard was colonized. The middle-class refugees who emigrated to America mainly sought freedom from interference by royal officials with their nonconformist religious practices. This they found as they carved their settlements out of the American wilderness. But they also sought an opportunity to achieve, by individual merit, the social prestige, political influence, and economic substance denied them in Europe. In the New World, where land was abundant and there for the clearing, the Colonists did manage to acquire a higher social and economic status. They also managed to acquire an amount of political privilege. The Colonists were successful in reaping the harvest of their industry and talent, free from restrictive state controls, because of a set of circumstances peculiar to the British North American Colonies.

Initial attempts to transplant the ancient social customs of Europe in the uncongenial New World climate failed. For more than a century after the first colonization of America, the British Crown was so absorbed with domestic strife and foreign wars that no firm control over the American plantations was asserted. Yankee traders ignored the imperial trade policies based on mercantilist principles. In frontier communities beyond the effective jurisdiction of British officials, the settlers worked out political practices not in accord with British policies. Royal governors found themselves, under the pressure of necessity, granting concession after concession to the Americans who demanded the relaxation or removal of imperial controls over various aspects of Colonial life. Through their own efforts, but largely by extralegal means, the Colonists were able to "liberalize" American life, so that individuals could obtain cherished privileges befitting their industry and talent. For decades the Colonists enjoyed the privileges they merited simply because British officials were in no position to deny them.

This so-called "policy of salutary neglect" ended with the French and Indian Wars. Out of the struggles of the seventeenth century in England, the Whig cause had emerged victorious. The powers of the king had been curbed; the leaders of Parliament had taken over the authority of the British Crown to rule. By the middle of the eighteenth century, the British Government was in a strong position at home and abroad. Government leaders took an increasing interest in Colonial affairs. Now that the British Government was able to enforce its mercantilist policies in the Colonies, it became determined to do so. It was the attempt by British rulers to assert their authority to govern the American Colonies as imperialist possessions that led to the War for American Independence.

It was expensive for the British government to administer affairs in the Americal Colonies. To help defray the costs of Colonial defense, Parliament, in 1765, passed the Stamp Act, imposing taxes on commercial transactions, licenses, legal instruments, and the like. This act touched off such a storm of protest in the Colonies that it was later repealed. But other Parliamentary actions offensive to British subjects in America followed. The Quartering Act (1765) provided that regular British troops should be housed and fed at the expense of American subjects. The Declaratory Act (1766) asserted the supremacy of Parliamentary authority over the Colonies and nullified Colonial legislation contrary to acts of Parliament. The Townshend Act (1767) imposed heavy duties on Colonial imports like tea and reorganized the customs collection to curb smuggling. The "Intolerable Acts" (1774) closed the Port of Boston in punishment for the "Tea Party," withdrew from Colonial bodies the authority to rule Massachusetts and placed it in the hands of the royal governor, and stripped Colonial courts of their jurisdiction to hear cases involving offenses against the British Crown. The Quebec Act (1774) established the Catholic religion in French Canada and set aside Colonial claims to Western territories in favor of Canadian claims.

When the British government tried, seriously for the first time, to rule the Colonies, the vested interests of Americans were

9

in jeopardy. Political privileges they had long enjoyed were denied by the British Crown. Their overseas trade was curtailed; their cost of living was raised; their economic growth was hampered. The westward movement of Colonials was retarded. The British policies aroused the deep resentment of Americans who had become accustomed to an uncommon amount of individual freedom in conducting their religious, social, political, and economic affairs. The Colonists came to fear and hate the symbol of British authority, King George.

As the Colonists came to realize that their vital interests were jeopardized by the policies of the Empire, they demanded that British interference in Colonial life cease, or at least be restrained. Their demands were ignored. The Colonists resolved to defend their interests. The question was how. Their stubborn resistance to British actions was countered by severe reprisals. They decided eventually, and reluctantly, to use force if necessary.

But during the critical period prior to the Declaration of Independence, the Colonists were by no means like-minded about how to resist British authority. In fact some—the Tories who later became Loyalists—expressed British views and defended British policies. Others, likewise relatively few in number but very articulate, voiced radical Republican views. They wanted full independence from Britain. But most Colonists were moderate in their opinion. Like the Republicans, they strongly opposed British policies. But like the Tories, they also opposed an outright break with the mother country. They were conciliatory in attitude, anxious to avoid violence, and asked simply that the British Government modify its policies to satisfy the interests of the King's subjects in America. However, as events moved toward open hostilities, moderate opinion was overwhelmed. Sentimental loyalty to king and country gave way to bitter hatred of the British monarch and his Parliament. Republican views, summed up in the Declaration of Independence in 1776, were then adopted by the most influential Colonial leaders.

4·

As the crisis developed in America, the Colonial leaders were confronted by the difficult problem of justifying their resistance to British authority. The Colonies were a part of the British Empire; the Colonists were subjects of the British king and were bound by acts of Parliament. At the same time the American Colonists found the British policies, even though in accord with law and custom, intolerable. But on what grounds could the Colonists justify their resistance to British rule?

At first they appealed to the original charters and the British constitution, alleging that the offensive actions by British officials were unconstitutional. The charters, they argued, were granted by the Crown, not Parliament. These charters gave American subjects of the King the venerable rights of Englishmen. A recognized right is to be taxed only by an assembly of one's representatives; another is trial by a jury of one's peers. Under the charters, the Colonists were entitled to regulate their own internal affairs, subject to the approval of the Crown. Since Americans were not represented in the Parliament, the British Government could not tax the Colonists—only the Colonial legislatures could do that, constitutionally. Since the Parliamentary acts implementing imperial policies violated the solemn contracts between the Crown and his American subjects, such acts were contrary to the "higher law" of the British constitution. In short, the Colonists were not bound to obey British officials acting "unconstitutionally."

These arguments appealing to the royal charters and the British constitution proved singularly unconvincing. The difficulty was that they rested on conceptions alien to British thought and practice. What the Colonists were tacitly assuming was that a constitution cannot be altered by a legislative enactment. In the seventeenth century, during the struggle with James I and prior to the civil wars, the notion of a "higher law" had been expressed by Chief Justice Coke; he contended that the king is bound by the common law of the realm. But the Glorious Revolution of 1689 had established the principle of parliamentary sovereignty: the king is subject to the higher law of the British constitution, but as the Parliament may determine. From the British point of view, the parliamentary acts the Colonists protested against were clearly constitutional.

Similarly the conception of representation the Colonists insisted on was unfamiliar to the British. In the British view the members of Parliament, Lords and Commons, speak for the entire British people. It really makes no difference who elects a member or where he lives or what his "interests" are. The Parliament is composed of respectable Englishmen who virtually represent all subjects of the British Crown.

This doctrine of virtual representation was quite alien to Colonial experience. In America, the practice was for residents of a territorial constituency to elect one of their number to represent the community in the Colonial assembly. Seats were apportioned on a geographical basis, and a residence requirement for representatives became fixed in custom. Elections were held frequently for short terms of office; by the election the constituents passed on the representative's record. In this conception of representation, the Americans were of course not represented in Parliament. But from the British viewpoint, they were.

Eventually the Colonists were confronted with a situation where they could make no persuasive case justifying their resistance to imperial authority in terms of British law. As a final resort they appealed, as had the English Whigs a century before, to an argument claiming an "extralegal" right of revolution.

This doctrine of revolution was derived from the natural rights–social contract theory espoused by "enlightened" seventeenth- and eighteenth-century Liberal thinkers. The fundamental rights of man, the Colonists contended, are prescribed by the laws of nature. These natural rights are inalienable and inviolable. Government is constituted by men to secure their rights. Each individual agrees to yield up to a common authority his right of "self-help" to protect himself. Thus authority is instrumental to the preservation of individual rights; government is a means to that end. In case of conflict between the end of natural rights and the means of constituted government, the end takes precedence. So long as government fulfills its proper function of preserving rights, its authority is legitimate. But when government itself subverts the rights of citizens, it acts without authority. Its actions depend on force, not law.

The British government, the Colonists charged, had violated the fundamental rights of Americans. Since it had no such authority, British rule was mere usurpation. By its illicit actions the British government had abrogated the social compact on which its authority depended. The Colonists had no recourse but to withdraw their consent to British rule and resort to their natural right of self-help. The Colonists had to, in John Locke's words, "appeal to Heaven"—revolt against British rule.

By this appeal to natural law, the Revolutionists could justify their resistance to British rule in America. Since the British government no longer had a right to rule, the American Colonists had a right to resist, to meet force with force. In the hands of the American Liberals this doctrine proved to be a potent ideological weapon for undermining British authority in the Colonies.

5.

We must remember that historically the aim of Liberals had been to subject the royal executive to legal restraints. In England the dynastic kings had asserted "prerogative" powers, authority supposed to be inherent in the royal office, hence not subject to parliamentary restrictions. It was the heavyhanded use of prerogative powers by the Stuarts to violate ancient liberties of Englishmen that provoked the constitutional crisis in seventeenth-century England. The dynastic kings had justified their actions on the grounds that they had a divine right to rule. In this conception the king was accountable only to God, the sole source of authority.

Liberal thinkers sought to discredit this theory of the divine right of kings by an alternative theory of authority, the natural rights–social contract theory. According to this theory, which was predicated on natural-law assumptions, no person has a divinely ordained right to rule another. Rather, each person has a natural right to rule himself. Individuals can remove themselves from this state of nature by a social compact under which they pool their respective rights to rule themselves in a common authority supreme in the society. In this way they form themselves a "sovereign people." In a sense the voice of God is spoken only by the sovereign people, who are the source of authority. The sovereign people constitute government to preserve the rights of individuals. The instrument for expressing the will of the sovereign is a constitution, the "people's law." By the constitution, public offices are created and vested with authority. But the authority of rulers to govern is strictly limited by the "higher law" of the constitution. This is the Liberal formulation of a doctrine of popular sovereignty.

This doctrine that the people are the source of sovereign authority and the government is their constituted agent could readily be used to justify a popular revolution, where a dynastic king refused to concede that his authority to rule was constitutionally limited. But alone it could not so easily be used to justify constitutional restraints imposed by a parliament on the royal executive to prevent the infringement of the liberties of subjects. To achieve this aim of curbing the authority of a king, Liberal thinkers such as John Locke devised an ingenious formula known as the theory of the "mixed" constitution.

The idea of a constitution in which the different principles of rule are combined is an ancient one. Greek and Roman philosophers had discussed it at length, and one Stoic thinker, Polybius, had made it the cornerstone of his political thought. The idea was revived by the Enlightenment thinkers in the seventeenth century. However, the definitive modern statement of the theory of the mixed constitution was by a French philosopher, the Baron de Montesquieu. Montesquieu elaborated his theory in a famous eighteenth-century political treatise, *The Spirit of the Laws*.

Montesquieu's theory was designed to provide an answer for a question which disturbed generations of Liberals: What is the best form of government for preserving individual liberty? For Montesquieu as for other eighteenth-century Liberals, this was mainly a problem of preventing the royal executive from violating the rights of subjects.

Montesquieu was concerned only about what he called "political liberty." He identified three forms of liberty: "Natural liberty" is the license to do what one desires; such liberty is impossible in any society. "Civil liberty" is the right to do what one pleases without injuring others. Natural law and social custom prescribe such liberty, but it cannot be assured in the absence of law. "Political liberty" is the right to do what the law permits. Such liberty presumes a civil society in which authority to make and enforce law is recognized.

Liberty, Montesquieu contended, results when the laws, not men, govern. Thus a dilemma: To have liberty, there must be law; to have law, there must be government—authority to make and enforce the law. But government, which is indispensable for liberty, is also dangerous as well, for rulers tend to abuse their office and violate the liberty of subjects. The question is how to constitute a government of law—how to make *rulers* subject to law?

Montesquieu's answer was of course: by a mixed constitution. His analysis rests on the classic definition of the three forms of rule: by the one, the few, and the many. For each there is a corrupt as well as a lawful form. Rule by one man according to law is monarchy; the virtue is honor. Government by a few, under law, is aristocracy; the virtue is moderation. Government by the many, under law, is democracy; the virtue is equality. With corrupt forms, rule is not according to law; despotic rule is for the benefit of a part rather than the whole society. The difficulty is that in practice each pure form tends to degenerate into its corrupt form, where the vice peculiar to that form of rule replaces its virtue. For example, aristocracy gives way to oligarchy, democracy to mob rule.

The only solution is to constitute a government in which all three principles of rule are combined, yet none prevails. In this way the virtue of each form can be secured in the governmental system, while the vices of all are avoided. With such a mixed constitution, the three principles balanced in the one system, rule is according to law and the liberty of individuals is preserved.

So argued Montesquieu.

6.

When the Liberals had sought to protect the liberties of subjects by imposing restraints on the royal executive, this theory of the mixed constitution served their purpose well. It did justify parliamentary checks on the king. But the theory could be turned with equal effect to justify curbs on the popular branch of government, the legislature.

Prior to the American Revolution, the branch of government most feared by the Colonists was the executive. The Colonial governors, as agents of the British Crown, were charged with the responsibility for administering those laws the Americans found so offensive. The Colonial legislatures, in contrast, were regarded as friends of liberty. After the Declaration of Independence, the new states, on instruction from the Continental Congress, adopted constitutions providing for systems of popular government. In these early state constitutions the powers of the governors were rigidly circumscribed and the rights of citizens were clearly set forth. In arranging the offices, the balance was heavily in favor of the popularly elected legislature. These new state governments, under popular control, proceeded to do the bidding of the people. Extensive reforms equalizing social, economic, and political opportunity were enacted. Some reforms affected property ownership, much to the alarm of those prosperous American leaders who were accustomed to dominating Colonial life.

By the time of the Philadelphia Convention in 1787, many delegates representing the propertied interests expressed grave reservations about the radical state experiments with popular government. In his *Notes on the Convention,* James Madison recorded numerous expressions of hostility toward popular rule uttered by the delegates, and included a number of his own. The delegates readily confessed their fear of "the great beast, the People." The rich are few and the poor are many; the majority seek through control of government to profit at the expense of the wealthy few. "The evils we experience," Elbridge Gerry of Massachusetts declared, "flow from the excess of democracy." For them the problem was how, in a political system founded on the principle of popular sovereignty, to protect the interests of a propertied minority from depredations by the "untutored masses."

The indigenous American Liberals who were later called "Federalists" worked out a solution for this problem at the Philadelphia Convention. Early in the deliberations, Roger Sherman of Connecticut (in a speech opposing popular election of members of the legislature) pointed the way: "The people ... should have as little to do as may be about the Government." Federalists like James Madison, Alexander Hamilton, and John Jay—authors of the *Federalist Papers*—and John Adams and John Marshall disagreed on some points, but on the big question they shared a single answer: the control of government should not get into the hands of the common people. The Federalist formula was to constitute a political system in which the people cannot effectively use the instrument of government to serve their needs.

The Federalists embraced Montesquieu's theory of the mixed constitution as "the sacred maxim of all free government." They reformulated his theory, extended it, and applied it to the American scene, incorporating the theory of separation of powers and checks and balances as an integral part of the Federalist formula.

The best way to make government subject to law, the Federalist contended, is to separate the powers of government among the branches of government. There are three functions: to make laws, to administer them, and to judge disputes arising under the laws. If two or more functions are concentrated in a single branch, government is then above the law. The government is sovereign, not the people, and liberty suffers. Therefore each function should be vested in a separate branch—the legislature, the executive, and the judiciary.

Yet if the functions are completely separate, the government cannot achieve its purpose; the system cannot allow effective rule. There is a middle way. The powers of government must be balanced and checked, as well as separated. Each branch should have sufficient power to perform its function independent of the other. In addition, each branch should have enough power to prevent the abuse of authority by the other branches. Because with the separation of power and checks and balances no branch can act without the cooperation of the other two except to perform its legitimate function, each branch is made subject to law. Each branch serves as a watchdog of the Constitution, to assure that rule is according to law. For example, the executive is independent to perform the function of administering the law, but for any other purpose it is dependent on the legislature and the judiciary. The Federalists concluded that a government of laws can and should be established by separating the functions of government among the three branches so that each branch checks and balances the other two.

The Federalists were responsible for drafting the United States Constitution and getting it ratified. They wrote the principles of separation of powers and checks and balances into the Constitution as part of their formula to curb the popular influence in government. The first three Articles describe the functions of the Congress, the President, and the Courts, respectively. Throughout the document we find provisions facilitating a check by one branch on the others, such as the Congressional power to impeach the President and Federal judges, and the President's power to appoint judges only with the advice and consent of the Senate.

But it was a popularly elected legislature that the Federalists feared most. Bitter experience had taught them that a legislature under popular control could harm the interests of the "better" classes. So in the original Constitution we find the Congress divided into two houses, with the members of the Senate, ostensibly representatives of the states, indirectly selected by state governments. The powers of the President and the judiciary—reflecting the monarchical and aristocratic principles—are extensive and rest on an independent constitutional base. The President is chosen by an electoral college removed from popular control, and the chief executive has veto power over Congressional enactments. Federal judges are appointed by the President with the concurrence of the Senate for life terms ("good behavior"). Thus the judiciary is almost entirely insulated from the influence of the electorate.

The more extreme Federalists like Alexander Hamilton were unable to gain acceptance for a system where the people had no voice whatsoever in the general government. For political reasons, they had to make compromises. But in securing the adoption of the United States Constitution, the Federalists were remarkably successful in creating a new central government well removed from the influence of the citizenry. This government, safe in the hands of the rich and the wellborn, could serve as a powerful check on state governments under popular control.

The Federal Constitution is an impressive political monument to the elitist convictions of those native American Liberals, the Federalists. For the Federalist formula, true to Liberal tenets, established a system of elite rule, traditionally the stock in trade of middle-class Liberals.

7.

It was the anti-Federalists, under Thomas Jefferson's leadership, who first advocated the practice of popular government on an extended scale.

Many prominent revolutionary leaders opposed the adoption of the Constitution. Patrick Henry, Governor of Virginia, and Richard Henry Lee, who originally proposed in the Continental Congress that a Declaration of Independence be drafted, refused to serve as delegates to the Convention and vigorously fought ratification in the Virginia House of Burgesses. Even of the fifty-five delegates who attended the Philadelphia Convention, only thirty-nine finally signed the draft. Within the states, opposition to the Constitution was widespread; ratification carried in several states (New York and Virginia) only by a bare plurality of votes. Those revolutionary leaders who fought adoption condemned the Constitution as a clever conspiracy to rob the American people of the fruits of their victory over British tyranny.

Other revolutionary leaders, Jefferson among them, accepted the idea of a constitution but were displeased by the Philadelphia Convention's handiwork. They believed that some central government was necessary to protect the states against foreign aggression and to regulate certain interstate affairs. But the Jeffersonians objected to many provisions of the original draft constitution. They contended that the new general government posed a threat to the liberties of citizens, that the Constitution vested too much authority in the general government at the expense of the states. It was the Jeffersonians, not the Federalists, who were responsible for appending the Bill of Rights to the Constitution, made in some states a condition of ratification. The Jeffersonians were the legitimate heirs of the radical Republicanism of the American Revolution. What the Jeffersonian Republicans feared was that a general government so removed from popular control would become a servant of the wealthy few, a fountain of special privilege.

During the administrations of Presidents George Washington and John Adams, some of the worst fears of the Republicans were realized. Federalist policies on the national debt, the tariff, and the National Bank—all sponsored by Alexander Hamilton—did grant privileges to moneyed commercial interests. The Republicans attacked such policies, and they also promoted the Kentucky Resolutions (secretly drafted by Jefferson) and the Virginia Resolutions denouncing the Alien and Sedition Acts of 1798 as an abuse of the constitutional powers of the general government.

The sharp political conflict which developed between the Federalists and the Republicans reflected two contrary views of popular government. The question at stake was the extent to which the people—the "sovereign people"—should play a role in governing themselves. Should the people be ruled by their "betters," or should they rule themselves?

The Federalists, who identified their interests with a prosperous minority, feared and distrusted the common citizens more than the officials of the Federal government insulated from popular influence. The Federalists ardently supported the Constitution as a device to prevent a majority of the people from using government to serve their needs. In the new Federal system the general government, remote from the citizenry, functioned as a check on the movement for self-government that was sweeping the states.

The Republicans, in contrast, identified themselves with the interests of a majority of the American people. They had greater confidence in the governed than in their self-chosen rulers. Jefferson believed that the American citizen could and should play a prominent role in his government.

For Jefferson, American society provided a firm foundation for popular government because a majority of the population was composed of small farmers. In Jefferson's time the country was predominantly agrarian and landholding was widely distributed. Most Americans were farmers who worked their own land. There was relatively little commerce or manufacture, and none in the sense of mass industrial production and distribution in national and international markets. The commercial interests were a small minority, and localized in a few cities along the Atlantic seaboard. Manufacture was mainly on a handicraft basis, with the farmer a versatile part-time "mechanic." Exchange was on a semibarter basis. The typical economic unit was a village community surrounded by small farms, and these farming communities were virtually self-contained economic units.

For Jefferson such a society of "freehold" farmers was a good society, wherein free men could govern themselves. A farmer who owns his land is economically independent, beholden to no one. He can make political judgments free from economic coercion. His interest is to wrest a living from nature, not to profit from the labor of others. With his stake in the community, the farmer is anxious to maintain law and order, to protect the rights of persons and property, to promote the general welfare of the community. He is a stable, solid, sober, free American citizen. In such an agrarian society, popular government is both possible and desirable.

But the Republicans of Jefferson's persuasion assumed that popular government meant the government of the local farming community. Their only experience with central government had been with the British authorities. Consequently, though they accepted the Constitution, they never believed that the Federal government could serve as a clean and sharp instrument for popular rule. At best it could be kept from serving the special interests of a wealthy few. The remedy was to put friends of popular government in control of the Federal government, persons who would not abuse the authority of their office. It was of course the Republicans who led the movement to oust the Federalists from control of the general government by electing Jefferson to the Presidency in 1800.

With Jefferson's election, the Republicans did succeed in gaining control of the executive and the legislative branches. But the Federalists managed to maintain control of the judiciary. Just before President Adams went out of office, John Marshall was appointed Chief Justice of the United States. The Supreme Court under Marshall's domination became the last Federalist stronghold. The politicians on the Court perpetuated the Federalist formula, in some cases rewriting the Constitution to do so, for several decades after the Federalist Party was so discredited at the polls that it ceased to be a significant force in state and national elections.

Thus was the stage set by Liberals for the rise of the Democratic movement, in reaction against the indigenous American form of Liberalism. It was in reaction against Federalist beliefs about the exercise of authority that the Democratic movement arose in America.

We must bear in mind that the great transformation which produced American Democracy was a fundamental change in attitude about the proper role of the governed in the exercise of authority. The Federalists believed that the people should be ruled by their "betters," the "natural aristocrats." Eventually this view was abandoned as the Democratic alternative, that the people should rule themselves, gained acceptance. This change in attitude marked a transition from a situation where participation in the exercise of authority was limited to a few eminent leaders, to a situation where virtually everyone enjoys the same privileges, where the "common man" (and woman) has equal opportunity to play a central and decisive role in making decisions about the exercise of authority. I am not suggesting that today all authority in this country is exercised in accord with Democratic principles. However, Democratic beliefs are so widely accepted that few Americans try to justify the exercise of authority contrary to Democratic principles. With the growth of the Democratic movement in this country, elite rule founded on Liberal beliefs has gradually declined, as people have more and more demanded that authority be exercised Democratically.

8.

Liberalism, then, is a creed and movement that the Democrat rejects. And so does the Catholic, we shall see. Neither accepts distinctive Liberal beliefs and practices.

But to understand the alternatives to Liberalism, we must know what the Democrat and the Catholic are for, as well as what they are against. What beliefs and principles does the Democrat accept? And the Catholic? What is the relation between Catholic teachings and Democratic principles?

About this contemporary issue there appear to be two "classic" positions which recent American writers have expressed. One extreme is that Catholicism and Democracy are incompatible, inherently so: a devout Catholic cannot possibly be a true Democrat.

A few years ago, a group of writers launched an unusually bitter attack against the Roman Church in the United States, advancing this view. Just as in the decade following the First World War, when the Ku Klux Klan whipped up anti-Catholic sentiment, so in the years after the Second World War we have again witnessed a wave of anti-Catholic agitation. The leading propaganda organs for spreading anti-Catholicism in past years have been the "liberal" journals of opinion like the *Nation* and the *New Republic*. In an article in the *New Republic* in the spring of 1943, George P. West proposed that "liberal" groups organize themselves to resist Catholic influence in this country. In the next issue an Italian refugee scholar, Gaetano Salvemini, bitterly attacked the Pope as a "friend of Fascism." These articles touched off a spirited journalistic hassle over Catholicism.

The writer who eventually emerged as the high priest of American anti-Catholicism was a lawyer, government official, and publicist, Paul Blanshard, one of the most hostile critics of Catholicism to appear in many decades. In a series of articles which were published in the *Nation* during the fall of 1947, he ridiculed views imputed to "The Church" about "medicine, sex, and education." A few months later, during the spring of 1948 in a second series, Blanshard advanced the near-hysterical charge that "Catholic power"—by which he apparently meant the American hierarchy and clergy under Papal dictate—threatens to destroy "the American way of life." Later he elaborated his indictment in two well-known and highly controversial books— *American Freedom and Catholic Power* (1949) and *Communism, Democracy, and Catholic Power* (1951).

Defenders of Catholicism have displayed little diffidence in replying to the critics of the Church. A barrage of articles by Catholic writers detailing a rebuttal to the charges against the Church appeared in many journals, especially Catholic publications like *America* and *Commonweal*. A Jesuit priest and eminent Thomist philosopher, Father John Courtney Murray, wrote dozens of tracts carefully explaining the Church's teachings and cogently defending Catholicism as an integral part of American life. An extensive answer to Blanshard's thesis, a definitive Catholic answer, was set forth by James M. O'Neill in *Catholicism and the American Tradition* (1953).

But Catholic writers have not been content merely to answer charges. They have moved on to elaborate the other "classic" position: that Democracy is founded on Christian moral beliefs. Unless a person accepts the religious teachings of the one true Church, he cannot possibly believe in and practice Democracy.

The foremost Democratic thinker to serve as a Catholic apologist is, as well, one of the ablest contemporary political theorists

—Don Luigi Sturzo, an Italian priest. Sturzo was a founder of the original Italian Christian Democratic movement (the Popular Party) after the First World War. He early denounced Mussolini and the Italian Fascist regime and was forced into exile, where he has spent his later years. Sturzo has expounded his views about Catholicism and Democracy in dozens of articles and a number of books which have appeared during the past three decades.

It is Sturzo's view that Christianity and Democracy are founded on respect for the human personality and both presuppose a moral freedom for persons. Between Catholic teachings and Democratic principles there is no conflict. Indeed it is the Christian religion which supplies the moral foundations for Democracy.

This view has also been expressed by an American Catholic layman, Emmet John Hughes in *The Church and Liberal Society* (1944). Hughes differentiates between "Liberalism" and "Democracy" and argues that Democracy's base is "religious and specifically Christian in essence." Religious skepticism, encouraged by such secular creeds as Liberalism and its perverse offspring, Socialism, has weakened the moral foundations of Democracy. But Liberalism and Socialism are now bankrupt. Only the Church has the moral and intellectual vigor to restore moral foundations for Democracy. "The faith of Democracy can be made lastingly strong by the faith of the Church."

What does all this mean? Some claim that Democracy and Catholicism are incompatible, others that they are inseparable. It is at least a plausible hypothesis that both these extreme views are untenable: that neither is Democracy inherently at conflict with Catholicism, nor is it predicated on Catholic dogma. This hypothesis is worth examining. To decide whether it is valid, we must inspect with care the theory and practice exhibited by Catholics and Democrats.

In this undertaking we are at the outset faced with a difficulty of identifying "orthodox" Catholic, and Democratic, beliefs and principles. Nowhere can we find Catholicism neatly packaged and labeled as genuine. In fact the question of what are Catholic views is vigorously disputed, especially by non-Catholics who have never troubled to find out. What are Democratic views is a no less disputed question.

These disputes are nourished by misunderstandings over the use of terms. Argument over what a term *really* means is a quite sterile, and futile, intellectual pursuit. Words derive their meanings from those who use them. What is important is to know how a person is using a term.

Therefore my next task shall be to explain what I understand by Democracy and Catholicism. I shall formulate my conceptions of Democratic and Catholic beliefs and principles and shall give the warrant for my conceptions. Others may have rather different notions. This need cause no difficulty, provided we understand one another. But I shall regard these conceptions I formulate as equivalents for the terms "Democracy" and "Catholicism." Then I shall proceed to the main task: to determine the relation between them.

Chapter Two

THE DEMOCRATIC TRADITION

I.

In formulating an authentic conception of Democratic beliefs and principles, we are faced with a curious situation. Perhaps no subject has attracted so much comment from so many writers within the past few decades as "democracy." Hundreds of books and articles have appeared in recent years, treating—if we are to judge from their titles—some aspect of the subject. Yet despite this voluminous literature, no statement of Democratic theory or practice is generally accepted as definitive.

What is Democracy? A collection of definitions merely reveals that the word is used to express widely varied conceptions. It is sometimes used to describe an existing governmental system. The British and American systems, strikingly unlike though they are in structure and operation, are often said to be "democratic governments." The term is sometimes used to describe a type of society: France and Italy are called "Western Democracies," in contrast to the Communist dictatorships of Eastern Europe. Other times democracy is used to describe a social creed summing up the aspirations of a movement, such as "Social Democracy" or "Christian Democracy."

This semantic confusion is further compounded by the practice of using the term within different frames of reference. In some cases Democracy is supposed to signify what actually exists, a picture of the present now lived. In other cases it is supposed to signify what ought to exist but actually does not; perhaps a picture of a past now gone, or a dream of a future someday to be realized.

Of course such variant usage makes for lively controversy over what Democracy *really* is. It is evident that, whatever it "is," Democracy is a good thing. The term has become one of approbation. Few are the theories or practices, beliefs or principles, that some champion has not tried to qualify as *"really* Democratic." Liberals, socialists, atheists, religionists, conservatives, radicals, individualists, collectivists, capitalists, unionists, constitutionalists, totalitarians—all want the Democratic label attached to their cause. Even the Communists claim that Soviet dictatorship is the only "true, proletarian democracy—people's democracy"; both Hitler and Mussolini boasted that their brands of totalitarianism were "higher," "more real" forms of Democracy. It seems that only a few esthetes and cranks who make a profession of snobbery relish the charge that they are "un-Democratic." Democracy may not be the order of our day, but it is certainly a symbol, whatever it signifies, dripping with prestige value.

Nothing would be gained in this study by contributing further to the prevailing confusion about the meaning of this word. Let me simply explain my usage of the term, and why I use it this way.

I shall rely on a historic meaning of "Democracy." As long ago as ancient Greece, as early as Plato's *Republic,* we find philosophers trying to classify the different ways by which authority can be exercised. Plato started the fashion of classifying forms of rule on the basis of participation in the exercise of authority. Rule by one person he called "monarchy"; rule by a few, "aristocracy"; and rule by the many, "democracy." He derived the term from the Greek words for people (*demos*) and rule (*kratia*) —literally, "rule by the people."

29

In the eighteenth century, when again the custom of classifying forms of rule was in vogue, American writers apparently used the term to mean simply "popular rule." In the *Federalist Paper No. 10* (1787), James Madison describes "pure democracy" as "a society consisting of a small number of citizens who assemble and administer the government in person." Madison, expressing a widespread attitude of his set, dismissed democracy as a bad form of rule, making for "turbulence and contention" in government. Perhaps because democracy was then a term of opprobrium, Thomas Jefferson avoided using it; instead he called "a government by its citizens in mass, acting directly and personally, according to rules established by the majority" (*Letter to Taylor,* 1816) a "republic." But once he does refer to a democracy as "the only pure form of republic" (*Letter to Tiffany,* 1816).

By the time Andrew Jackson had risen to power, democracy, no longer a term of reproach in this country, meant for most Americans "government constituted and administered by the people themselves." The followers of Old Hickory proudly called themselves Jacksonian Democrats. It was this phenomenon of Jacksonian Democracy that Alexis de Tocqueville tried to portray, in the 1830s, to his French compatriots. This conception of democracy was given a familiar statement by a little-known American writer a decade before Abraham Lincoln delivered his Gettysburg Address. In a discourse before the Maryland Historical Society in December, 1853, George Burnap defined "pure democracy" as "the government of the people, for the people, and by the people" (*The Origins of American Democracy,* 1853, p. 16).

2.

We find that American writers, though they have expressed rather different attitudes toward popular rule, have recognized Democracy as a form of rule by the people. What they all evidently accept is a notion of Democracy as a particular way of exercising authority. In this conception, Democracy is a process by which questions about the exercise of authority are decided.

Let us look at the situation this way. In our society important decisions about the exercise of authority over us are made every day. These decisions affect our daily lives most intimately. They determine where we can live, how we can live, what our income can be, how much of our income we can spend as we choose, where we can go, how we can spend our time, and so on. These decisions are made by many different "authorities." Some decisions are made by the Congress, the state legislatures, and local assemblies. Some are made by the President and his numerous aides and advisors and assistants, by governors, mayors, city managers, by Supreme Court justices, other judges, commissioners, and justices of the peace. A host of decisions are made by lesser officials and employees of county, municipal, state, and Federal governments.

At the same time, many decisions about the exercise of authority are not made under government auspices at all. They are made by such agencies as executive committees of political parties, lobbyists in consultation with the officers of special-interest organizations, directors of professional associations, executive secretaries of trade or labor organizations, governing boards of churches, trustees of nonprofit foundations, the staff members of publishing firms, advertising agencies, and manufacturing concerns. Of course the management personnel of business enterprises make some of the most important decisions of our society.

These numerous decisions which so intimately affect our daily lives are made not only by many different "authorities" but also in many different ways. In the various decision-making processes, the persons affected by decisions about the exercise of authority play widely varied roles. Perhaps they play a commanding role,

31

like the members of the Westside Civic Improvement League. Or perhaps they have no influential role whatsoever; they are subject to a system of elite rule.

But it is significant that in our society at least some decisions about the exercise of authority are made by the persons over whom the authority is exercised. They are made by the members of organized groups according to certain accepted rules. These rules are prescribed by certain principles—Democratic principles: (1) that authority to make decisions binding on the members is located in the group itself; (2) that in arriving at a group decision, each member counts for one and no more than one; and (3) that the group's decision is finally determined by a vote of a majority.

Let us call a decision-making process governed by these principles "Democratic" and agree that decisions made this way are made "Democratically." In this sense Democracy describes neither "what exists" nor "what ought to exist," strictly speaking. It is a conception of a way decisions *can* be made: "what *could* exist," and perhaps does to some extent if not entirely. But meaningful use of this term does not depend on the extent to which decisions are actually made by a Democratic process. Nor does it depend on demonstration of a contention that decisions *ought* to be made in a Democratic way. Operationally defined, a given decision-making process is Democratic to the extent that Democratic principles are actually followed. In this sense, then, Democracy is a sort of a model process, a set of rules prescribing practices which *can* be followed in making decisions.

To what extent are decisions in this country in fact made by a Democratic process? Of course many political decisions are. We elect our representatives to legislative assemblies and our other government officials by procedures characteristically Democratic. Government boards and commissions ordinarily arrive at their decisions in a Democratic way. Most public agencies at the local and state levels of government, such as school boards and planning agencies, generally follow Democratic procedures in their decision-making.

Perhaps the Democratic practices of numerous private, "extra-legal" groups who make decisions binding on their membership are even more important in our lives. In fact the Democratic decision-making process is most extensively used by the memberships of those diverse voluntary groups—economic, social, political, cultural, educational, professional, religious, civic, recreational—which flourish in every American community. Councils of labor unions, directorates of corporations, trustees of charitable foundations, executive boards of service clubs, committees of party organizations—these are the bodies where Democratic decision-making is most common. The experience of most Americans with the Democratic process is actually acquired, not by participation in governmental affairs, but through membership in such voluntary associations as the Kiwanis Club, the Business and Professional Women, the Parent-Teachers Association, the Izaak Walton League, the League of Women Voters, the American Civil Liberties Union, the many Community Chest agencies —organizations like the Westside Civic Improvement League.

The relatively extensive and apparently increasing use of a Democratic process of group decision-making in certain areas of American life has led some to describe the United States as a "Democracy." This usage is understandable; but if the term is meant to characterize American life, it is, of course, rather misleading. The whole of our national existence is obviously not guided by Democratic principles. We have already seen that the American political system designed in 1787 at Philadelphia was not intended to be Democratic; the founders of our constitutional scheme deliberately sought to curb the rule by the people. Nor was the system as it worked out in practice Democratic. During a century and a half of American political development, reform groups have struggled to change features of our political system to make it conform more closely to Democratic principles.

These struggles have not yet ended. Despite the impressive achievements of such movements, American governments do not now entirely provide a Democratic system of rule. In fact some distinctive features of our political system do violence to Democratic principles. The practice of judicial review and the institution of the Electoral College are examples. Perhaps such features of our system can be justified on some grounds, but surely they cannot be justified on the ground that they conform to Democratic principles.

So is the situation, too, with many political decisions made under private as well as under public auspices. Many such decisions, though they may vitally affect the lives of American citizens, are not now arrived at by Democratic procedures. In many important areas of American life, no serious effort has yet been made even to structure decision-making processes on a group basis, let alone along Democratic lines.

However, for our purpose it is significant that in present-day American society some important and many not so important decisions about the exercise of authority are made by processes prescribed by Democratic principles. It is to such group decision-making processes that I refer when I use the term "Democracy." So let it be clear: what I mean by Democracy is a process of making decisions about the exercise of authority according to the principles of popular sovereignty, political equality, and majority rule, as American thinkers have understood those principles.

3.

We have already seen that the idea of Democracy is as old as ancient Greece. We find too that Roman and medieval thinkers were familiar with the idea of popular rule, and that throughout the modern period, since the Reformation, political thinkers have discussed Democratic ideas. However, until recent times, most political thinkers considered Democratic rule only for the purpose of condemning it. Even in the late eighteenth century, most political leaders agreed with James Madison that rule by the people, one of the "pure" forms of rule, should be avoided in a well-ordered polity like the government of the United States.

General acceptance of Democratic theory and practice is then a recent historical development. It is a development of the last few centuries. And it was in this "New World" country where Democratic beliefs and principles first gained acceptance, under the impact of circumstances native to America.

To our forebears, the early settlers in the New World, the only familiar and accepted form of rule was by an elite. For many centuries in Europe, aristocrats had governed the less fortunate members of societies, and it was an elite, albeit one of religious merit, not of land or birth or wealth, that first governed in early America. Claims by a religious elite to rule we do not today take seriously, but other forms of elite rule are familiar items in our everyday experience. But so is Democratic rule, and it is Democratic rule that we most widely accept, and prefer. The story of how this change has come about, with various forms of elite rule being abandoned in favor of Democratic rule, I shall attempt now to sketch.

The story of the Democratic movement in America is our most famous epic. Yet it is a peculiar story indeed. It is not a saga of great men or grand designs. It is a simple story of plain people faced with everyday tasks, working out, as they went along generation after generation, new and better ways of doing unspectacular jobs. Now, in retrospect, we realize that what the American people worked out is the most significant political invention of our modern world. Yet it is a dramatic story, strangely, with few stars and no plot.

This is not to say that the Democratic movement in America discloses no pattern. It does show a distinctive pattern. As attitudes about the role of the governed in decision-making have changed, so have the practices. But the growing acceptance of

35

Democracy has been most gradual. At no point has there been a sharp and sudden break with the past. Instead the changes have come piecemeal: a slow but steady extension of more and more privileges, to more and more members of American society, in more and more areas of American life.

Perhaps this growth of Democracy has been so gradual because American Democracy has not evolved from fabricating novel beliefs and practices. Rather the pattern of acceptance has been for familiar ones to be more widely extended and applied. The comment is often made, frequently with a sneer, that American Democrats have made few "original" contributions to political thought. It is true that for the most part they have been leaders rather than theorists, men of action rather than academic philosophers. But it is also true that Democratic theory has tended, quite naturally, to follow instead of precede Democratic practice. Democratic doctrines have appeared as generalizations describing principles already accepted on a limited scale. The principles were familiar to many Americans who accepted them as guiding rules in much of their everyday lives when the doctrines were first espoused. What was new was their application to an unfamiliar area of decision-making. Because of the mode of its development, American Democracy bears an empirical character which is still a distinguishing mark.

The gradualness of the transition from elite to popular rule, as Democratic principles have been accepted for more and more areas of American life, is symbolized in the drift of Thomas Jefferson's thinking over the years, compared with that of his contemporaries. Jefferson's tendency was to extend ever more widely, to apply ever more broadly, the same beliefs and principles he espoused in his youth. Many of Jefferson's contemporaries shared his principles, but narrowly applied. As times changed Jefferson was prepared to extend and apply them as few others in his day were. For example, the Federalist Alexander Hamilton accepted as did Jefferson the principle of popular sovereignty. The Revolutionists declared that the authority to make decisions binding on the citizens is located in the people. This principle they accepted in claiming that the British government lacked authority to legislate for the American Colonies and that the Colonists had a right to resist British rule by means of force. The Federalists accepted this principle but applied it only so far as the exercise of "constituent" authority was concerned. In the Constitution, Article V provides that only the sovereign people have authority to amend the higher law. This amending process is, as Jefferson once pointed out, a peaceable equivalent, in a constituted society, of revolution. It is the prescribed procedure by which the people exercise supreme authority. But Federalists like Hamilton who agreed that only the sovereign people can enact the higher law of the Constitution refused to accept the same principle when applied to decisions about the exercise of governmental authority. They maintained that even decisions about who should occupy public office should be made by a select few who were specially qualified. On the other hand, Jefferson contended that such decisions should be made, not by a minority of "natural aristocrats," but by a majority of the people. He wanted to apply the principle of popular sovereignty in an area of decision-making where the Federalists refused to accept it.

What does this mean? That the general pattern of Democratic development in America has been for principles of decision-making already operative in a familiar area of experience to be adopted in another area, where decisions were previously made by some elitist process. This development has not been devoid of scheme. The pattern of acceptance of Democratic principles shows two definite directions of movement. Democratic principles accepted as rules in extralegal, voluntary associations have been adopted to govern the decision-making processes in the more official organizations of public life. The direction of movement has been from private to governmental organizations. Also, the principles accepted in the local community have been projected to regulate the practices at higher levels of organization.

Here the direction of movement has been from the local to the state to the national level. The dual trend has been from the local voluntary association to the national government. But this trend has not yet run its course, with the result that today the principles of elite rule are more evident in the official structure and functioning of the Federal government than in any other area of American public life.

4.

But where did this all begin?

Perhaps it would come as something of a shock to the members of the Westside Civic Improvement League to learn that the first American Democrat was a rebellious clergyman who didn't like the rule of Puritan theocrats, but such is the case.

Elite rule was first abandoned and Democratic principles of decision-making were first accepted in the government of church congregations. The paramount role of religion in American life, starting with the early settlements of the seventeenth century, has understandably evoked a wealth of comment. America is a product of the modern age, and in the forefront of advances in modern life has been religious protest. The dynastic system was initially challenged by Liberal dissenters in the area of the authority of the established churches. Similarly, it was in the area of church government where elite rule was first broken in America, and popular rule instituted.

The case for Democratic rule in religious organization was summed up in 1717 by a Colonial clergyman, John Wise, in a tract, *A Vindication of the Government of New England Churches.* By Wise's time the practice of vesting ecclesiastical authority in a few "elders" had been gradually abandoned in Colonial churches. The early Puritans, followers of John Calvin, had employed an elitist mode of church government, justified by their theocratic teachings. The Puritans held that true religion

38

is primary in the life of Christians; that authority is divinely prescribed for the care of man's spiritual and temporal needs in accord with God's will; that a few "elect of God" have a divine right to exercise authority; and that civil authority is subordinate to ecclesiastical authority, just as the needs of the immortal soul are superior to those of the mortal body. In the theocratic theory, the first duty of civil rulers is the care of religion and morals, under instructions from the church elders.

Though in the earliest Colonial settlements this doctrine, that authority is a monopoly of a religious elite, was in some form generally taken for granted, the Puritans found it most difficult to carry out in practice. Frequently the ruling elders disagreed among themselves about exactly what God's will prescribed. Frequently too those who likewise professed to be guided by the inner light of divine grace charge that the ruling elite confused God's will with their own interests. Under the circumstances, the practical difficulties of the theocratic scheme encouraged separatism. The opportunity to migrate was ever present for hardy souls willing to brave once again "the howling wilderness." After the first successful rebellion against theocratic rule led by Roger Williams (1602–1682), who protested against church interference in civil affairs and domination of the entire community by a self-chosen religious elite, it became common for discontented factions to break away from older communities and found new settlements more to their liking.

When members of these Protestant sects formed their churches, it was the custom to use the instrument of the "covenant." A church covenant was a contract prescribing the congregation's "discipline," the rules which each person, upon acceptance into membership, swore to abide by. For the exercise of church authority these congregations, which originated in protest against elite rule, quite naturally adopted, as the remaining alternative, the practice of making decisions by direct vote of the entire membership. It was this widely prevalent "congregational church discipline," where the church membership, in conformity with

39

Democratic principles, directly exercised the ecclesiastical authority binding on the congregation, that John Wise proposed to vindicate in his tract.

Members of Congregational churches readily applied the principles they had developed for governing their common religious affairs to other community affairs. Why not? When exercising the authority of other voluntary associations, social or economic, perhaps, the Colonists used the decision-making process most familiar to them. They ran their churches as they pleased, Democratically. They similarly adopted a Democratic process when exercising civil authority, which more often than not in frontier settlements was extralegal anyway. In theory the British Crown ruled, but actually, we have seen, in their village communities the Colonists ruled themselves.

The tendency for the decision-making process devised for voluntary groups to be used in exercising civil authority was encouraged by the practice of government agencies to assume responsibility for functions originally performed by voluntary associations. As communities became more firmly established and better organized, informal private associations yielded up their responsibilities to government bodies. Care of the poor and instruction in the schools are examples. At one time both functions were church functions; later local government took them over. When such functions were acquired by civil authorities, the public agencies, whether a school board, a welfare agency, a public works commission, or a park district, continued, quite understandably, to use the already established decision-making process. Thus was Democratic rule infiltrated into a governing system originally founded on elitist principles.

By the time of the American Revolution, the practice of making decisions binding on the members of the community by group discussion and vote had become, in the course of about a century, a habit deeply ingrained in Americans. It was to be expected that after the Declaration of Independence the new governments, successors to the volunteer citizens' committees and patriotic societies of the Revolution, would be constituted on principles of Democratic rule.

Since then the same pattern of Democratic development has persisted: every reform enacted to Democratize the exercise of governmental authority has been anticipated in the practice of voluntary associations, which have pioneered in the acceptance and use of a Democratic decision-making process.

5.

We have so far said that in many American communities the principles of popular self-government were firmly established before the Revolution. In fact it was those policies of the British Crown which had the effect of stripping the Colonists of the decision-making authority they customarily exercised that spurred American resistance to imperial rule. It was to be expected that after the Declaration of Independence attempts would be made to constitute the new state governments on Democratic principles. For just as the Democratic decision-making process was accepted for voluntary associations before it was adopted for exercising governmental authority, so was it used in local communities long before attempts were made to project Democratic principles to govern the exercise of authority at higher levels of organization.

This trend is strikingly evident in the movement to Democratize the state governments in the decades following the Revolution. In the eighteenth century many Americans understandably felt that the decision-making process used so extensively in local communities was not well suited for the state governments. Certainly it was unsuitable for the new general government. In fact the suggestion that the authority of the general government should be exercised according to Democratic principles was regarded by the founders of our Constitution as singularly radical and somewhat ridiculous, a form of patent political heresy. Why they felt this way is easy to understand.

Perhaps today, accustomed as we are to the telephone, the telegraph, and radio communication, and to rapid automobile, rail, and air transportation, it is difficult for us to imagine a situation where the central focus of American life was necessarily the local community, and very likely a small farming village at that, quite isolated, psychologically as well as physically, from the rest of the country. In this situation, most activity, not only political but social and economic as well, was conducted locally.

It was in such situations, to suit the needs of small farmers whose frame of life was a rude frontier community, that Democracy originated. Democratic beliefs were first articulated by plain men of the soil under the influence of frontier conditions. Democratic principles were first practiced in agrarian communites, self-contained, self-sufficient communities. Because Democracy became accepted by the American people long before this country was transformed into an industrialized, urbanized, continental nation, even today Democratic beliefs and principles still bear the stamp of the frontier village, a mark of fundamental contrast, incidentally, to European experience with Democracy.

In view of the origins of American Democracy, it is understandable why most early American leaders assumed that Democracy was not possible, even if desirable, above the level of the local community. In the early days of the Republic, for most Americans the state government was distant, with the capital city perhaps several days' hard ride away. The Federal government was little more than an idea nowhere embodied in the daily lives of American citizens. The center of all life was the local community.

So we find that Thomas Jefferson, ardent champion of Democracy though he was, believed that self-government and local

42

government were two sides of the same coin. He assumed that Democracy would thrive depending on the amount of governing authority exercised in the local community.

The aim of popular government, Jefferson held, is to serve the needs of the people. As servants and dutiful agents of the public, government officials should convert the popular desires into government policy. How can the people best make the government do their bidding? The more distant that government is from the people, Jefferson argued, the more difficult it is for the people to have their desires expressed in government policy. Where the relation between the public official and the citizen is direct and intimate, the popular will can be readily discerned, and the people can see to it that the public official serves the interests of the community. At the local level, therefore, popular self-government is most feasible. At the state level, where the principle of representation is required as well, Democratic rule is difficult, though Democratic principles should be utilized to the limit. But at the Federal level, Democracy is virtually impossible. Perhaps the general government can be prevented from serving as a tool for minority privilege, but never can it be converted into a fit instrument for popular rule. In nature and structure it is inherently un-Democratic. Jefferson therefore concluded that the authority of the local community, where Democratic rule is possible, should be supreme; minimum authority should be vested in the general government; the maximum should remain with the local community.

Later reformers sought to Democratize the Federal government, but only after Democratic reforms had already been achieved to some extent at the state level of government.

The movement to Democratize the state governments took the form of agitation for constitutional change, necessarily so. In this country from the beginning the tension of Democratic reform has been between constitutional principles and Democratic beliefs. Of course American Democracy for a century and a half

43

has developed within the context of our constitutional system. It has developed in spite of the hostile scheme concocted by the Federalists. We have seen that their deliberate aim was to prevent the people from speaking in a clear and decisive voice through the instrument of government. This aim was skillfully promoted by the Federalist formula of constitutional restraints. Institutional barriers against popular influence in governmental affairs were written into the United States Constitution and in state constitutions patterned after the same principles. Hence revisions in our constitutional arrangements have been required for the achievement of Democratic reforms. American Democrats have never repudiated the constitutional system, though they have condemned many elitist features of it and have demanded revisions to allow more popular participation in the exercise of authority. Hence as Democracy has advanced, constitutional principles have been revised to conform better to Democratic beliefs about the exercise of authority.

It is significant that the leadership for the first Democratic reform movement, and the impetus behind it, came from the newer Western regions of the states and of the country. In those states admitted to the Union after the Federal Constitution was adopted—such states as Kentucky, Tennessee, Ohio, Indiana, Illinois, Michigan, Wisconsin, for the most part carved out of the Northwest Territory—Democracy was never regarded as a heresy. In the states along the frontier, Democratic beliefs were, for reasons we shall see in a moment, enthusiastically espoused. Democratic principles were readily written into the new state constitutions, enabling the citizens to exert the greatest possible influence in governmental affairs. In the older states, conventions were called to rewrite the constitutions along more Democratic lines. In the decade of the 1820s, New York, Virginia, and Massachusetts convened constitutional conventions for this purpose. To the extent that Federalist principles had been abandoned in the state governments in favor of popular rule, this reform movement had borne fruit by 1830.

6.

It was during the period between Jefferson and Jackson that Democratic beliefs and principles became so widely accepted in this country that an American political ideology, Democratic in character, attracted the attention of foreign observers. The Jeffersonian Republicans, reacting against Federalism, launched a reform movement which swept the country during the first three decades of the century. But it was the achievement of the Jacksonian Democrats to enact the most vital reforms required for Democratic rule in the states. Andrew Jackson's election to the Presidency in 1828 symbolized victory in the first great struggle for Democratic reforms. It is understandable why Jackson's election marked a new era in American politics.

Before Jackson's election, the Federal government had been dominated by what was called the "Washington dynasty," the political leaders of the nation's capital. Presidential candidates had customarily been nominated by Congressional caucuses, operating quite independently of public opinion, and had been elected by an Electoral College without any popular mandate. But with Jackson this pattern changed. He was not an outstanding figure in Washington politics so much as he was a popular national leader, a military hero. He was also prominent in state politics and had a considerable reputation in the Western section of the country. His political strength lay outside Washington, in his mass appeal for the "common man."

Jackson too, like Jefferson, championed the interests of the small farmer, but Jackson's election signified the national triumph of the beliefs and principles of the settlers of the "new West." The West of Jefferson's day had become by the Jacksonian era part of the East. The new West was the Mississippi Valley basin. It differed from the earlier frontier regions in several notable respects. The settlers in the Mississippi regions had strong nationalist sentiment, compared with the established residents in the older states. The settlers had broken the ties with their native states but had not yet acquired a strong sense of state patriotism. Many had lived in Federal territories before statehood was granted and were accustomed to look to the nation's capitol for political favor. They were less parochial in outlook and their national allegiance was stronger than was the case with the citizens of the original states.

Also in the attitudes of the settlers of the new West equalitarian sentiment was especially strong. The leveling influence of the frontier precluded any vested interests or established classes. Commerce was undeveloped and monetary wealth was of little importance in a frontier community where there was not much to market. The frontier compelled an equality of merit of a special sort. No man was another man's better. All were farmers searching for land and an opportunity to build a new life by their sweat and toil.

In the absence of any recognized "natural" aristocracy, the distinction between those who exercised authority and those over whom it was exercised was virtually obliterated. Everyone participated in the process of governing. Public officials were unavoidably drawn from the ranks of the "common people"—the only people in a frontier community.

The ideal of the new West was that of the "self-made man"— who took advantage of the opportunity that nature provided and through industry and skill accomplished practical tasks. The prime job on the frontier was to convert the wilderness into a habitable country. What was admired was a person's ability to perform this job. His family, his "station," his wealth, his learning, these counted for little compared with his prowess in the frontier arts.

On the other hand, what the Western farmer feared and hated most was "privilege"—advantage for a special few at the expense of others. It was popularly believed that the real producer of wealth in society is the farmer. He extracts wealth from the land.

Those who distribute goods and perform services, those who engage in trade and banking, are not "productive." They do not labor. They produce nothing but consume much; they are social parasites who profit from the labor of others. Commerce and banking were quite naturally identified with the Eastern "interests," a wealthy minority who acquired their substance, it was assumed, through some sort of special, and vicious, privilege. No decent man could earn a fortune in gold.

Here the interests of the Western settler coincided with those of craftsmen—"mechanics"—and farmers elsewhere in the country. All worked for a living, and most were self-employed "laborers." It was these plain people, enjoying no particular social or economic distinction, who rallied to support Jackson as the defender of the "People" against the "Interests," symbolized by the National Bank.

As a matter of fact, prior to the Jacksonian reforms commercial interests did receive privileges from government. The legislatures, the supposed link between the electorate and the government, dominated political affairs at the state and also at the Federal levels of government. The legislature controlled most public offices, either through the practice of nominating candidates in caucus or through actual legislative election or appointment. At the same time "representatives" tended to be drawn from the "natural aristocracy." They were inclined to be unresponsive to popular desires and susceptible to influence from well-placed special interests, notably banking and commercial interests seeking preferment from government. Hence the popular influence in governmental affairs was remote and indirect at best. Even qualified voters, after casting their ballots for their legislative representatives, exerted scant influence. The Congress especially was regarded as a stronghold of minority privilege, jeopardizing the welfare of the states and their citizens.

Consequently we find that the aim of the Jacksonian Democrats was to make government—including the Federal government—subject to popular control; to see to it that government was run for the benefit of a majority of the American people rather than a minority—for the farmers rather than the commercial interests. The immediate problem for the Jacksonians was how to break the hold of special interests on government officials by curbing the influence of the corrupt legislators. How to make public officials responsible to a majority of the people?

The Jacksonian ideal was the free expression of the desires of the people in all government affairs—in all three branches of government. The goal was to make every public official, whether a legislator, an administrator, or a judge, a dutiful public servant, obedient to the will of a majority of citizens.

For the Jacksonian Democrats, concerned as they were about the hold of an unresponsive legislature on the government, the practice of direct election of the executive officials was most important. By popular election, the position of the executive could be strengthened at the expense of the legislature, for then the executive would have a mandate from the voters. With this electoral support, he could exercise control over appointments and could use his veto power to curb legislative action. The scheme was to make the executive independent of the legislature and directly responsible to the electorate. The Jacksonian conception of the executive was of a strong and independent, popularly elected leader to serve as a check on the legislature and the courts, both regarded as easy prey to influence from special interests.

It was in this pattern that Andrew Jackson set the character of the Presidential office, not to encourage the expansion of Federal powers but to redress the balance among the three branches. In fact several of Jackson's famous vetoes were of bills to expand Federal powers, bills which, in his view, granted privileges to special interest at public expense. Jackson felt quite justified in asserting the authority of his office against the Congress and the courts for he regarded himself, with some justification, as a representative of a majority of the people, defending the public interest.

7.

What the Jacksonian Democrats generally protested against was elite rule founded on Federalist principles. What they wanted was for government to serve the interests of a majority of the people. To this end they demanded that the privileges enjoyed by a few be extended to the many, so that all could participate equally in political affairs. This desire for greater equality of opportunity has supplied the impetus for Democratic reform in this country.

From time to time as the Democratic movement has advanced and matured, the demand for political equality has taken on a somewhat different character. Here again the pattern of acceptance is set by the direction of movement: from voting, to popular election, to officeholding, to direct participation in the decision-making processes of government. This pattern of acceptance of Democratic principles reveals a kind of logic of development.

In the strategy to equalize political opportunity, the initial move by the reformers was to demand a "democratic franchise" —universal suffrage for all adult, white males. In a scheme of popular government, where the public official is separated from the citizenry, the vote is of course vitally important. It is the link between the citizen and the government. It is the means by which the citizen can express his desires in electing public officials and can impose sanctions on them for the conduct of public affairs.

Prior to the adoption of the Democratic franchise, religious qualifications for voting were not uncommon and property qualifications were quite general. Also, the franchise was "restricted," so that a person who was qualified to vote in one election might not be qualified to vote in some other. For example, many persons who could vote in elections for state assemblymen were not

49

qualified to vote for members of the upper house of the state legislature.

Adoption of the Democratic franchise meant that such religious qualifications for voting as still existed were abolished, and property qualifications were abolished too. It also meant a single set of voting qualifications. If a person could vote in any election, he could vote in all. This Democratic franchise had become widely accepted, as a result of new states adopting constitutions and older states amending theirs, by the 1830s. Many years later reformers succeeded in extending the suffrage to persons without regard to race, color, or previous condition of servitude, at least in law if not in practice. Woman suffrage came finally in the years of the First World War.

Franchise reform opened the way for other demands for equalizing political privileges. One was the privilege to be elected to public office. Before the Jacksonian Democrats had done their work, a significant distinction was drawn between the voter and the public official who was supposed to represent him. Public office was largely monopolized by members of the "natural aristocracy," the few persons of outstanding wealth and education. In part this was because qualifications for holding office were set so much higher than voting qualifications that many citizens were ineligible. What the Democratic reformers demanded was "equal qualifications for office": generally, that any eligible voter be qualified to hold any post of public trust and responsibility; specifically, that any voter in a constituency be entitled to represent the district in the legislature.

Closely connected with this was the demand for popular election of all public officials. Until the Democratic reforms were achieved, executive and judicial offices for the most part were not elective. The officials were appointed or indirectly elected by a legislature. Democratic reformers insisted that the principle of popular election, already accepted for the lower house of the legislature, be extended to include executive and judicial offices as well as the upper house. They wished to make every public official periodically accountable to a majority of the voters.

Such reforms, calling for equal qualifications for office and popular election of public officials, were adopted many years ago for state governments. Most American voters are now qualified to hold state and local offices. But at the national level, where the Federalists embalmed the distinction between voting and officeholding in the Constitution, these reforms, as others, have never been fully achieved.

In fact it was long after Democratic reforms were widely accepted for the government of states that any serious attempt was made to Democratize the Federal government. This attempt, despite the efforts of many reform movements, has been something less than successful.

At the present time many millions of American voters are not qualified to serve in the House of Representatives or the Senate, let alone the Presidency. It was less than fifty years ago that the practice of popular election of United States Senators was finally accepted. Only two members of the Federal executive are elected, and then only indirectly by the Electoral College. Most candidates for state and local offices are now nominated by the voters in a direct party primary election, but not candidates for the Presidency and the Vice Presidency of the United States. They are picked at national conventions where delegates may plainly ignore the desires of the voters. And even though generations of American political leaders have entered into a conspiracy to prevent the Electoral College system from working the way the Philadelphia Convention intended, it is still possible for a candidate to be elected President of the United States while his opponent receives a majority of the votes cast. It is not only possible; it has happened. It could not happen in the election of a mayor or a state governor, but it can happen in a Presidential election. And of course all Federal judges are appointed by the chief executive with Senate confirmation, without regard for the desires of the electorate.

The pattern of Democratic development, for elite rule to be displaced by Democratic rule, is general in American political life, perhaps, but far from complete.

8.

But the story of the Democratic movement does not end with the triumph of the Jacksonian Democrats. The general character of American state governments was then set along Democratic lines, as earlier the character of local governments had been. But from Jackson's day to the present, reformers have attempted to gain ever wider acceptance of Democratic principles. These attempts have met with some successes as well as many failures.

During the middle decades of the nineteenth century, Jacksonian Democracy was predominant. Democracy in America had arrived, as Alexis de Tocqueville testified. Democratic beliefs were so widely accepted that few who doubted them dared to state their views frankly in public, and certainly not if they desired to participate in American political life.

Yet during this period there was slight advance in Democratic practice. The movement to Democratize state governments had borne fruit. The serious attempt to Democratize the Federal government was yet to come. Democrats were still content that Federal offices be in the safe hands of other Democrats, so that state governments could proceed to serve the needs of the people without interference or handicap from Washington.

In fact during this period the energies of most American political leaders were absorbed by the two great issues of the Civil War: slavery and union. Should men own other men as chattel? What should the nature of the union be? For years these issues were treated separately; a states' rightist might also be anti-slave. But then the issues acquired a sectional significance, dividing the North and the South.

However, during this period, after the triumph of Jacksonian Democracy, for the first time the problems of Democratic theory and practice were seriously probed and debated. These discussions were largely inspired by the great controversy over slavery and union. Henry David Thoreau and John C. Calhoun framed and explored the central issue in Democratic theory: What is the relation between majority rule and minority rights? This issue depended on the Democratic doctrine of consent: Democratic rule is legitimate only so long as the ruled consent to the authority exercised over them. In the practice of local communities, this problem of consent was never particularly troublesome. But when placed in the context of state—and Federal—government, founded on constitutions, the problem posed immense and perplexing difficulties.

In his *Essay on Civil Disobedience* (1849) Thoreau, imbued with abolitionist sentiments and a Puritan conscience, argued that a majority has no right to rule a minority against their consent. No man can determine the rightness of another man's conduct. Only the individual can decide for himself moral questions, be they political or otherwise. As a moral agent, the individual is sovereign.

In his *Disquisition on Government* (1850) Calhoun, as devoted to the Democratic tradition as he was loyal to the South with its "peculiar institution," argued that majority rule can work in practice only so long as the majority's decision benefits the entire community. To the extent that a numerical majority equates its special interests with the authority of government, rule cannot be Democratic, for to that extent the minority will refuse consent to the government's action. Calhoun offered his principle of "concurrent majorities" as the remedy for this practical difficulty of Democratic rule. By this principle any important minority interest would have a veto on a government action.

The main forum for the great controversy was the United States Senate. Here men like Calhoun, Henry Clay, Jefferson Davis, and Daniel Webster not only debated the issues of the day. They also discussed the principles and practices of Democratic rule. But the grave issues which divided the North and the South were not settled, unfortunately, by words and votes.

53

The controversy over slavery and union split the Democratic tradition into the "states rights" and the "national democracy" wings, eventually identified with the Southern and Northern causes, respectively. Southern apologists, who inherited Thomas Jefferson's agrarianism, insisted that slavery, like so many other matters the Federal government sought to control, was properly a question for local jurisdictions to determine. Abe Lincoln of Illinois, a proponent of "national democracy," contended that slavery was a matter of national concern—a nation could not survive half slave and half free. The matter should be determined by a majority of the American people, and the Federal government should implement the nation's policy.

In the carnage of the War between the States the great experiment in popular government survived its most severe trial. The North, of course, emerged victorious. At least the nation, if not its Democratic heritage, was preserved intact. The Democratic movement did not recover from the shock of the Civil War until long after Reconstruction had spent its course. Then Democratic beliefs were reformulated, and Democratic practices revised, adapted to the radically different circumstances of late-nineteenth-century life. These circumstances provoked new crises to be weathered in the development of the American Democratic tradition. In a sense these crises have not yet receded into American history. Democratic theory and practice designed for the frontier community have not yet been suitably redesigned to meet the needs of urban communities dispersed over a vast continental nation.

9.

The decades after the Civil War witnessed an accelerated expansion of the nation, rapidly and radically transforming the character of American life. The population of the United States between 1850 and 1900 jumped from 23 to 75 millions, largely because of the huge influx of European immigrants. As the Far West was settled and the Western boundaries were pushed to the Pacific Ocean, America became a continental nation. Railroads were built and telegraph lines were strung, enabling rapid transcontinental communication and travel. In the short space of a few decades manufacture and commerce on a mass scale for a national market appeared on the American scene. Eastern mill towns became, in less than a generation, thriving metropolitan centers of industry. This country was becoming the industrialized, urbanized, continental nation that it is today. American life was being integrated economically, as the war had integrated it politically.

For above all it was an age of enormous economic expansion for the American nation. This expansion did not result from "natural causes." It was made possible by the modern business corporation, a creation of American governments.

In the first half of the nineteenth century the typical form of business enterprise was the individual firm or private partnership, often a family enterprise. By such small-scale businesses most commerce and manufacture were conducted. The exception was the limited-liability joint stock company (such as the Bank of the United States) chartered by a special act of a legislature. But "corporations" enjoying government franchises were few in number before the states passed general incorporation acts in the decades around the Civil War. Under these acts any group of persons could, by complying with certain standard statutory requirements, organize a company with the legal advantages of chartered corporations; the company was "incorporated" under state laws. This collectivized form of business enterprise, privileged by government, proved popular when the country's economy was being expanded and industrialized. A small owner-operated firm could not undertake enterprises requiring vast outlays of capital and big payrolls; large-scale corporate enter-

55

prise was almost imperative for the development of such industries as railroads, steel, mining, oil, banking, insurance, shipping, and utilities.

Corporate enterprise flourished and the great industrial empires were founded in a congenial political climate. The American constitutional system encouraged large-scale enterprise and public policy stimulated corporate growth. Under the Constitution, the Federal government was vested with authority to regulate interstate commerce, but any regulation of economic affairs in the interest of public health, safety, or welfare fell within the "police-power" jurisdiction of the several states. However, the regulatory legislation enacted by the states was with fair consistency ruled unconstitutional by the Supreme Court of the United States after the Court invented the doctrine that a corporation is a person entitled to judicial protection against unconstitutional laws. Moreover no state alone was a match for a giant corporation, which was capitalized at millions of dollars in stock held by hundreds of absentee owners, and which conducted a network of operations throughout the entire country. At the same time, government policy in the form of tax advantages, bankruptcy proceedings, legal exemptions, direct subsidies, protective tariffs, public works, and government contracts served to grant additional privileges to corporate enterprise that no small unincorporated business could equally enjoy. In fact a small company, family owned and operated, could not compete successfully with a giant corporation engaged in the mass production and distribution of goods on a national scale. Government policies favoring large-scale corporate enterprise, combined with government inaction in controlling economic affairs in the public interest, allowed the "captains of industry" to amass great wealth and great power, such as had never before been known in this country. The few aggressive, ambitious men who guided the destinies of huge corporate interests acquired this wealth and power not simply because they were endowed with remarkable skill and energy in collectivized processes of producing and distributing goods and services. They also had unusual ability to manipulate for their private advantage, with callousness as well as shrewdness, other persons and things, including government.

The radically altered complexion of American politics following the Civil War made possible the "Gilded Age." For a generation the Southern agrarian interests were neutralized as a force in national politics; Northerners dominated. The "freesoil" farmers of the Middle West, nourished in the traditions of Jackson and Lincoln, were becoming an increasingly important political force, but their era of domination was still to come. It was the corporate business interests of the industrial, urban Northeast who exerted the greatest influence in national politics. But in this section of the country the great bulk of the population who labored in the shops and mills and offices were not politically effective. A gulf separated the voters from their government. In metropolitan centers political life was controlled by the leaders of party organizations. These political "machines," thriving on unassimilated immigrants and underprivileged workers, well oiled by patronage and graft, were headed by politicians whose profession it was to buy and sell political influence for a profit. Business was brisk and lucrative with the captains of industry whose fortunes depended on special privileges which only government could grant. Governmental officials were enlisted, as mercenaries, in the struggle to exploit American society for the benefit of private interests. The political system constituted on Democratic principles to serve the needs of agrarian communities was perverted to serve the special interests of a few whose great wealth enabled them to purchase political favor at the expense of the public. The public was truly damned.

For many millions of citizens the dream of America as the land of opportunity, free of vested privilege, faded with the rise of corporate enterprise. In the midst of enormous newly created industrial wealth, poverty was the lot of the many who labored in the factory and on the farm. Labor was regarded as just another commodity to be bought in the market for as little as the traffic would bear. More and more immigrants were imported from Europe to work in the factories, crowded into the slums of mill towns to work long hours under miserable conditions for pitiable wages. American citizens were used as mere pawns in a struggle for greater wealth and power. The glaring fact was that American life had become characterized by inequality of opportunity. The land of promise was becoming a land of the privileged few and the dispossessed many, socially and economically as well as politically. Democracy was being displaced by plutocracy.

10.

The betrayal of the American dream did not go unchallenged. Farmers, factory workers, white-collar employees, merchants, professional men—members of the great American middle class—all suffered from the consequences of the reign of corporate wealth. Their economic and social status was being undermined. Worst of all, their political privileges were being denied. As the cherished Democratic principles were corrupted, tensions within American society were aggravated. Once again spokesmen for the "common man" charged that government was being used as a tool to serve the special interests of a few at the expense of a majority of the people. "Steal a loaf of bread and go to jail; steal a railroad and go to the Senate." Against the changing order of life, where an economically privileged few were coming to dominate American society, arose the movements of protest, inspired by nostalgia for a paradise lost.

These protest movements of the late nineteenth century reflected a variety of attitudes—social and sectional—and took on rather different forms. But all called for drastic reforms in the new condition of American life. The Grangers, the Knights of Labor, the Single Taxers, the Free Silverites, the Bellamy Nationalists, the Populists—all these movements shared a common goal. It was a radical goal, perhaps—to restore equality of opportunity by ending special privilege for a wealthy few—but it certainly was not a goal alien to America. The principle of equality has suffused the Democratic movement since its inception. What these reform groups wanted to do was to restore on a national scale a condition of social, economic, and political equality which characterized American life before the Civil War.

How to equalize opportunity? This question divided the protest movements. Some, like the Bellamy Nationalists, advocated a root-and-branch reconstruction of the system. Others, like the Single Taxers, demanded changes in certain public policies, without sweeping modifications in the system. Throughout the era of the protest movements, a gradual transformation in thought about the nature of the problem of reform and its solution was under way. Familiar conceptions inherited from an agrarian society were abandoned in favor of newer conceptions suited to the changes that were occurring in American life. For example, in the earlier agrarian society the problem of equalizing the distribution of wealth could be, and for the most part was, resolved by government aiding the farmers to increase their production. So long as the consumer and the producer were one and the same, wealth distribution could be equalized in this way. In the new industrial society, governments continued to aid producers of wealth by granting special privileges to corporate enterprise. But with highly collectivized industrial enterprise and specialization of task, with absentee ownership and a controlled market, wealth production was separated from consumption of goods by a great void. As the share of a few increased, the share of the many in the wealth produced declined. In such a society resolving the problem of equalizing wealth had to be tackled at the point of distribution as well as production, and in novel ways. Government had to regulate private enterprise in the public interest. Government had to provide needed services for the public to consume. In an urban, industrialized, collectivized society, where economic interdependence is the rule rather than the exception, government must assume new functions and play new roles. Similarly with the problem of equalizing social and political privileges. The old formulas no longer worked and the old conceptions no longer applied. A new program of Democratic reform had to be devised.

With the Progressive movement, it was. The movements of protest matured as they mounted over the years. Few achieved their immediate goals, and most died out after a brief history of glory. But eventually these many varied efforts to enact Democratic reforms culminated in the Progressive movement, which reached the peak of its influence in the years around the First World War.

The Progressives were animated by a vision: a prosperous industrial nation of urban dwellers with a pattern of life of a Democratic community—that pattern which Jefferson, Jackson, and Lincoln sought to institute, cultivate, and protect. The Progressives demanded that Democratic principles be elaborated and extended to pervade social and economic affairs and, most of all, political affairs at the national as well as the local and state levels of government. In a Democratic society, government should be an effective instrument for serving the needs of a majority of the people. Democratic government should be used to enact those changes in economic and social affairs desired by a majority of the citizens.

Not all the reforms advocated by the Progressives were achieved, Teddy Roosevelt's "New Nationalism" and Woodrow Wilson's "New Freedom" notwithstanding. In fact the Progressives were least successful at the national level of government. For example, they failed, as other Democratic reform movements before them had, to abolish the practice of judicial review. But the reforms achieved as a result of the Progressives' effort brought about notable changes in American life: extensive government regulation of business in the public interest, social and labor legislation, woman suffrage, graduated income tax, direct election of United States Senators, and the "direct democracy" reforms—such as the party primary, the initiative, the referendum, and the recall. These were most fully articulated by Progressives like "Fighting Bob" LaFollette, Hiram Johnson, George Norris, Teddy Roosevelt, and their kindred political spirits. And it was through the hard work of the Progressives in the cities and the states that such reforms were finally enacted. The American political system, particularly in the areas of local and state government, is today constituted along more Democratic lines, and today better serves the needs of the American people, thanks to the labor of a generation of Progressive reformers.

Democratic reform was stymied during the hectic years of the First World War. The Progressive movement, its work still not finished, failed to survive the stress of the war years and the severe reaction of the twenties. Peace and prosperity—what appeared to be "normalcy"—were back, to dull American appetites for reform until the crash of 1929. Early Progressive leaders died broken men, like Bob LaFollette; or perhaps they turned down the easy path of respectable conservatism, like Hiram Johnson; or possibly they weathered the drought until the rains of the New Deal fell once again on American political soil, bringing new life to Democratic reform. George Norris was among these old Progressives who lived to see the new successes.

Solid advances in Democratizing American life were made during the desperate years of the thirties, as the Roosevelt administrations strained to lift the nation out of the great depression. To relieve the distress of farmers, unemployment of workers, and paralysis of business, the New Deal launched temporary, stop-gap, emergency programs. It also enacted long overdue economic and social reforms. For the first time in our history, the national government frankly assumed responsibility for providing greater equality of economic opportunity for the underprivileged members of our society, for protecting the plain citizen against catastrophes beyond his power to avoid, and for supplying the public with needed services that private enterprise and other governments were unable or unwilling to provide.

Political reforms were overshadowed by the social and economic crisis, but they were not ignored. The successes of the New Deal are symbolized by the Tennessee Valley Authority, one of its finest achievements and the realization of the dream of one old Progressive—George Norris. The TVA harnessed the resources of a river valley and put these to work for the people of a region. It made possible low-cost electric power and also enriched the lives of millions of citizens by programs for flood control, wildlife conservation, recreational facilities, navigation, and land use. But most important, the TVA introduced a method of administering the authority of the national government that enormously increased citizen participation in public affairs. In his testament, *TVA: Democracy on the March* (1944), David Lilienthal tells the story of how the Democratic decision-making process became accepted and was used in another area of American life. It is a story which certainly deserves a place in the annals of Democratic reform.

Still today there is, of course, on the agenda of American Democracy much unfinished business for future reform movements to transact. In many vital areas of our national life elite rule prevails and Democratic principles are not yet, centuries after their design, fully accepted. In no area of American life is this so glaringly evident as in the conduct of the national government. Examples of violations of Democratic principles in the decision-making processes used in the three branches of the government are too numerous to mention. Examples are fewer, though still disturbingly numerous, in the conduct of local and state governmental affairs, where the lead of voluntary community groups like the Westside Civic Improvement League has yet to be followed.

Even so, over the years the Democratic process of decision-making has become ever more widely accepted; it has been refined, elaborated, adapted, extended; it has been applied in more and more areas of public life. Perhaps the doctrines of popular sovereignty, political equality, and majority rule are not much talked about by our fellow citizens, at least not in theoretical terms. But Democratic precepts based on them are followed from custom and habit in the daily life of virtually every citizen. Though Democracy in America has not yet arrived, it is well on its way.

II.

In Europe the Democratic movement developed more recently and its course has been markedly influenced by American experience. When Alexis de Tocqueville first reported to the French people that Democracy in America was here to stay and really not too bad after all, European political leaders ridiculed the American system. Democratic rule was with remarkable uniformity condemned by nineteenth-century political leaders of varied outlooks, the most scathing terms being used by British Liberals.

The British ruling class which rose to power after the Glorious Revolution succeeded in denying political privileges to prosperous members of the new middle class created by the Industrial Revolution until the so-called "Great Reform" of 1832. The Reform Bill, enacted by a Whig ministry of Earl Grey after a period of grim crisis, abolished the "rotten boroughs" and other abuses of the electoral system which enabled the landed aristocracy to dominate British political life. Also by this act, which set relatively high property qualifications for voting, the franchise was granted to affluent business and professional people, the profit-takers from industrial enterprise. Not so fortunate were the common people who neither owned nor rented property of substantial value. Indeed by the 1832 reform only a few hundred thousand voters, virtually all prosperous residents of borough constituencies, were added to the rolls: an aristocracy of land gave way to an aristocracy of industrial wealth.

In the years following, spokesmen for the new working class, the employees of middle-class businessmen, agitated for further franchise reform without avail. The Chartist movement, the first mass Democratic movement in Britain, was formed to secure extension of the privileges gained in 1832 by members of the middle class to the common people. In the 1840s many thousands of Britishers signed the "People's Charter" petitioning Parliament for electoral reform. The famous "six points" called for such radical changes as universal manhood suffrage, equal electoral districts, secret ballot, annual elections, abolition of property qualifications for public office, and payment of salaries to members of Parliament. But the movement proved abortive. It was regarded by middle-class leaders as dangerously subversive of British institutions and was forcibly, in fact brutally and ruthlessly, crushed by a British Government firmly in the control of middle-class Liberals.

It was not until Benjamin Disraeli, the Tory Democrat, secured passage of the franchise-reform bill of 1867 that members of the British working class, the skilled craftsmen in the boroughs, were first granted the privilege of voting in Parliamentary elections. Other acts followed, extending the franchise to more and more British subjects. By the Representation of the People Act of 1918, some women were allowed to vote; the "Equal Franchise" Act of 1928 removed the remaining restrictions on woman suffrage. While less than 4 per cent of the British population were allowed to vote in 1832 (during the heyday of Jacksonian Democracy in America), today more than 60 per cent of the British people enjoy the suffrage. But it was not until 1945, when a British Labour Government passed an act based on the principle "one person, one vote," that a Democratic franchise was finally accepted in Great Britain. By this act, "plural voting," the practice which allowed a person to cast two ballots in the same election if he held certain university degrees or owned property in a second constituency, was abolished, as was the "restricted franchise," which prevented persons qualified to vote in Parliamentary elections from voting in local elections because of property qualifications. Significantly enough, it was the Tories who took the first important step in the direction of a Democratic franchise and the Socialists, speaking for the urban industrial workers, who were eventually responsible for Democratizing the British political system, over the frenetic opposition of middle-class Liberals, ever true to their belief in elite rule.

On the Continent, Democracy has traditionally been a minor political force. In the United States and Great Britain, political life has not been seriously disrupted in recent times by disagreement over the character of the regime; on this question, a consensus is shared by all political groups. But not so in other countries. Continental Europeans in particular have engaged in bitter and violent controversy over such fundamental issues as the status of the monarchy, of the church, and of property. European proponents of Democracy, controversialists too, have been united less by allegiance to a set of political practices than by concern to propagate a creed. In the absence of functioning systems of Democratic rule and in the presence of virile traditions of elite rule, Continental Europeans have characteristically entertained a conception of Democracy as an ideal goal somehow to be realized, rather than as a method of decision-making to be somewhat improved and extended.

Until the late nineteenth century, no political system on the Continent could in any significant way be described as Democratic; Democratic principles simply were not accepted. The possible exception was Switzerland, where the local governing unit, the commune, dates from the Helvetic Republic of 1798. Following the Napoleonic Wars, a system which allowed some popular control was gradually developed in Swiss cantons, a development accelerated after the adoption of the Swiss Federal Constitution in 1848, when the principle of universal manhood suffrage was adopted.

In France the Democratic dream proclaimed during the Revolution was stillborn. For a hundred years, one system of elite rule succeeded another. Finally after the Franco-Prussian War in the 1870s, the Second Empire was overthrown and the Third Republic was established. It provided for a system of parliamentary government superficially resembling the British system. In Italy a similar development occurred, though in neither France nor Italy was popular influence in governmental affairs an actuality. In the Scandinavian and Low Countries, political systems approximating British experience and partly incorporating Democratic principles in the exercise of authority gradually gained some acceptance by the period of the First World War.

But in Central and Eastern Europe, Democratic sentiment was nowhere strong and experience with functioning Democratic systems was, at most, scant.

12.

Nevertheless, down through the First World War it seemed that the "irresistible movement of Democracy" was sweeping everything else aside. Popular rule seemed to be supplanting aristocratic rule everywhere. The war was ostensibly fought, by Americans at least, as President Wilson declared, "to make the world safe for Democracy." The world was made "safe" by the victory of the Allied powers, which added credence for the popular belief that Democracy and progress go hand in hand. The Armistice heralded an era of experimentation with popular government in Europe. Old regimes were overthrown and new governments to some extent constituted on Democratic principles were set up. The principles were gaining acceptance, or so it seemed.

Actually they were not, for the practices did not follow. In countries like Germany these experiments soon failed, as the pattern of political conduct reverted to elitist standards. One by one the postwar regimes fell from power, some by their own weight, to be replaced by dictatorships. In Russia, the Bolsheviks established a Communist regime, setting a fashion in dictatorial rule. In Italy, the Fascists led by Mussolini converted an enfeebled parliamentary regime into a totalitarian dictatorship ruled by a party elite. Later in Germany the Nazis did likewise. Anti-Democratic movements thrived throughout the interlude between the two World Wars.

By the time the Second World War broke out with Hitler's invasion of Poland, Democracy was everywhere in the world on the defensive, trying to fend off the attacks from totalitarian movements, whether of the Communist, Fascist, or Nazi variety. Even in the United States and Great Britain, strongholds of twentieth-century Democracy, totalitarianism posed a menacing threat. Only twenty years after the Armistice, it seemed that progress went hand in hand with elite rule—what's more, a most extreme kind of elite rule.

But out of the ordeal of the Second World War the United States and Great Britain emerged with their political systems still intact. The integrity of Democratic beliefs and the vitality of Democratic principles may have been damaged; the forms of rule remained, apparently unshaken. After the hostilities were over, in many countries experimentation with popular government began anew. Within the past decade substantial advances in developing working systems of popular government have been made in some Continental countries. But Soviet Russia, too, survived the trial of war. In Central and Eastern Europe the new regimes, precariously founded and plagued by crises, were soon destroyed and replaced by Communist dictatorships. In France, Italy, Germany, and other European countries, parliamentary regimes instituted after the end of the war are still functioning. Even these regimes are not yet firmly founded. The period of test to see whether they can withstand the assaults of elitist movements from within and without is not at an end.

So today we find the Democratic movement confronted

throughout the world by a formidable totalitarian enemy. Soviet Communism, the most widely prevalent and virile contemporary form of elite rule, has already become entrenched in many countries, and not only European countries. In all parts of the world strong Communist movements are active, threatening popular as well as reactionary regimes. Today we find Democracy and Communism embroiled in a titanic struggle for the hearts and minds of the people of the world.

Another political force of major proportions in Europe as elsewhere in the world, a movement which, like Democracy, is firmly anti-Communist, is Roman Catholicism. With the rise of totalitarian dictatorship in this century, the Catholic movement has become not weaker but stronger. It has become an even more significant movement politically than it was a half century ago.

It would appear that Catholicism is a natural ally for Democracy in the world-wide struggle against Communism. But a question disturbing some minds is whether Catholicism is a friend or enemy of Democracy, as we have come to think of it here in the United States. Catholicism is no doubt incompatible with Communism. But is it at all compatible with Democracy?

The first step in answering this question is to get clear what Catholicism means in our world today.

Chapter Three

THE CATHOLIC TRADITION

I.

What is Catholicism?

In formulating an authentic conception of Catholic teachings of political significance, we are again, as we were in our task of describing Democracy, faced with a curious situation. Exactly what the teachings of the Roman Catholic Church are is not a simple and easy question to answer. But in this quest we do have more reliable signposts to mark our path than we did in our search for an authentic conception of Democracy.

Though much confusion surrounds the answer to this question, it is significant that this confusion is mainly in the minds of non-Catholics. It results from certain popular misconceptions about the role of the Church in political affairs and about the relation between the Church's officialdom and the lay communicants. Let us clear up these quite unnecessary misconceptions and set matters straight about what Catholic teachings are.

It is a mistake to assume that a proposal espoused by a Catholic is prescribed by the Church as part of its official program. After all, the Roman Church includes many millions of members. But some rabid anti-Catholics have made this error of equating the proposals sponsored by one or a few Catholics with the "orthodox" teachings of the Church. A notable offender on this score has been the American Protestant writer Paul Blanshard; I mentioned him earlier as the author of recent books and magazine articles attacking the Church. Morris Rubin, the editor of the *Progressive Magazine,* once remarked to me that "anti-Catholicism" seems to be "the anti-Semitism of the American Liberal." Certainly Blanshard's virulent attacks against the Church are reminiscent of the hysterical anti-Semitic propaganda that the Nazis engaged in. In his *American Freedom and Catholic Power* (1949) Blanshard goes so far as to impute to Catholicism certain teachings which the Church has never endorsed, in fact views which prominent Catholic officials have explicitly disavowed, even condemned. What Blanshard mistakenly assumes to be "Catholicism" is for the most part, it seems, what Blanshard opposes rather than what Catholics favor.

We should be extremely careful to avoid confusing a political view expressed by some Catholics with the Church's theory of practice for the simple reason that the Church officially endorses no political doctrine or program or movement. Strictly speaking, there is no "orthodox" political belief which a Catholic communicant must accept as a requirement of his religious faith. Catholic dogma does not concern political matters. The doctrine or Papal infallibility, which was first declared in 1870 after many months of debate at the Twentieth Ecumenical Vatican Council, extends only to "questions of faith and morals." Even then, a belief has the status of dogma only when the Pope, as the "spiritual head of the Church Universal," has issued an *ex cathedra* pronouncement on the question. On such questions, Catholic communicants are obliged to accept the declared belief as dogma. Failure to do so invites discipline from the Church, including the extreme sanction of excommunication, the Church's ultimate "spiritual sword." But a Catholic is subject to Church discipline only on a question of faith and morals.

On other questions, including political questions, we find no official Catholic beliefs. Indeed for every political view advanced by a Catholic, there is no doubt another Catholic who rejects it. Some of the most severe and incisive criticism of political causes seeming to have Catholic auspices have actually come from other Catholics.

At the same time, members of the Church hierarchy do, of course, issue pronouncements on political questions. A prominent Church dignitary, perhaps even the head of the hierarchy, may grant or withhold his blessings from a political cause. But Papal pronouncements on such matters are "guiding" only, as statements of the foremost Catholic teacher of the day. As is so often the case, while a teacher may teach, the student may not learn.

The fact is that within the Church hierarchy, as well as the lay Catholic community, there is widespread disagreement on many political questions, just as on others there is an impressive consensus. This complicated unity in diversity is not at all puzzling, provided one understands how the massive organization of the Roman Church functions in resolving differences among its vast membership.

The process by which a Papal pronouncement is obtained on a disputed question is involved and deliberate. It is analogous to the American judicial process by which a Supreme Court ruling on an undecided question of constitutional law is obtained. When an issue is raised, lay and ecclesiastical Catholic leaders undertake discussion of it in an effort to resolve the differences of opinion. What is under debate is the bearing of Catholic teachings on the issue. The more stubborn issues are referred up through the levels of the hierarchy, perhaps from the parish ultimately to the Papal Court. There Vatican officials consider the question further until a decision is arrived at. Then the Pope may make a public statement on the question, perhaps in the form of an "encyclical letter" addressed to the Church's faithful. Once a Papal pronouncement has been made, each member of the hierarchy—especially the bishop—is responsible for interpreting and applying the Church's instructions for the congregation under his jurisdiction. This process of resolving differences within the

Church is concluded only after exhaustive examination of the question at issue. The process, which is not necessarily a formal one at all, may take years, even decades, before it is concluded by a Papal pronouncement.

Let us bear in mind, therefore, that a Catholic must accept no political belief as dogma. At the same time, on many political matters Catholic leaders do share a consensus, perhaps signified by a Papal pronouncement. Indeed we find that Catholics rather generally accept as "sound Catholic teachings" the political beliefs enunciated by the Papacy and propagated by high churchmen. These beliefs are supposed to be not only compatible with Christian dogma but also warrantedly derived from the Church's religious teachings. However, such acceptance does not depend on Papal fiat; no religious requirement is involved. The acceptance depends, quite understandably, on a reasoned and deliberate judgment by a Catholic that the beliefs are proper ones for a member of the faith.

Misconceptions about "what Catholics *really* believe" take on a seeming plausibility unless one bears in mind, too, a venerable policy of the Church in instructing its communicants. This policy rests on familiar Christian tenets. It is believed that men are stained by original sin; the purpose of life on this earth is to allow men an opportunity to redeem their souls; they can achieve salvation through the mediation of Jesus Christ, the Savior; the Church's task is to perform Christ's mission. However, the Church does not secure salvation for its communicants; each Christian must work out his own peace with God. Instead, the Church's function is to assist the faithful in their search for salvation by providing them with opportunity for instruction in Christian belief and for guidance in Christian living. It is up to the communicant to take advantage of this opportunity.

Accordingly, what the Church offers its communicants is general statements of belief and principle. These are not enunciated at the convenience or whim of the hierarchy. They are declared in response to felt need on the part of the Church's faithful who are confronted by a problem and seek religious guidance in solving it. This instruction the Church offers. But the Church does not itself attempt to solve its communicants' problems by presenting detailed prescriptions about what they should do. It is the moral responsibility of each Catholic to apply the Church's teachings for himself in living his own life.

Let us now sum up the situation. Even though there are no "orthodox" Catholic political views or programs or movements, there is a set of Catholic beliefs and principles bearing on present-day political affairs. These are beliefs and principles which have received Papal blessing and have been accepted by Catholic leaders to the extent that none denies that they are "authentically Catholic." Such beliefs and principles about which a consensus does exist among prominent Catholic spokesmen we can properly impute to Catholicism. These beliefs and principles are what I mean by "Catholic teachings." Any other theory or practice ascribed to by some Catholics, but without Papal sanction and without general acceptance by Catholics, we cannot properly regard as "Catholicism."

Let us next determine what these Catholic beliefs and principles of present-day political significance are. This story, like so many stories of modern political developments, begins with the Protestant Reformation.

2.

We have seen that the domination of Roman Catholicism over Christian Europe was ended during the Protestant Reformation, with the dismemberment of Christendom into separate religious movements. Reformation theologians like Martin Luther and John Calvin not only challenged the authority of the Church hierarchy headed by the Pope, but also repudiated Catholic dogma. As Protestant sects broke away from the Mother Church to form independent religious congregations, each with its "re-

73

formed" theology, both Catholic teachings and the Universal Church itself were abandoned, at least in parts of Europe, not to be restored even during the Counter Reformation.

We have seen too that this dismemberment of Christendom during the sixteenth century coincided with the rise of the dynastic nation state. While the transformation in religion took the form of fragmenting Christian Europe into numerous smaller parochial churches, the political transformation took the opposite form of consolidating peoples along territorial lines. Strong royal families forged a few large, powerful dynastic states, each regime dominated by the hereditary head of the ruling house. The authority of this dynastic king, undisputed ruler of the realm, extended well into the province of religious affairs. In all dynastic states the religious affiliation of the royal family determined which sect was to be the state church. The church was subordinated to the civil power, with the king the actual if not the titular head of the national church and with the church a department of the royal state. So, with the breakup of the Catholic Church, religious sects tended to acquire national lines; in some cases (as in England) a Protestant sect became the established church of the realm. In most countries of Northern and Western Europe sectarian Protestant churches became dominant; in those countries Catholicism became a minority, and unofficial, religious faith. In most countries of Central and Southern Europe the Catholic Church managed to retain its dominant position and Roman Catholicism continued as the "state religion."

In all dynastic states the national church, whether Catholic or Protestant, was a natural ally of the royal regime. The church was dependent on the state for its revenue and was itself a large landholder; clergymen were virtual employees of the state and some indeed held high posts in the royal administration. The close association of "altar and throne" meant that members of the church hierarchy were called upon to defend the *status quo* of the monarchy and nobility, and this in the interest of protecting the religious establishment itself. Because of this intimate relation

74

between church and state, the established church was regarded by those thinkers and leaders hostile to the dynastic system as a defender of reaction and an enemy of progress. In France, especially, the Roman Catholic Church, linked as it was so closely to the regime, was quite properly regarded as a stronghold of royalist sentiment. When the *ancien regime* of the Bourbons was swept away during the French Revolution, the revolutionists understandably singled out the Church hierarchy for particularly severe reprisals.

During the nineteenth century, when the impact of Liberalism was felt in practice as well as thought and the social consequences of the Industrial Revolution were revealed in European development, the role of "established" religion in social and political affairs underwent a marked change. As the middle class rose to dominance at the expense of the landed nobility, and as Liberal constitutional governments replaced dynastic regimes, the political influence of the church, as a component of the state, declined. Yet as the national churches were stripped of their temporal wealth and power, they became more potent religious forces. Churchmen could and did turn their attention more and more to spiritual matters, but also to the imperatives of Christian ethics for the social problems wrought by the Industrial Revolution. No longer apologists for the regime, churchmen could and did become spokesmen for the great mass of underprivileged citizens at whose expense the tremendous material advances of the nineteenth century were gained. Churchmen became leaders of social-reform movements dedicated to improving the lot of the working classes.

This changed role of organized religion in social and political affairs did not come suddenly or without diligent pioneering effort by those advanced churchmen, Catholic and Protestant, who realized that religious leaders could ill afford to ignore the plight of underpriviliged Christian workers. The Church of England, traditionally identified with the Crown and the Tory party of the landed nobility, experienced a changed role under

75

the pressure of nineteenth-century circumstances. Discontented factions within the hierarchy led social-reform movements which, though at first frowned on by the leadership, the Church eventually adopted as its own. In the 1840s a group of socially conscious Anglicans, like the clergyman Charles Kingsley, espoused the cause of the Chartists, in defiance of their superiors within the hierarchy and in the face of the complacent middle-class rulers. They founded the Christian Socialist movement in England, established educational institutes for workingmen, and generally agitated and promoted the cause of reform in British society with the aim of improving the lot of the working classes.

In the Catholic Church the change came slowly too, even painfully, and only after a protracted contest within the hierarchy itself. But outstanding clerics and laymen who championed "social Catholicism" throughout the century labored to turn the attention of Catholics toward the social and economic problems of the workers. Efforts by these "social Catholics" to apply Christian principles to modern affairs were not in vain. Eventually it became clear to all that the Church must either accommodate itself to new ideas and conditions or else suffer a serious loss of prestige and influence among the mass of peoples who were employees.

Perhaps the significance of this struggle within the Catholic Church over its proper role in social and political affairs can be best understood in terms of the relation between Catholicism and two other nineteenth-century movements—Liberalism and Socialism. Catholics have traditionally displayed hostility toward middle-class Liberalism as well as working-class Socialism, and for substantially the same reason. It is true that both movements were virulently anticlerical, but Catholic opposition cannot be explained so simply as mere political expediency. Catholic opposition is founded on the historic teachings of the Church of Rome. Both the Liberal and Socialist creeds rest on principles contrary to the natural-law teachings of the Church.

3.

What all Catholics share, of course, is the religious dogma of the Roman Church. But they also share a Roman Catholic philosophy. In the course of its long life the Church has accumulated not only a massive corpus of theological and canonical writings but also a close-knit and systematic philosophical system at least complementary with Catholic dogma. This philosophy was definitively formulated during the Middle Ages by the greatest Scholastic philosopher of the Church, St. Thomas Aquinas.

The philosophy of Aquinas represents an effort to harmonize the "revealed truth" of the Scriptures with "natural truth," and to do this through the exercise of "philosophic reason." Supposing that all knowledge is of a single piece and that faith complements reason, St. Thomas set as his goal a universal synthesis combining classical pagan, especially Aristotelian, theories which commend themselves to "reason," and Christian teachings as elaborated by Catholic theologians, notably the early Church fathers such as St. Augustine. This Thomist philosophy, though devised in the thirteenth century, has had a profound influence on all modern Catholic thought; the philosophy of the "Angelic Doctor" has been adopted as the semi-official philosophy of the Church. In an encyclical *Aeterni Patris* ("Christian Philosophy," 1879) Pope Leo XIII declared that the major tenets of this *philosophia perennis* are constituent doctrines in modern Catholic thought.

The point of departure for a Catholic thinker is a theory of "law" which is basic in Thomist philosophy. Though essentially religious in character, this theory reveals marks of Aristotelian metaphysics and medieval legalism as well as of Christian dogma. Like other Christian thinkers, St. Thomas deemed that the universe is ordered by the will of an omniscient, all-powerful

God. Like other medieval thinkers, he conceived of law not in the sense of man-made enactments by a legislature or court, but rather as rules, normative in content, which pervade the universe. St. Thomas defined law as "the rule and measure of acts"; by law he meant nothing less than divine prescription governing the universe, including man, society, and, by analogy, the physical world. By definition God's law is "true" in that it is rationally, morally, and empirically valid, independent of human choice or action. All law is thus part of the divinely ordained, hence harmonious, system willed by God to rule the animate and (analogically) the inanimate world. Though all of one piece, this law of God is made manifest in different ways. Hence St. Thomas classified law not as to kind but as to form (or "level") of manifestation. The highest form of law, the perfect law, the first law of the universe which is the *summa* of all other law, is, in Thomist terms, "eternal law"—the reason of God. The will of God made manifest as revealed truth in the Scriptures is "divine law." "Natural law" is "the rule of conduct which is prescribed to us by the Creator in the constitution of the nature with which He has endowed us." A fourth category, "human law," is the man-applied principles of natural law, adjusted to a particular time and place.

For St. Thomas, then, natural law is a guide to how men should act rather than a description of how they do act. Following Aristotle, St. Thomas conceived of "nature" not as the primitive but rather as the ultimate in development. Nature implies a set of underlying purposes toward which an entity is directed by the will of God, the "Author of Nature." Natural law is but evidence of the rational will of God at work in the world, ordering the moral universe which He has created. God has endowed man with an immortal soul; His command is that man's purpose on earth is to seek salvation of his soul. The merciful and providential God has endowed man too with the capacity for achieving salvation, as well as the duty to do so. He has implanted in man's nature the moral law and has granted man the gift of reason. Indeed it is the rational faculty and the possession of a soul which sets man apart from other animals; man possesses "the full perfection of animal nature," but it is reason which "makes a human being human, and distinguishes him essentially and completely from the brutes." Through exercise of his reason, man can discover the law which "orders our nature," and he can act accordingly, in conformance with law. When man acts rationally, he acts right, as God intended man to act, in accord with his nature, and in so doing he obeys natural law—the universal, supreme, moral standard for human action.

From the Thomist theory of a rational man in a moral universe ordered by divinely ordained natural law, the Catholic thinker derives his views regarding the "true nature" of man and society. Implicit in this conception is a doctrine of human rights and duties. As a creature of God, each person is endowed "by nature" with rights so essential to the purpose of human life that they are inseparable from him. Of all man's natural rights, the most fundamental is the right to life as the Creator intended; from this all other rights are in a sense derivative. If man is to fulfill the purpose of his existence in this world, his material and spiritual needs must be satisfied; thus each person has a natural right to satisfy these needs. All specific natural rights of man in Catholic theory are grounded in these fundamental human needs.

But the Catholic thinker holds that as man has natural rights so has he God-given duties equally essential to his nature. Indeed men have been granted rights so that they can perform their duties to God. Duties are inseparable from rights; one implies the other. Since natural rights and duties are rooted in natural law and are therefore part of the moral order of the universe, both are inviolate. If a person's natural rights or duties are infringed or abrogated by human action, the person is prevented from performing his prime duty to obey the will of God. So the Catholic argues that neither the rights nor duties of man can be impaired by human action or law without contravening the moral law of nature. It follows that human law, if it is to be true law, must conform to the imperatives of the divinely ordained natural law.

This Catholic doctrine of natural rights and duties, unlike Enlightenment theories, does not presuppose a "state of nature" wherein isolated individuals supposedly live a primitive existence prior to forming or entering into society. Indeed in the Catholic conception the only "natural" condition of human life is in a community with others, as a member of society. The Catholic thinker holds, as Aristotle held, that man is by nature a social animal: "In the plan of the Creator, society is a natural means which man can and must use to reach his destined end." Society is willed by God for a purpose—to provide for human needs, because alone and unaided man cannot satisfy either his spiritual or his material needs. It follows that society is a moral organism devoted to the common needs of its members, and that the natural rights of persons derived from human needs are not against society, but in accord with the common good.

4.

Based as it is on the Thomist theory of natural law, the Catholic critique of modern creeds is substantially the same today as it was a century ago when Pope Pius IX in his famous "Syllabus of Errors" identified for condemnation those doctrines of Liberalism and Socialism and other modern creeds which the Church regarded as "errors." Subsequent Popes have reiterated the basic charges alleged by Pius IX.

The general Catholic thesis in criticism of Liberalism and Socialism can be summed up as follows: (1) The critical situation of modern society is a result of the intellectual ascendancy of Liberalism and the application of Liberal principles in social, economic, and political life. (2) The alternative solutions to modern problems offered by such creeds as Socialism are unacceptable, because they aggravate rather than remedy the ills of society. (3) The only real cure for the modern situation is a reconstruction of society according to Christian principles, a reconstruction which would include both a reformation in the realm of religious beliefs and a renovation of social institutions.

Implicit in this thesis, which appears as a constant theme in modern Catholic writings, is a plea to men of good will to rally to the standard of the Catholic Church, a plea which is, of course, most pointedly addressed to Protestants to return to the fold of the Mother Church. For this thesis rests on an underlying assumption which supplies an element of unity for the entire Catholic critique of Liberalism and Socialism. It is that the root of modern difficulties is to be found in religious and moral beliefs, and that any adequate solution of the difficulties must accordingly include the realm of faith and morals. The character of this assumption becomes evident in elaborations of the Catholic thesis in criticism of modern creeds, for Catholic thinkers present a distinctive analysis of the course of modern developments, an analysis in the light of which all non-Catholic doctrines appear as forms of heresy.

According to the Catholic analysis, modern evils such as international wars, civil conflicts, and economic disorders have all resulted from the repudiation of the teachings of the Roman Church. The troubles began in the sixteenth century when Reformation theologians not only challenged the institutional dominance of the Universal Church, but also undermined the intellectual foundations on which Christian faith and morals rest. The Reformation marked the beginning of an intellectual revolt which spread from theology to all realms of thought and practice. Out of this revolution came the Enlightenment, an intellectual movement which reached its ripest development and bore its bitterest fruit in the nineteenth century. The basic tenet of the Enlightenment was "naturalism," a denial of the supernatural realm. Acceptance of this tenet is tantamount to rejecting the Christian conviction that moral principles should guide and control all human affairs. The fundamental assumption of naturalism, the Catholic critic charges, is that "human nature and human reason ought in all things to be master and guide." By this assumption man's physical or animal nature is stressed, to the neglect of the spiritual; denied is belief in divine purpose, immortality of the soul, original sin, and the efficacy of grace and prayer. By denying the intimate relation between faith and reason, all revealed truth of the supernatural order is ignored. In its stead human reason, unaided by faith, is asserted to be the supreme source and judge of all truth. By his insistence on viewing the universe solely in material terms, the naturalist repudiates the central truth that the world is a moral order governed by natural law according to divine reason.

The consequence of accepting the naturalistic tenet is to remove the religious basis—the only adequate basis—for public and private morality. Every man accordingly becomes a force unto himself, bound only by the laws of his own choosing. Society becomes a conventional rather than a natural association of persons, and for material and secular rather than spiritual and religious purposes. Self-interest and expediency are glorified at the cost of the common good and social justice; authority is held to depend on consent rather than duty; marriage is regarded as a civil contract rather than a religious sacrament; liberty is confused with license as men demand rights but refuse to perform duties. A life of virtue gives way to a life of pleasure, dedicated to the pursuit of worldly aims.

The product of the Enlightenment was "Liberalism," founded on naturalistic error. It was the separation of religion from the total life of man as a member of society that resulted in the moral and intellectual bankruptcy of Liberal society. It was in reaction against the degradation and corruption of human affairs spawned by Liberal teachings that Socialism and other such creeds appeared. But these creeds, though the criticisms of Liberal errors may be sound and the revulsion against Liberal society warranted, are themselves founded on error; they perpetuate rather than repudiate the errors of naturalism. So the Church must condemn certain doctrines shared alike by the Liberal and Socialist traditions, as well as certain doctrines peculiar to one tradition or the other. For to rid modern society of the evils which plague it, to restore order and harmony and justice in human affairs, all false teachings, Liberal and Socialist as well as the totalitarian creeds following in their wake, must be abandoned.

5.

In the early decades of the nineteenth century, European Catholics lived in the shadow of the French Revolution. By midcentury the full impact of another "revolution," which proved to have an even more profound influence on the lives of Europeans, was increasingly being felt. The implications of industrial capitalism for Catholic teachings and practice attracted the attention of a growing number of churchmen. Industrial capitalism tremendously augmented the wealth of nations, but at the same time for many members of society its result was a miserable condition of life. Conditions wrought by the new economic system posed in shocking form what came to be called the "social question." The overriding problem was how to improve the lot of industrial working classes. Catholic reform movements arose, as did European Socialism, in an effort to resolve this problem through social reform. Indeed the extent and vigor of "social Catholicism" in various countries can almost be measured by the degree to which economic life was transformed by industrial capitalism, and this even though all Catholic movements for reform of that system have simultaneously been concerned with the unfortunate lot of peasants and non-industrial workers generally.

The memory of the reign of terror faded slowly from the

minds of devout Catholics on the Continent. Those socially conscious Catholic leaders who insisted that somehow the lot of the impoverished industrial workers must be improved were at first often regarded with grave suspicion by the highest officials of the Roman Church. Consequently, during the nineteenth century, there emerged a twofold division in Catholic opinion, symbolized by Catholic reaction and Catholic reform. "Conservative" Catholics not only clung tenaciously to their monarchist convictions but generally were hostile to "new" ideas espoused by middle-class Liberals as well as working-class Socialists, and to the changes called for in the *status quo* by those movements. In contrast, practices sanctioned by the established system the "social Catholics" condemned as contrary to Christian principles. As imperatives of Christian teachings they advocated social and economic reform.

In the decades immediately following Waterloo, Catholic reaction dominated Catholic opinion. The antipathy shared by conservatives toward reform was encouraged, or at least not discouraged, by Pope Pius IX, who occupied the Holy See from 1846 until 1878. But the influence of "social Catholicism" gradually ascended, so that even before the end of the century Catholic social movements received not only the blessings but also the firm backing of the Supreme Pontiff at Rome.

The elevation to the Papacy in 1878 of Leo XIII as successor to Pius IX marked a victory for the "social Catholics" who had pioneered the reform movements. It was under the tutelage of Leo XIII, "the workingman's Pope," that the Catholic Church assumed its new role as a champion of social reform. Social Catholicism, no longer the unrequited labor of a minority of advanced clerics and laymen, took on a new character and acquired considerably enlarged dimensions. Guided by Pope Leo's pronouncements, lay and ecclesiastical leaders throughout the Catholic world engaged in concerted action to promote the Church's reform program. The climax came in 1891 with the publication of *Rerum Novarum* ("The Condition of Labor").

In his famous encyclical Leo XIII set forth definitively and force-fully the Catholic criticisms of Liberalism and Socialism and the alternative program of reform sponsored by the Catholic Church. The principles espoused by Leo XIII were reaffirmed and refined and extended by later Pontiffs. By 1931, when Pius XI published *Quadragesimo Anno* ("Reconstructing the Social Order") to commemorate the fortieth anniversary of his predecessor's famous encyclical, several generations of Catholic social reformers had achieved notable successes in propagating, and to some extent in applying, Catholic social principles.

The Vatican's assumption of social-reform leadership climaxed the longtime efforts of many "social Catholics" to "reconstruct" modern society according to Christian principles. The earliest precursors of Leo XIII were two Frenchmen. In 1834 a royalist, Count Alban de Villeneuve-Bargemont (1784–1850), published his three-volume *Christian Political Economy,* a critique of classical political economy from the standpoint of Christian ethics. It is claimed that his writings and his lifetime advocacy of legislation to curb the social evils of the industrial system had a pronounced influence on Pope Leo. The influence of Frederic Ozanam (1813–1853), a Sorbonne professor and a founder of the Society of St. Vincent de Paul for charitable assistance to the poor, was of a somewhat different order. He attacked the Manchester school of political economy and advocated social reform in the interest of the working classes. He also contended, in contrast to Villeneuve-Bargemont, that Christianity and Democracy are inseparable. Ozanam was the forerunner of the movement which ultimately came to be called "Christian Democracy." Another outstanding figure in the development of French social Catholicism was the Dominican priest and associate of Lammenais and Montalambert, Jean Baptiste Lacordaire (1802–1861), a friend and biographer of Ozanam. During the Third Republic, Comte Albert de Mun (1841–1914), for many years a member of Parliament, was a foremost social Catholic leader. De Mun headed the committee which in the 1870s founded the Catholic

Workingmen's Clubs, and he was the founder of the Catholic youth movement in France.

In Germany the pioneer of social reform was Bishop Wilhelm Emmanuel von Ketteler (1811–1877), a friend of the Socialist Ferdinand Lasalle and an outstanding German political figure during the third quarter of the century. Trained as a lawyer and diplomat, von Ketteler finally entered the priesthood and rose rapidly in the German hierarchy as a champion of working-class interests as well as a defender of the Church against the Prussian *Kulturkampf* of Bismarck. Bishop Ketteler sponsored the founding of the Catholic Center Party and was himself elected a member of the Reichstag in 1871. In his *Christianity and the Labor Question,* Ketteler advocated a "social-action" program of "corporate self-help"—the formation of trade unions and co-operative societies—along with social legislation as means for improving the status of industrial workers.

A "romantic" school of Austrian Catholics which advocated a return to a precapitalist guild system was headed by Baron Karl von Vogelsang (1818–1891). Through the Fribourg Union, composed largely of members of this school, von Vogelsang had a pronounced influence in France, Switzerland, and Germany and was the intellectual godfather of the later Catholic corporative movement. In Switzerland a prince of the Church, Gaspard Cardinal Mermillod (1824–1892), was patron of the Fribourg Union (*Union Catholique d' Etudes Sociales et Economiques*), an international group of Catholic social thinkers formed in the 1880s. The Union supposedly paved the way, through the preparation of memoranda on social questions for the Vatican, for the promulgation of *Rerum Novarum*. A Swiss professor influenced by Bishop Ketteler, Gaspard Decurtins (1855–1918), was the international leader of the Catholic labor movement.

In Italy Catholic social movements were retarded by the belated unification of the country and were complicated by bitter controversy over the role of the Pope as a secular ruler. But the Sicilian priest Gioachino Ventura (1792–1861) and Guiseppe

Toniolo (1845–1918), a professor of economics at the University of Pisa and "the scholar, the theoretician, and the apostle of Christian Democracy," made outstanding contributions. In more recent decades Don Luigi Sturzo (1871–), founder of the Italian Popular (Christian Democratic) Party and after 1926 a refugee from the Fascist regime, has perhaps been the foremost international leader, intellectual as well as political, of Catholic social movements.

The influence of social Catholicism in Spain, overwhelmingly Catholic as well as predominantly agrarian, even today remains negligible.

In Great Britain and the United States social Catholicism has for the most part been overshadowed by non-Catholic reform movements. In both countries Catholic social reform developed slowly, in part because Catholics composed a minority of the population, in part because Catholic reform activities have traditionally been the work of outstanding individuals who joined hands with non-Catholics to promote common aims. But several Anglo-American Catholics have played significant roles as reform leaders. Henry Edward Cardinal Manning (1808–1892), a friend of Henry George, became a recognized champion of working-class interests after he intervened in behalf of the workers in the London Dockers Strike of 1889. The first prominent American Catholic to distinguish himself as a reform leader was James Cardinal Gibbons (1834–1921), Archbishop of Baltimore, who risked Papal censure to plead, in the face of hostility displayed by many members of the hierarchy, especially in Canada, the cause of the newly formed Knights of Labor, the forerunner of the American labor-union movement. More recently "the foremost academician of the American Catholic social movement" has been the late Monsignor John A. Ryan (1869–1945), a professor of moral theology who became the first director of the Social Action Department of the National Catholic Welfare Conference after its creation in 1919. Father Ryan wrote extensively on the economic and social aspects of Catholic teachings.

6.

Catholic criticisms of Liberal and Socialist theory and practice are of course based on an alternative set of principles which Catholic reformers insist on invoking for social and economic affairs. Taken altogether these principles define the ideal Christian social order. This ideal would be realized in practice—presumably this is the ultimate goal of all Catholic reform—if human relations in all societies, from the family to the international community, were ordered according to Christian principles. For the Christian social order is, in the Catholic view, part of a divinely ordained moral order of the universe, and those moral principles which animate the social order are derived from natural law.

It so happened that the resurgence of the Catholic Church as a champion of social reform coincided with a general revival of European interest in medieval life. This display of interest indicated in part a reaction, in some quarters quite severe, against the prevailing beliefs and principles which set the character of nineteenth-century life. To many social thinkers, the guild system appeared as a welcome alternative to the extremes of Liberal practice and Socialist theory. In his encyclical *Rerum Novarum,* Leo XIII, always outspoken in his admiration for medieval culture, issued a call for a return to principles of the guild system in order to remedy the ills of modern industrial society. In later encyclicals, notably *Quadragesimo Anno,* his successors reaffirmed and elaborated the social principles Leo initially set forth in the name of the Church.

The medieval Thomist dream was an organic community in which each and every member cooperated to promote the common good. Undoubtedly this dream was never actually realized, but it served as a normative model for appraising beliefs and principles. It was supposed that each member should perform a useful function appropriate to his social station, and that he should perform his function in association with his fellows. For each social rank or class, there was a corresponding economic function; for each function, there was an appropriate group organization or "order." Thus the proper basis for organizing economic life was assumed to be the "functional association." These "corporations" were regarded not simply as legal fictions, like the limited-liability joint stock company, but as essential forms of social life. The members were supposedly joined together by a community of interests primarily economic but embodying implications for all aspects of life. Since economic activity was supposed to be regulated by accepted principles of right and wrong to which all persons were expected to conform, the corporations, though semi-independent and self-governing groups, were expected to function in harmony for the common good. Thus group cooperation, not individual competition, should be the guiding principle of economic life, and human needs, not gain, should direct the production of goods and services.

Neither Pope Leo nor his followers ever demanded that modern life be completely reconstructed to restore the medieval scheme. But they did urge both that certain prevailing social and economic principles be abandoned and that certain principles of the guild system, after necessary adaptation to suit the circumstances of industrial societies, be reestablished. Consequently Catholic thinkers have invoked essentially medieval, as well as religious, conceptions to substantiate their positions in discussing modern social and economic problems, whether in propounding the Church's doctrines or in criticizing alternatives.

In Catholic teachings the right ordering of human affairs according to natural law is "justice." Since each person is endowed with dignity as a son of God, each member of society is obliged to live justly and is entitled to just treatment at the hands of his fellows. When rights and duties of all persons are recognized, observed, and fulfilled, as natural law requires, then justice prevails in society. Like other aspects of human existence, social life is ordered by principles of justice, and those principles especially applied to social and economic relations are termed by Catholic thinkers "the principles of social justice." Hence it is these principles which specify the ideal Christian social order.

Though Pope Pius XI did not coin the term, "social justice" has become a common concept with Catholic thinkers only as a result of his frequent use of it. But the meaning of the concept has been imprecise and has been a subject of some controversy among Catholic thinkers. Traditionally, Catholic thinkers distinguished between "commutative," "legal," and "distributive" justice, depending on the set of human relations involved. Commutative (or individual) justice concerns the relations between persons equal in dignity, and the object is the good of each; this usage is sometimes described as "strict justice." Both legal and distributive justice concern political relations of persons and the state. According to legal justice a person is obliged to pay the state its due, that is, to obey the law. According to distributive justice, the state is obliged to assign (or "distribute") in fair proportions the benefits and burdens of membership in civil society. Certain recent Catholic writers tend to equate legal justice (and others, distributive justice) with the newer concept of social justice. However, in its broadest sense the concept appears to include both legal and distributive justice and to embrace as well an additional set of human relations, namely, the social and economic relations of groups, including the state. Father John A. Ryan accordingly defines social justice as "that form of justice which impels men to promote the common good; that is, the welfare of the community as such, as a unified entity, and also the common good as comprising the welfare of all members of society."

7.

Catholic thinkers consistently maintain that a Christian social order cannot be established unless social institutions are shaped and activities directed by the principles of social justice. Yet exactly what these principles are is not at all clear. Pius XI often spoke of "the laws of social justice," and other Catholic thinkers frequently refer to various "essential principles." But nowhere do we find a systematic, full, and definitive formulation of the principles of social justice. The closest approximation is contained in a brief and sketchy pamphlet, *Introduction to Social Justice* (1948), by an American priest, Father William Ferree. In the absence of an authoritative formulation, I offer the following statement, gleaned from Catholic writings, particularly papal encyclicals. As far as I can tell it includes at least the more important principles. For convenience I have grouped them according to what appear to be the three key concepts—"common good," "functional association," and "subsidiarity."

1. Common Good. The principle which prescribes the proper end of social life is implicit in the Catholic notion about the natural purpose of human society. The end of man on earth is to achieve the highest good. A person can attain his fullest development only in association with others, as a member of society. The purpose of a society is to promote the end common to the members. A true society is thus a moral organism dedicated to fostering the good life for its members.

Men have varied needs, and for them to be adequately satisfied varied functions must be performed. These varied functions are performed by different members of society. Social functions can be ordered as to their importance to the group, but the functions performed within a society are interdependent. No matter how menial, the contribution of each member is essential for the good of all. Each member, by performing his appropriate social function, contributes to the satisfaction of needs of others. Since each member has needs which must be satisfied for his own good, and since the good of all is inseparable from the good of each, society must bear responsibility for adequate satisfaction of every member's legitimate needs. At the same time, the common good of the group takes precedence over any special interest of a member.

Hence it is a fundamental principle of the Christian social order that "the common good of all society must be kept inviolate."

2. Functional Association. The common good is best advanced when the parts function in harmony for the good of the whole. Since the good of each depends on the efforts of all, each person should, in performing his function in society, cooperate with the other members. So to promote most effectively the purpose common to them, persons must associate. They must organize themselves as members of functional groups. For example, all persons engaged in a distinctive type of economic activity should organize themselves as members of vocational associations. Employees should form labor unions and employers should form corresponding trade associations. These employer and employee associations should in turn be federated in a vocational "corporation"; the purpose of this corporation is of course to further the common good of all persons engaged in that industry. The vocational corporations representing the many different economic functions should be joined together, as a federation of federations, in a "chamber of corporations." Thus the proper unit of social organization is the functional association devoted to the common good of the members.

3. Subsidiarity. For every human need, spiritual or temporal, God has also provided man with the means of satisfaction. Since human needs must be satisfied through functional associations, in any society the members, taken altogether, possess ample authority to attain their common purpose. A functional association has authority to regulate the affairs of its members, to the extent (no more or less) that they bear on the purpose of the group. Take as an example again a vocational association. The association has authority to settle such matters as rates of wages, hours of work, conditions of employment, participation in management, standards of quality, and prices for the commodity or service produced.

Just as the social functions of persons can be ranked in the order of their importance, functional associations, too, are of unequal status; some are superior, some inferior, in relation to others. So just as the members of a society are ordered by rank, functional associations should be ordered hierarchically. In every society there must be a ruling part to exercise the authority of the group. In a functional association, authority may be vested in offices such as a governing board or council, composed of persons chosen by the members to represent them. A higher organization should coordinate and supervise the activities of a lesser organization, to ensure that the common good of the society is properly fostered. It should also aid and assist a lesser organization. But no functional association dedicated to the common good should be interfered with in promoting the common purpose of its members. A higher organization should not itself undertake to perform a function appropriately the function of a lesser organization. (For the benefit of the members of the Westside Civic Improvement League—*this* is the principle of sub sidiarity.)

A comment about these principles is in order. The principles of social justice, prescribing the character of an ideal Christian order, are clearly derived from Catholic teachings. They imply that certain social and economic practices now followed should be abandoned and others instituted. They call for what might be termed "institutional reform."

But we must remember that these principles are mainly moral in content. They declare what persons *should* do as members of society, if they choose to live a Christian life. This emphasis on faith and morals is the most significant feature of these teachings, for in the Catholic view the prime task and mission of the Church is to restore Christian beliefs to their rightful place in human affairs.

Consequently we find that Catholic proposals for changes in social and economic practices are ordinarily coupled with a claim that "moral reformation" is a necessary condition for successful social reform. The outward forms of society can perhaps be changed by legislation or decree, but this is not enough. It is the hearts and minds of men that must be reformed. Men must abandon false beliefs which allow them to do injustice to their fellow men. They must embrace those true beliefs about social justice which are grounded on religious teachings.

8.

It is clear that Catholics share an impressive consensus on the principles of social justice. But it is also clear that from this fact we cannot infer that every political program or movement sponsored by Catholics is a faithful representation of the Church's teachings. We have already seen that, in a strict sense, no such program or movement can claim to be genuinely Catholic, since the Church makes no official endorsement of political causes.

But this is not the significant point. Even though the underlying Catholic beliefs and principles are everywhere the same, we find that reform programs advanced by Catholics throughout the world differ rather markedly. And this is to be expected.

Roman Catholicism is a world-wide religious faith; it has millions of followers and they live in almost every country. The Church embraces a multiplicity of races and nations at stages of development from that of the most primitive African tribe to the intricate urban civilization of the most highly advanced industrial nation. In some countries, like Italy, the population is overwhelmingly of the Catholic religion, while in other countries, like Great Britain, Catholics form only a minority sect. In some countries, like Germany, economic life is collectivized, thoroughly organized, and industrialized, while in others, like Mexico, an antiquated agrarian economy still remains. In some countries, like the United States, a virile tradition of popular government exists, while in others, like Spain, authoritarian rule is the only familiar form. In some countries, like France, a bitter heritage of anticlericalism agitates political life, while in others, like Portugal, such animosity toward the institution of the Church is strikingly absent—the Church may even enjoy great prestige and favor, as it does in Eire. The circumstances of Catholic lives span every possibility.

This means that the political problems which confront Catholics vary from time to time and place to place, and vary tremendously. So do the actual conditions under which those problems must be solved. For the Italian Catholic, political circumstances are not the same as they are for the Englishman— or the German, the Mexican, the American, the Spaniard, the Frenchman, the Portuguese, or the Irishman. Each is confronted with problems and conditions peculiar to his time and place. This great variety and diversity of circumstances pose for Catholic reformers—who share uniform Catholic principles—a practical question: How, in a given situation, can Catholic principles be best promoted? By what method of action can Catholic reform goals be best advanced?

To this question the Church offers no rigid answer. In fact Church officials avoid specifying any actions which Catholics must take. The question of how to apply general Catholic principles to specific problems of local concern, how to adapt those principles to circumstances set by time and place—this question each Catholic must answer for himself. Of course local Church officials may, in their role of teachers, urge or dissuade reformers of Catholic faith. They may, in their role of spiritual advisors, offer religious and moral counsel. But the Church does not prescribe the reform program, nor does it exert control over the reform movement of Catholic inspiration. It is not simply that the Church may not sponsor a reform program advocated by Catholics. The Church may oppose it. In some instances the Vatican or lesser ecclesiastical offices have found it necessary to repudiate, by public statement, a program or movement claiming Catholic sponsorship. But this merely illustrates the point: Different Catholic groups may advocate different reform programs, but the Church has none of its own.

95

Consequently, we find that so-called "Catholic reform programs" differ in significant respects and enjoy varying degrees of acceptance among Catholics. For us the critically important question is whether any program authentically based on Catholic teachings is also genuinely Democratic in character. Are the programs and movements sponsored by Catholics who are patently non-Democratic, perhaps even anti-Democratic, to be explained by Catholic teachings? Are the programs and movements sponsored by Catholics who are apparently Democratic also to be explained by Catholic teachings? Do the Church's teachings prevent or require a Catholic to embrace Democratic beliefs and principles? Or do those teachings simply allow a Catholic who so chooses to accept Democratic theory and practice?

An answer to this question is perhaps suggested—at least the issue is clearly drawn—by the program and movement called "Christian Democracy."

Chapter Four

CHRISTIAN DEMOCRACY

I.

Christian Democracy is for our purpose the most significant Catholic reform movement. But it is not the only such movement. Among Catholics there appear to be three main schools of opinion about how the goal of social justice can be best realized. Each school has attracted widespread support from Roman Catholics and has inspired a reform movement of important dimensions. These movements are (1) Catholic Corporativism, (2) Social Action, and (3) Christian Democracy.

Historically the oldest school is Catholic Social Action. It originated in the early nineteenth century when churchmen became increasingly concerned about the "social question." Corporativism developed later, with a growing reaction against the social consequences of industrial capitalism and with a revival of interest in medieval life. The program did not bear fruit until after the First World War. During the second half of the nineteenth century, some Catholic political organizations first appeared, but these were merely forerunners of the Christian Democratic movement. Christian Democracy developed most recently, with the growth of political parties avowedly of Christian inspiration, formed for the purpose of participating in parliamentary politics.

The movement has flourished only in the years after the Second World War.

These programs and movements are distinct, but they are not mutually exclusive. Actually their aims are complementary. It is principally in emphasis and on methods where they differ. The differences reflect three diverse sets of circumstances under which Catholic reformers have found it necessary to work. Let us take a closer look at these three Catholic reform movements— Corporativism, Social Action, and particularly Christian Democracy.

2.

A century ago in Europe, Liberalism was the creed of the age, and Socialism was the most discussed challenge to the order of the day. It was as a more acceptable alternative to both the Liberal and Socialist schemes that Catholic Corporativism was first championed.

The Catholic Corporativist program calls for sweeping changes in modern life. To achieve the ideal of a Christian social order, the corporativist contends, a wholesale reorganization of present-day society is required. It must be reconstructed according to corporative principles. Only in such a society, founded on the principles of social justice, can the common good be best advanced.

The influence of Catholic Corporativism has varied widely from country to country. Certain conditions seem to favor a reception of corporativism, while others definitely do not. In countries where the population is overwhelmingly of the Catholic faith, corporativism has enjoyed its greatest vogue by far. But interestingly enough in Ireland, one of the best contemporary examples of a Catholic state, the influence of corporativism has been slight.

The Irish Constitution of 1937, which was prepared under the personal supervision of Eamon De Valera, provides for a parliamentary system of government founded on Catholic principles. The preamble acknowledges the nation's obligation to the "Divine Lord, Jesus Christ, who sustained our fathers through centuries of trial"; the language and content of the articles pertaining to property, education, marriage and the family, religious worship, and social policy are manifestly inspired by Catholic teachings. The Constitution grants a "special position" to the Church, even though it is not "established" and other religious denominations are explicitly recognized. But most significantly, what the Constitution does not provide for is any thoroughgoing system of "social reconstruction." The corporative influence is revealed only in a diluted form, in a scheme for functional representation used to elect the members of local councils and representatives in the "second (upper) chamber" of Parliament. Incidentally, it is interesting that the first President of Eire was a Protestant, Douglas Hyde.

While not all Catholic states are founded on corporative principles, neither are all corporative states founded on Catholic principles. The most famous corporative experiment in recent times has been the Fascist regime in Italy. But this brand of corporativism was sharply, even severely and bitterly, criticized by Catholic spokesmen. They recognized that while a corporative system of economic and social organization can be employed as a device to achieve a Christian social order, it can also be used for contrary purposes. Consequently they have generally been quite anxious to draw a clear distinction between "state corporativism," especially of the Fascist variety, and Catholic "corporativism by association." Catholics have charged that state corporativism of the sort instituted by Mussolini is corporative only in structure; it lacks the essential qualities of Catholic corporativism since the system is not devoted to the goal of social justice. Such corporativism has been condemned in very outspoken terms by some Catholic leaders, including the Pope.

In his famous encyclical *Quadragesimo Anno* (1931), Pope

99

Pius XI, after briefly referring to the newly announced Italian corporative scheme—a Fascist decree of 1930 creating a Council of Corporations had not yet gone into effect—pleaded for a "sane corporative system." He voiced the fear of many Catholics that "the new syndical and corporative order savors too much of an involved and political system of administration; that... it rather serves particular political ends than leads to the reconstruction and promotion of a better social order." In another encyclical published only a few weeks later, *Non Abbiamo Bisogno* ("The Conflict in Italy," 1931), again the Pope drew a line separating Catholic teachings from Fascist practices; the occasion for the encyclical was a wave of repressive police measures taken by the Fascists against Italian Catholic leaders. The Pope denounced the Fascist demonstrations as "definitely anti-Catholic and decidedly anti-religious... police measures having been put into effect with their accompaniment and consequence of acts of violence and of irreverence" by "a regime based on an ideology which clearly resolves itself into a true and pagan worship of the state." Then the Pope took pains to explain that what he was condemning was only "that much in the program and in the action of the party which We have seen and have understood to be contrary to Catholic doctrine and to Catholic practice and therefore irreconcilable with the name and with the profession of Catholics."

Catholic critics have stressed several specific objections to Fascist corporativism. One is that a system imposed from above and dependent on state power is too rigid to serve the needs of varied functional groups; such a system fails to do the necessary job. Another is that such a system easily lends itself to abuse. Under state corporativism, functional groups are not independent and self-governing organizations; instead of the state merely coordinating the activities of groups to secure the common good, it dominates the system for the political advantage of the regime. In other words, state corporativism is contrary to Catholic principles of "corporativism by association."

So it seems that, in addition to a mainly Catholic population, other conditions must exist as well for "corporativism by association" to take root. In countries where the vestiges of medievalism are rare, such as the United States and Canada, no Corporative ideas have had marked influence. In Great Britain, France, and Germany corporative ideas have enjoyed an amount of popularity, though not necessarily in a Catholic form. Guild Socialism in England and Syndicalism in France have perhaps attracted larger followings than Catholic Corporativism. The influence of the Catholic brand of corporativism has been most noticeable in those mainly Catholic countries where no anticlerical faction seriously threatens political domination, where economic life is not highly industrialized—and where no strong tradition of popular government exists. In a few countries—Austria and Portugal are examples—the influence of Catholic Corporativism has been pronounced.

The authenticity of the Austrian and Portuguese experiments with corporativism has been seriously questioned by some Catholic writers. However, Austria and Portugal do present instances of what appear to be Catholic corporative principles in action, comprehensively applied on a national scale. The ambitious reforms attempted in the early 1930s by the Christian Socialist regime in Austria were short-lived, in fact abortive. But about the same time, the Portuguese corporative system was established; it has now been in effect for two decades. It is no doubt the most outstanding as well as the most successful example of the ordering of an entire nation's social and economic life according to corporative principles which are ostensibly Catholic. Therefore it warrants our inspection.

3.

The situation in Portugal prior to the establishment of the corporative system invited sweeping reforms. Following the revolution in 1910, a republican regime was set up. Republican leaders proved unable to operate the new parliamentary system successfully. During its sixteen years of life, there were forty-three different ministries. Chronic political instability was accompanied by steadily mounting economic and social distress. In May, 1926, a military junta seized control, abolished the parliamentary regime, and established a dictatorship for the professed purpose of restoring stability to Portuguese life. In April, 1928, the military clique finally installed as Minister of Finance Dr. Antonio de Oliveira Salazar (1889–   ), a professor of political economy at the University of Coimbra and an intellectual leader of the Catholic Center Party. His fiscal reforms met with striking success; in July, 1932, he became prime minister. In March, 1933 (the month Franklin Delano Roosevelt was inaugurated President of the United States), Salazar promulgated a new corporative constitution; in a plebiscite a huge vote was cast for its adoption. The following September he issued a series of decrees known as the Statute of Labor, thus establishing the Portuguese *Estado Novo*.

Salazar's deliberate attempt was to establish a system patterned after the principles enunciated in papal encyclicals, yet fashioned in harmony with the Portuguese culture. "We seek," he once said, "to construct a social and corporative State corresponding exactly with the natural structure of society." The 1933 constitution defines the *Estado Novo* as "a unitary and corporative Republic." As contemplated in the constitution, the entire social and economic life of Portugal, from the local to the national level, would be organized on a "functional" basis. The upper house of Parliament, for example, is a Chamber of Corporations, composed of representatives of social, economic, and cultural groups. But even though this constitution has been in effect for more than two decades, Salazar himself has admitted that the corporative system has not yet been fully realized in practice. At the same time, it is obvious that so far substantial changes have occurred.

It is generally recognized that the Austrian corporative scheme exhibited definite "Fascistic" tendencies, to say the least; most paraphernalia of the totalitarian state were readily evident under the short-lived regime which ended when Austrian Nazis assassinated Chancellor Dollfuss. But the theory and practice of Salazar's regime as well have evoked much controversy, among Catholics as well as non-Catholics. The issue is whether the *Estado Novo* is a true Portuguese expression of Catholic teachings or just another "Fascist" regime.

Salazar's regime is in practice, at least pending a full establishment of the corporative system, a dictatorship. Salazar's critics have likened his regime to the Italian Fascist state and have compared him to Mussolini. They have pointed to the curbs on the press, to the absence of independent trade unions and the prohibitions against strikes and lockouts, to the ban on organized political opposition and the dominance of the official "National Union" movement, to the obviously sympathetic policy toward the Spanish regime of Generalissimo Franco, to the close liaison between the state and the Church. Salazar's regime, they have concluded, is a "clerical Fascist dictatorship."

Apologists for the *Estado Novo* have contended that the authoritarian practices must be explained by Portuguese experience under the republic. The dictatorship is temporarily necessary for rebuilding Portuguese society and for constructing the corporative system contemplated by the constitution. But this is merely a transitional phase prior to the emergence of a genuine constitutional government headed by a strong executive. One British observer, Michael Derrick, in a book entitled *The Portugal of Salazar* (1938), contended that "Portugal is not Fascist," on the grounds that (1) totalitarianism is repudiated in theory and does not exist in practice; (2) the Portuguese corporative system is fundamentally unlike the Fascist "state corporativism"; (3) Salazar's regime has never allied with totalitarian powers but instead has openly shown sympathy for the Western "democracies."

According to Derrick, the regime is authoritarian but it is not totalitarian. The state does recognize individual rights and does not invade the legitimate jurisdiction of the family, the Church, or the local community. Each functional association is an independent expression of group interests and is vested with authority sufficient to accomplish its proper purpose; the function of the state is limited to directing and integrating corporative life for the common good. Contrary to the charge of the critics, the "National Union" is not a totalitarian party; it is a movement open to all members of the nation. The Union is not a popular base for a dictator's power but was created by Salazar after the regime was established to encourage the mass of Portuguese people to participate in public affairs. To compare Salazar to Mussolini is to ignore the vast differences between the two men, differences which suggest the essential contrast between the two regimes. Salazar is a mild-mannered and retiring scholar who was called upon to assume power during a national crisis and did so only reluctantly. He has labored diligently to provide Portugal with an orderly and stable government and has made no effort to exploit his great authority for personal ends.

So the apologists have concluded that Salazar's regime represents a sincere if not perfect effort to apply Christian principles in solving the vexing problems peculiar to Portugal. If the Portuguese experiment has departed from strict Catholic teachings, it is not because the goal of social justice has been perverted but rather because unique circumstances have made necessary the use of unfortunate methods for establishing a corporative system, or, for that matter, any other stable system of government in Portugal.

Just what are the facts of the case? What is the significance of the *Estado Novo* for Catholic corporative teachings?

Salazar's theoretical statements of the principles of his regime certainly seem to conform to Catholic doctrines and to conflict with Democratic principles. In a collection of speeches published under the English title of *Doctrine and Action* (1939), Salazar remarked that "we are anti-parliamentarians, anti-democrats, anti-liberals." Liberal parliamentary Democracy failed in Portugal, he charged, because it was contrary to the nation's traditions and alien to its culture. The *Estado Novo* is an effort to construct a Christian social order suited to Portuguese circumstances; the regime represents an application of Catholic principles, adapted to a peculiar set of problems and conditions.

At the same time, Salazar distinguished his regime as fundamentally unlike the one-party totalitarian dictatorships. He expressed rather sharp criticism of the Nazi, Fascist, and Communist doctrines. Totalitarianism, he charged, is "essentially pagan." Granted, a government must have at its disposal enough authority to rule effectively, there are still definite limits on state action and these limits should be defined in a constitution. Salazar also condemned the use of violence and terror as political techniques, repudiated the aggressive nationalism of the Fascists, and severely condemned the Nazi racial doctrines.

Even so, some Catholic critics refuse to accept the Portuguese regime as a genuine expression of Catholic principles. Don Luigi Sturzo not only condemned the Fascist "Corporative State" as a "mere technique for power" exploited by Mussolini and his henchmen; he also branded the Portuguese scheme (and the Austrian) as "semifascist" state corporativism. A few Catholics, like Sturzo, insist that corporativism is not at all a suitable program for achieving a Christian social order. They point out that no thoroughgoing reformation in faith and morals has occurred in modern society. They admit that in practice corporativism is contrary to Democratic principles, but they deny that corporativism is an authentic Catholic reform program. For these critics, the goal of social justice must be promoted by other means.

4.

The reform program of Catholic Corporativism, whatever its character, may be well suited to the needs and conditions of certain countries, but for many others it is clearly not. In these countries Catholics have used different means to promote the goal of a Christian social order. One such reform program, espoused by Catholic reformers with the blessings of the Vatican, is "Social Action."

This term Catholic writers have used in various ways. Historically it was used loosely and broadly to include any sort of Catholic "temporal" (in contrast to "spiritual") activity carried on out of religious zeal. Such activity began, we have seen, in the nineteenth century with reform agitation by socially conscious churchmen who wanted to improve the unfortunate lot of the industrial working classes. This activity was apparently inspired by a fear that the great mass of peoples were turning away from the Church toward Socialism in the hope of improving their material welfare. It was in an effort to counteract the influence of Socialist ideas and movements among Catholic workers that Church leaders proposed social and economic reforms, professedly applying Christian ethics to problems fomented by industrial capitalism.

Since Social Action began as a Catholic movement to combat Socialist influences, its leaders quite understandably adopted tactics used by the Socialist opposition. The early Socialists were inclined to advocate "direct-action" methods to achieve their aims. Instead of trying to persuade a hostile regime to accept working-class reforms, the Socialist techniques were to propagandize, organize, and agitate the workers. Political involvement was avoided because it ordinarily meant trouble. Social Action leaders similarly tried to promote their reform aims by propagating Catholic principles, by organizing associations of Catholic laymen, and by agitating for specific social and economic changes in the system—always staying clear of the political arena. Historically, then, Social Action represents an attempt to apply Christian principles directly in solving everyday social and economic problems, without the intervention of government.

Perhaps we should digress a moment to clarify the present-day meaning of Social Action. Years ago the reform activity by Catholics who were propagating the principles of social justice and promoting social movements was called "Catholic Socialism." This term Francisco Nitti used in his historical account of such activity during the nineteenth century—*Catholic Socialism* (1895). However, the term fell into ill repute, perhaps because it smacked of Marxism. Later the nonpolitical "beneficent Christian action on behalf of the people"—the great majority, that is— was called "Christian Democracy." This term Leo XIII used in his encyclical *Graves de Communi* ("Christian Democracy," 1901); the encyclical was promulgated to end a controversy over an Italian reform group, *Democrazia Christiana,* accused of Socialist leanings. But more recently the term Christian Democracy has been reserved for the political activity of parliamentary parties of Catholic inspiration. The nonpolitical reform activity has been called "Social Action." This usage was common with Pope Pius X, who spoke of Social Action as simply "the Christian solution of the social problem." In an encyclical *Il Fermo Proposito* ("On Christian Social Action," 1905) he particularly stressed the nonpolitical character of Social Action.

The story of the early Social Action movement is in a sense a chapter in the history of the European labor movement. In its beginnings the principal Social Action reform aim was to relieve the distress of industrial workers. The program naturally centered on labor questions. Associations of workers were early recognized as necessary means for promoting the welfare of workers. Thanks to the pioneering efforts of many reformers, including Catholics like Bishop Ketteler and Comte de Mun, "workingmen's associations" were formed during the mid-nineteenth century. These "unions" eventually flourished in industrialized countries, despite the initial hostility of government officials and the public generally. Catholic opposition to organized labor declined after the publication of *Rerum Novarum* (1891). In that encyclical the Pope declared that the right of workers to organize functional associations is grounded in natural law. During the pontificate of Benedict XV, the view that social justice requires labor unions became so widely accepted among Catholics that lay resistance to organized labor virtually disappeared.

However, in the last quarter of the nineteenth century the European labor movement came under the domination of Socialist, Communist, and Syndicalist leadership. A few labor unions were founded on a religious basis and continued to thrive free of antireligious influence. But most of the labor movement on the Continent, in contrast to this country, took on a strong antireligious bent. Then the Church urged that Catholic workers form separate unions; the Church's view on the matter was set forth years ago by Pope Pius X in a letter on labor unions to the German hierarchy, *Singulari Quandam* (1912). So in some countries Catholic workers formed "Christian Trade Unions," ordinarily by secession from the Socialist-dominated organizations. In English-speaking countries, where the labor movement is traditionally non-Marxist and nonrevolutionary, Catholic workers belong to the regular labor unions, which have no religious character. The Church does not object to these "mixed" or "neutral" unions where separate Christian unions are not necessary or feasible. Even so, Catholic workers are still urged to form another association for promoting Christian teachings, while remaining members in good standing in their regular unions. For example, in this country an Association of Catholic Trade Unionists was organized in 1937 on the implied instructions of Pope Pius XI. It is composed of Catholic workers who are members of "neutral" unions; the purpose of the Association is to provide religious instruction for Catholic workers. The Association has not been especially active except in New York City and Detroit, where the members have attempted to implement a program calling for greater intraunion democracy and elimination of racketeering and Communist influence in the labor unions.

The Catholic Social Action movement originated with a reform program for the benefit of industrial workers, but over the years it expanded to embrace many other programs. It early included reforms to advance the welfare of agricultural workers. In fact the Social Action movement has long been strong among peasants, who still make up the bulk of workers in some European countries. In Germany, Austria, Belgium, Italy, and the predominantly Catholic countries, peasant leagues were formed decades ago under Catholic auspices. These organizations, sometimes termed the "white cooperatives," promote collective marketing, purchasing, credit, and insurance schemes for the benefit of their members.

Along with the peasant and labor-union efforts, the Social Action program included sponsorship of youth and women's groups. In 1868 an Italian Youth Association was formed with the sanction of Pope Pius IX; in 1874 the organization held its first national congress at Venice. In France, Comte de Mun actively encouraged the formation of Catholic youth organizations during the 1880s. In the years around the turn of this century, similar organizations were founded in most European countries.

Perhaps the best-known Catholic youth group is the "Jocists" (Jeunesse Ouvrière Chrétienne). This organization was founded in 1919 by a Belgian priest, Canon Joseph Cardijn; it was composed of young Catholic workers dedicated to applying Catholic principles to social problems. It is a mass movement, yet the underlying aim appears to be to train leaders who will serve as cadres for other lay organizations. Guided by religious teachings, these leaders make the Church's influence felt in many areas of social life. The movement spread rapidly, first to France, then to other countries; within a decade it included several hundred thousand members. The Jocists have almost become the prototype for contemporary Catholic Action organizations. A host of lay groups for women and adult workers, for students and peasants, and other groups both youth and adult, for men and women, all patterned after the Jocists, now exist throughout the world. What started as a modest program to help distressed industrial workers has now become an international social movement.

5.

It was during the pontificate of Pius XI that Social Action acquired a new character and the organizations to which it referred assumed semiofficial status as Church-endorsed movements. For with Pius XI, "Catholic Action" took on a technical meaning; Social Action became an aspect, though certainly the most important one, of "official Catholic Action." The major role in Social Action played by "the Pope of Catholic Action" began in December, 1922, with his first encyclical, *Ubi Arcano Dei* ("Peace of Christ in the Reign of Christ"). Provoked by the chaos and strife following in the wake of the First World War, this encyclical has been described as "a general call to Catholic Action"; the Pope declared that it marked "the beginning of a new era in the history of the Church." There followed a series of encyclicals and other public statements on the movement; Pius XI's last official act was to send a letter to the Philippine hierarchy exhorting them to promote Catholic Action as a means of fulfilling the Church's mission in that land. His successor, Pius XII, has continued the policy of vigorous Vatican support for the Catholic Action movement.

Under Pius XI's leadership "official Catholic Action" emerged as simultaneously a program, a method, and a movement. The program is of course essentially religious—"spiritual in nature yet temporal in effect." It is devoted to "moral reformation"—the conversion (or reconversion) of peoples to embrace and apply Christian teachings in their daily lives. The primary goal of Catholic Action is thus to develop a "Christian social conscience."

As a method, Catholic Action is nonpolitical, relying on direct-action tactics rather than political activity to achieve the movement's goals. This means, in practice, education, agitation, and propaganda by lay groups, combined with "good works." In fact the "actionists" have developed an "Inquiry Method" which is almost a formula for interrelating thought and action in applying Christian principles. The method is to study concrete problems, determine the Christian solution, and then to act accordingly—so the slogan (which originated with the Jocists): "Observe, Judge, Act." This method is combined with the "cell technique"—small groups are formed to train leaders; the members split apart and form other cells. In this way, through infiltration by trained leaders in many organizations, the influence of Catholic Action is exerted very widely if indirectly.

Though Catholic Action can be regarded as a method for advancing the program's aims, that method is used by organizations of Catholic laymen under the supervision of the hierarchy. Pope Pius XI defined Catholic Action as "the participation of the laity in the apostolate of the hierarchy"; certain Catholic writers appear to prefer the name "Lay Apostolate" to Catholic Action. As a movement, Catholic Action consists of numerous associations of Catholic laymen formed under Church auspices; these associations are the practical application of Catholic social principles by concerted group action. Two types of organizations are excluded—those which engage in political activity and those affiliated with non-Catholic groups. Separate organizations exist for the four divisions of Catholic laymen—men, women, young men, and young women; within each division there are various sections. The Jocists, for example, are now included in the worker's section of the young men's division. All these affiliated organizations, which together make up the present-day Catholic Action movement, seek to attain similar aims and use similar methods in their activities.

The precise form of Catholic Action organization varies somewhat from country to country, but the general pattern is everywhere the same. In parochial centers the work of Catholic Action groups is guided by the parish priest. However, the prime responsibility for Catholic Action rests with the bishop; hence the key center is the diocesan headquarters, immediately supervised by the bishop or his agent. At the national level there is ordinarily a secretariat. An international office is maintained at the Vatican.

In summary: Social Action obliges a lay Catholic, whatever his calling, to "live out" the moral precepts of the Christian faith in his daily affairs. This obligation is most significant in social and economic relations. Members of Social Action groups are expected to inculcate the principles of social justice in modern life. Social Action "seeks to imprint Christian principles on the whole social fabric, but is particularly interested in social legislation, social policy, and social systems."

6.

The Social Action movement appears to flourish with adversity for the Church. In fact it almost appears to be a defensive reaction by devout Catholics against the challenge offered by antireligious social and political movements. In countries like Ireland and Portugal where the Church enjoys the official blessings of the regimes in conducting its religious mission, the need for Social Action has not been pressing and Catholic Action is relatively undeveloped as a movement.

Nor has Catholic Action been seriously promoted in countries like the United States. Generally in the English-speaking nations the Catholics are a minority sect, yet they are free to practice their religion without political restrictions. In this country we have experienced waves of anti-Catholic agitation (such as the current one) from time to time, but politics is by custom divorced from religion and the government is neutral as far as the Church is concerned. No doubt the need for Social Action is present here, but it certainly is not acute. Hence, we find that in this country the influence of Catholic Action has been rather slight.

In the United States, Social Action has mainly taken the form of an education program, apparently designed in the main to acquaint lay leaders and the lesser clergy with Catholic social principles. The Social Action program in America is primarily the task of the Department of Social Action of the National Catholic Welfare Conference. This organization of the American hierarchy, with headquarters in Washington, D.C., was founded just after the First World War. During that war, a National Catholic Welfare Council was organized under the supervision of an Administrative Committee of American Bishops to assist the war effort. The organization was instituted on a permanent basis in September, 1919. In 1922 it was briefly suspended by the Vatican, then reinstated after the supremacy of bishops within their dioceses was explicitly recognized; the name was changed to the National Catholic Welfare Conference. Now the N.C.W.C. carries on many activities which in those countries where Catholic Action has been fully established are assigned to a national secretariat.

The initial aim of the Department of Social Action was to promote the "Bishops' Program" of 1919. This was a statement of Catholic social principles applied to the American scene. The statement was mainly derived from *Rerum Novarum* and was actually drafted by Father John A. Ryan, the first Director of the Department of Social Action. Since that pronouncement, the American hierarchy has from time to time enunciated proposals for social and economic reform and the Department has continued to be the national agency for promoting the bishops' programs. In performing its function the Department serves as a clearinghouse for publications and sponsors various activities by Catholics in the fields of labor and social welfare.

Another Social Action organization in this country is the National Catholic Rural Life Conference, with headquarters at Des Moines, Iowa. This is the American counterpart of the European Catholic peasant leagues. It publishes a monthly journal, *The Christian Farmer,* and generally carries on among agricultural groups activities like those of the Social Action Department of the N.C.W.C. Incidentally, one aim of the N.C.R.L.C.

(among many others) is to encourage owner-operated family farms.

Catholic Action in the United States has been, to say the least, a movement on a quite modest scale. However, in countries like Italy and France this is not the case. In such countries the populations, even though overwhelmingly of the Catholic faith, have displayed bitter anticlericalist sentiments. The regimes have pursued anti-Church policies. Socialist and Communist and other antireligious groups have attempted to woo workers away from the Church's influence. In the face of such hostility against Catholicism, the movement has thrived; Social Action organizations have achieved their greatest effect in those Continental countries where the Catholic religion has been under severe attack. We find that the influence of Catholic Action has been most marked during periods when the Church has suffered from disfavor by the constituted regime, and where, for one reason or another, Catholics have been unable to promote their reform programs openly in the political arena.

It is to be expected, therefore, that the historic home of Catholic Action is Italy. There tension between the Church and state has persisted for centuries to disrupt Italian political life. In Italy a national Catholic lay organization was founded in 1865. Later it was suppressed by the Italian government as a "subversive" organization. So was its successor, *Opera dei Congressi e dei Comitati Cattolici,* founded in 1881, but only after the *Opera* had stimulated study of the "social question" among Italian Catholics and had fostered numerous cooperative associations among workers and peasants. Other Italian regimes, including the Fascist, have vigorously fought the Catholic Action movement. Despite many setbacks, *L'Azione Cattolica* is now a strong, well-entrenched, highly developed movement in Italy, with a national secretariat and a full complement of lay organizations in all divisions. In France and Belgium, too, Social Action is today a vital and well-developed movement.

What is the significance of this Catholic reform program of Social Action? It is a program which, in Sturzo's words, "aims at the defense of the Christian spirit against anti-religious tendencies...." The movement has since its founding, and most particularly in recent decades, keenly competed with "left" political movements. Social Action has offered concrete, practical reform proposals inspired by Christian principles for alleviating the social and economic distress of the many members of modern societies.

Catholic apologists have firmly denied the charge often made by totalitarian rulers that Catholic Action is a disguised political movement, that it is a device used by the Church hierarchy to exert control over the laity for political purposes and thereby to advance in a covert manner the Church's political and social programs. But there appears to be some substance to the charge, even though strictly speaking it is not accurate. One observer, who terms Catholic Action "an instrument of totalitarian permeation," has claimed that Pius XI perfected the movement as a nonpolitical technique for combating antireligious regimes, notably the Italian Fascists. Perhaps this is the case. The totalitarian regimes pursued policies which do violence to Catholic social principles, and they repressed, as a matter of policy, any reform activity inspired by Christian principles. Certainly the Catholic Action movement has supplied formidable opposition to the spread of totalitarianism in recent decades. During the years of the underground resistance in the Second World War and in the postwar reconstruction period, this role of Social Action has become increasingly significant.

But of prime importance to us: Catholic Social Action is evidently neither pro-Democratic nor anti-Democratic. The movement has no particular political coloration at all.

7.

The most significant Catholic reform program by far is "Christian Democracy." It is also the most recently developed program. Like Catholic Action, the Christian Democratic movement evidences the contemporary resurgence of Catholicism as a social and political force. But unlike Catholic Action, the Christian Democratic program is frankly political. It is promoted by "confessional" party organizations which operate, alongside competing political parties, within established systems of popular government.

Christian Democracy has been described (by Anthony T. Bouscaren) as "a political movement based on the compatibility between Christianity and democracy, which seeks to apply new techniques to social and economic problems within the framework of constitutional, law-limited government." To realize a Christian social order is of course the goal of the movement. But the distinctive idea is about how to achieve it. The Christian Democrat believes that a proper method is organized political effort. The Church's reform program should be advanced by a party organization under Catholic leadership which participates in a political process structured along Democratic lines. For the Christian Democrat, as any other political leader who accepts the Democratic decision-making process, success depends on winning elections and controlling public offices. The Christian Democratic program can be achieved only to the extent that governmental policies are set by the principles of social justice.

The earliest proponent of the idea of Christian Democracy was apparently a Frenchman, Frederic Ozanam (1813–1853). Ozanam, a Sorbonne professor, was a founder of the Society of St. Vincent de Paul and a pioneering advocate of social legislation for the benefit of industrial workers. He also believed that Christianity and Democracy bear a peculiar affinity. They are more than just compatible; they are inexorably linked together. In 1848 he wrote: "Democracy is the natural goal of political progress"—a notion, incidentally, that Alexis de Tocqueville had advanced some years before, after his visit to the United States. And, said Ozanam: "God is guiding the world towards democracy." For him the Democratic credentials were authentically Christian; a Catholic is not "a democrat although a Christian, but a democrat because a Christian."

The most prominent contemporary Christian Democratic leader is the Sicilian priest Don Luigi Sturzo, a prolific author as well as a talented statesman and a brilliant thinker. Always a faithful apologist for the Church and always orthodox in his theology, Sturzo as a young man was nonetheless influenced by the "modernists." Modernism was a philosophical and theological movement of advanced Catholic intellectuals which gained some favor during the second half of the nineteenth century. The views of the modernists were eventually repudiated and denounced by the Vatican as founded on "error." An Italian leader of the movement, Romulo Murri, a personal friend of Sturzo, was in fact condemned by the Pope and left the Church.

Sturzo has explained his political career as an effort both to promote the Church's reform program and to combat the political influence of partisan groups who were avowedly antireligious. While still a student, Sturzo began his long career in politics. He started in local politics by organizing cooperatives among Italian peasants and aiding and counseling them in efforts to raise their incomes. For many years he served as Mayor of Caltagirone. He had held many other political posts when in January, 1919, he founded the Italian Popular Party. He led the *Popolari* until 1924, when it was suppressed by the Fascist regime and he was forced into exile. While in exile, he continued his work as the foremost intellectual leader of the Christian Democratic movement.

Despite efforts by Catholics like Sturzo, for years the Christian Democratic movement lacked the declared blessing of the Vatican. It was long after the Papacy had enthusiastically endorsed Social Action that it finally accepted as legitimate partisan political action by Catholics. The traditional policy of the Church was to discourage Catholic political organizations. In 1870 the Holy See imposed the *Non Expedit* ("It is not expedient") forbidding organized Catholic participation in Italian parliamentary elections. This move followed the suppression of religious congregations by Italian laws passed in the 1860s and the seizure of Rome by the Italian government. The Vatican's hostility to organized Catholic political action began to dissipate during the pontificate of Leo XIII, though under Pius X and Benedict XV the Vatican continued to issue stern pronouncements about partisan political action by organized Catholics.

In fact some early Christian Democratic groups in France and Italy were officially banned by the Vatican. Perhaps the best-known instance is that concerning *Le Sillon* ("The Furrow"). This organization was founded in 1894 as an outgrowth of Comte de Mun's *Ralliés* (Catholics rallying to the Republic during the Dreyfus incident). It started under the leadership of Marc Sangnier as a Catholic youth organization, but Protestants firmly committed to its principles of popular sovereignty, political equality, and natural rights were allowed to join. The Sillonistes held that democracy needs Christian principles to provide a moral basis for common action and public virtue. At the several national congresses, *Le Sillon* also championed, in the face of criticism from conservative Catholics, the cause of social legislation and workers' associations. In 1910 certain principles espoused by the Sillonistes were condemned by Pope Pius X as "modernist errors." Democracy as such was not denounced. However, Catholic principles of the divine origin of authority, of social hierarchy, and of rights and duties according to natural law were proclaimed as contrary to Sillonist principles. After the Papal condemnation, the movement was disbanded, but a successor, the League of the Young Republic, was formed in 1912.

Not until after the First World War, which brought the Bolshevik revolution and the establishment of other dictatorial regimes in the wake of the military victory of the Allied powers, was the ban against Catholic political action finally withdrawn. It was lifted at the urging of Sturzo; he states that in 1919 he was assured by the Vatican that the *Non Expedit* would not be an obstacle to founding an Italian Catholic party, provided it involved neither the Holy See nor the Catholic Action movement.

8.

The hesitant, reluctant modification by the Vatican of its policy against organized Catholic political action can be explained only by a combination of peculiar circumstances. Of course the activities of early Christian Democrats were bitterly opposed by conservative Catholics who feared the coming to power of the "masses." They had similarly opposed the initial efforts of the Social Action leaders. This conservative opposition was given some official support because certain early Christian Democrats espoused not only advanced political views but also philosophical positions which came to be associated with "modernism." At least as many early Christian Democratic leaders, however, were devout Catholics whose religious beliefs were above suspicion. Sturzo is an obvious example. But until Christian Democracy was disassociated with theological views of dubious orthodoxy, the movement was regarded with suspicion.

In addition, the anomalous position of the Pope as a temporal ruler in Italy complicated Vatican acceptance of Catholic political organizations. As long as the "Roman question" was outstanding, the Vatican displayed some anxiety to avoid any charge that the Church either subverted or collaborated with political regimes. In 1892 Leo XIII sent a letter to the French hierarchy urging them to obey dutifully the Republican regime, in spite of its ardent anticlericalism. In the encyclical *Graves de Communi,* primarily directed to Italian Catholics, again he declared that the Church's mission was nonpolitical; he exhorted Catholics to avoid involvement in partisan politics which would reflect adversely on the Church. The purpose of the encyclical, according to Sturzo, was to discourage certain political extremists in the

Catholic social movement and to prevent Social Action from becoming entangled with changes in political regimes. Leo XIII's successors found frequent occasions to reaffirm his warnings. Pope Pius XI was several times led to disclaim charges that the Italian hierarchy was politically partisan.

Even so, to understand fully the traditional Vatican policy toward Catholic political action, and especially to understand the delayed development of the Christian Democratic movement, we must appreciate the differences between Continental Democratic theory and practice and the Democracy of English-speaking countries. In the Anglo-American tradition, Democracy, though to an extent related to Liberalism, has never been characterized by anticlericalism, and no historic conflict has existed between Christian and Democratic groups. In contrast, Continental Liberals tended to oppose extending political privileges to the great mass of peoples and generally were less than enthusiastic about expanding popular influence in government. The Continental Democratic movement, as a result, received its strongest support from working-class groups which were at the same time hostile to Liberal theory and practice. Socialists identified themselves with "the people" and promoted the Democratic cause of government for the benefit of a majority of the people. Marxist parties in fact preempted the "Social Democratic" label. Consequently, in Europe Socialism has historically been linked with Democracy. But European Socialists have also been anticlericalist. The Church hierarchy therefore looked with misgivings, if not rank hostility, on any popular movement called "Democratic," just as it did on movements called "Socialist"—out of fear of atheism.

Perhaps the crucial factor in the development of the Christian Democratic movement was the pressing need for political organizations capable of defending the Church's interests and advancing the social-reform program. In a sense the opposition forced Catholic reformers to fight for their program in a political arena. Certainly the movement acquired its greatest strength in those

Continental European countries where devout Catholics were confronted by aggressive, well-organized, anticlericalist political antagonists.

We must remember that the political situation in many European countries contrasts rather sharply with that prevailing here in the United States. In this country a Catholic is not identified by his religious faith when he engages in political activity. He does so as an individual member of a political party. But in this country we have a two-party system. There are only two main parties, and they are not formed around controversial issues of profound import or around the interests of special groups. Rather, the Republican and Democratic parties are organized around broad and general questions of public policy which evoke the interest of a vast majority of the American people. Another way to put it is that the two parties are in substantial agreement on the fundamental issues of American political life.

In most European countries the situation is quite different. A multiparty system is characteristic of Continental politics. Instead of two large and popular parties, there are many minority parties. Each is organized around a few basic issues which divide the electorate, for example, such a question as whether the regime should be a monarchy or a republic. Hence the parties try, like pressure groups in this country, to promote the narrow special interests of their constituents. Many Continental parties have customarily included as features of their programs opposition to Church proposals. With the increasing parliamentary activity of anticlericalist Socialist, Communist, National Socialist, Liberal, and conservative factions after the First World War, organized political action by Catholics became imperative. Catholic Democrats particularly were more and more moved by the pressure of events to organize separate "confessional" parties. For they had to participate in parliamentary politics in order to promote social reforms as well as to protect the Church from political attacks. Sturzo once remarked, significantly, that Pius XI "displayed a rather favorable attitude towards intervention

of Catholics in the political field, in the attempt to oppose the
socialist wave."

9.

We find forerunners of the Christian Democratic movement, in the form of intellectual leaders and political organizations, fairly numerous before the First World War, but it was
not until after 1919 that the movement actually developed on
any scale. For the most part the Christian Democratic parties
were organized during the interval between the two World
Wars. Even then the movement progressed slowly. With the
spread of totalitarian dictatorships, the Catholic parties, along
with the other dissident political groups, were crushed. After VE
Day, the Christian Democratic parties reappeared as stronger
and better-disciplined organizations than their prewar counterparts. The development of the movement in France, Italy, and
Germany followed much the same lines.

The French Christian Democratic movement began under the
Third Republic with the formation of the Popular Liberal Party;
the party reached the peak of its prewar strength in the mid-1930s
—in 1934 it founded the journal *L'Aube*—but it was never a very
effective organization. During the Vichy regime, the party was, of
course, suppressed. With the liberation of France, it was re-formed
as the Popular Republican Movement (*Mouvement Républicain
Populaire*), supported by the French Catholic youth and labor
organizations. As part of the "Third Force," the MRP has had
members in important posts in many Fourth Republic ministries;
it has produced in Robert Schuman and Georges Bidault two
outstanding premiers.

The Italian Popular Party (*Partito Popolare Italiano*), founded
in 1919, won in its first election contest one-fifth of the seats in
the Italian Chamber to become the second largest party, next to
the Socialists. The *Popolari* was suppressed by the Fascist regime

122

in the mid-1920s. After the liberation of Italy, it was re-formed as the Christian Democratic Party. As the largest party in the Italian Parliament, the Christian Democrats, especially under the leadership of the late Alcide de Gasperi, have dominated the Italian government since 1945. The party is supported by the Catholic Association of Christian Workers (ACLI), founded in 1944. In the April, 1948, Italian elections the Christian Democrats polled almost a clear majority of the popular votes.

The German Center (Catholic) Party, which was originally founded during the period of Bismarck's dominance, became one of the stronger parties under the imperial regime. After the Armistice in 1918, the Center Party entered the three-party "Weimar Coalition" which prepared the constitution and dominated German politics during the abortive republic. The party was outlawed after the Nazi *coup d'état*. With the collapse of the Nazi regime, it was re-formed as the Christian Democratic Union under the leadership of Konrad Adenauer. The CDU, in alliance with the Bavarian Catholic Party (the Christian Social Union), has consistently polled a larger number of votes than any other party in West German elections. The Adenauer coalition has headed the Bonn government since its creation. The Christian Democrats did not retain the pre-Nazi party name, perhaps because in 1933 some Center Party members voted for Hitler's Enabling Act, perhaps because the CD leaders desired to make their party interdenominational as much as possible. The Bavarian Catholic Party's leadership has generally been more conservative than that of the CDU leaders, though a "Left Catholic" faction, led by a Munich attorney, Dr. Joseph Mueller, and supported by many clergymen, has increasingly exerted greater influence in political affairs.

Prior to the Communist *coups d'état* in Czechoslovakia, Poland, Hungary, Romania, and other Central and Eastern European countries, Catholic parties, now suppressed, were active. Elsewhere in Europe—in Austria, Belgium, Holland, Luxembourg, and Switzerland—Catholic parties more or less patterned after the Christian Democratic parties in Italy, France, and Germany have continued to participate with some success in parliamentary politics.

It is since the end of the Second World War, then, that the Christian Democratic movement has experienced its greatest growth. In postwar elections the Christian Democratic parties in Continental European countries have consistently polled from one-fifth to one-half the popular vote—an impressive share of the vote where many parties are competing for electoral favor. In the parliaments of those countries free of Soviet domination, Christian Democratic leaders have played prominent roles in shaping the regimes and directing the governments.

This remarkable postwar growth in influence of European Christian Democracy is attributable in part to the firm and steadfast opposition displayed by leading Christian Democrats to the totalitarian movements and regimes. To continue the fight against totalitarian dictatorships after the seizure of power, Christian Democratic leaders like Don Sturzo went either into exile or into the underground. Throughout the Second World War, the Christian Democrats supplied many leaders of the underground resistance movements and the "free governments" in exile. In the Italian resistance movement (*Giunta*) the largest group was De Gasperi's Christian Democrats; they fought alongside Communists and other partisan groups against the Fascists and the Nazis. Georges Bidault, the MRP leader, was chairman of the French National Resistance Council. The German Christian Democratic Union was originally formed by Konrad Adenauer as an underground resistance movement. The exemplary antitotalitarian record of these and other Christian Democratic leaders has undoubtedly contributed to the postwar successes of their parties, the initial nucleus of which was the resistance groups.

Perhaps as a result of the wartime experiences of their leaders, combined with the failure of the parties during the 1930s, the Christian Democratic parties developed since 1945 differ in several important respects from their prewar counterparts. Though the leadership and the membership continue to be overwhelmingly Catholic, the term "Catholic" is noticeably absent from the names of most postwar parties. They profess to be nonsectarian; Protestants who accept the Christian Democratic program are welcomed into membership. Moreover, the new Christian Democratic parties are more like mass movements than political factions, as European, or at least Continental, political parties have traditionally tended to be. Unlike political parties in this country, the Christian Democrats maintain auxiliary youth, women, and labor organizations for mobilizing electoral support. This custom has long prevailed in European politics. But like American parties, the Christian Democrats avoid special-interest demands and strive for a broad, popular appeal. In fact they, more than any other European political movement, resemble the parties in English-speaking countries.

Even as impressive as the Christian Democratic movement has been during the past decade, it promises to exert increasingly greater influence in European politics in the future, as the international movement grows and matures. In 1926 an International Secretariat of Democratic Parties of Christian Inspiration was founded under the tutelage of Don Sturzo, with headquarters in Paris. Several international congresses were held, attended by delegates from a number of different countries. But with the rise of the totalitarian dictatorships, the organization became virtually inactive although it remained in existence.

During the Second World War when many Christian Democratic leaders were exiled in London, the British "People and Freedom" group sponsored private meetings of anti-Fascist Christian Democrats from eleven countries. In November, 1940, the International Christian Democratic Union was formed with a headquarters in London. The Union adopted a constitution and elected officers, but while the war was on it functioned with slight effect.

In 1946 efforts to create a strong international federation of

Christian Democratic parties were blocked by French MRP leaders. They advocated a less formal, more private, association. In February, 1947, the Swiss Popular Party called a congress at Lucerne. This congress decided to accept a Belgian proposal calling for an informal organization of Christian Democratic leaders who would meet together to exchange views, rather than an international federation of parties. This organization, known as the *Nouvelles Equipes Internationales,* held its first conference at Liége in May, 1947. Subsequent congresses, to which fifteen countries have sent delegates or observers, have been held at Luxembourg and, in September, 1948, at the Hague. An office of the Secretary-General has been established at Paris.

10.

However, we must not assume that all European Christian Democratic leaders are like-minded on all questions, or that all party members endorse with equal enthusiasm the party programs. Actually the ideas and practices of the leaders vary somewhat. As in most other political movements, we find "radical" and "conservative" wings of opinion on about every question. At the same time most members of the principal Christian Democratic parties do seem to share some common views. This is despite the fact that the Christian Democratic parties in the different countries have not officially adopted a uniform program. What is significant is that the general orientation of the Christian Democratic parties, as reflected in their programs, is much the same if not identical.

For one thing, the Christian Democrats are characteristically "center" parties, as European political organizations are classified. This means that they accept the constituted regime, unlike the extreme "right" and "left" factions. Hence in their programs the Christian Democrats share a number of points with other center (or "third force") parties. In addition, the Christian Democratic programs contain some distinctive proposals.

Like other center parties, the Christian Democrats are committed to the principles of popular government. They advocate a parliamentary regime generally patterned after the British system of government, long the prototype for friends of popular government on the Continent. Hence the Christian Democrats oppose the extreme "right" and "left" groups which demand fundamental changes in the constitutions. They favor the constitutional guarantees of civil liberties, unrestricted popular elections, a head of state with secure tenure, a strong but politically responsible ministry, a bicameral legislature but with limited powers for the upper house, and decentralization of authority in the form of local "home rule." On questions of political forms, the Christian Democrats and other third-force parties may to some extent disagree on details, but we find no basic differences between them.

Similarly, again like other center parties, the Christian Democrats oppose the influence of the reactionary "left"—the Communists. If anything this opposition is more vigorous and uncompromising than that of other third-force groups. The Christian Democrats have consistently resisted Communist efforts to dictate domestic policy. They have also consistently tried to prevent any expansion of Soviet influence in foreign affairs. In the "cold war" the Christian Democrats have generally sought to stabilize East-West relations for the sake of world peace. But when a choice between supporting the United States or the Soviet Union has been required, the Christian Democrats, more often than other third-force parties, have aligned themselves on the side of the "Western Democracies." In fact, among European political leaders, the Christian Democrats are the Soviet Union's most severe critics and the United States' best friends.

Where the Christian Democratic programs are distinctive is in regard to the status of the Church and reform of the social and economic system. Present-day Christian Democratic parties are, as European Catholic parties have traditionally been, friendly to the religious institution of the Church. This does not mean that the Christian Democrats propose establishment of the Catholic Church or even preferred treatment for ecclesiastical officials. In fact, the Christian Democrats insist on a clear separation of Church and state. However, they do defend what they regard as the Church's legitimate interests and policies as they bear on politics. These pertain to matters which in the Catholic view concern faith and morals. For example, the Christian Democrats advocate provision for religious instruction in the schools, state support of parochial schools, recognition of marriage as a religious sacrament, stringent curbs on divorce, and freedom for the clergy and members of religious orders to carry on the Church's spiritual mission. While advocating such policies, the Christian Democrats do not uncompromisingly demand that they be adopted. What they do insist on is that the Church is a legitimate "society" and that its rights, as the rights of any other "natural society" (like the family and the labor union), must be dutifully respected by the government. The state must allow the Church to perform unhampered the function for which it properly exists.

Distinctive, too, is the Christian Democratic program for social and economic reform. This program is, of course, derived from the Catholic principles of social justice; it represents an attempt to apply these principles to contemporary social and economic problems. This means that the Christian Democrat rejects the competitive individualism of capitalism—advocated by the Liberal—and the rigid state collectivism of Socialism. Neither system advances the common good, in the Catholic view. For the Christian Democrat assumes that a properly ordered society is by definition pluralistic. Persons are members of various social groups, each of which exists to satisfy certain needs of its members. No "society"—the church and state included—has an exclusive claim on any person. At the same time, every person has rights and duties by virtue of his membership in "natural" social groups: as a member of a family, a functional association, a civil community—and a church and a state. The peculiar role of the state is to serve as regulator and coordinator of the many "societies"—to assure that the rights of members are protected and that their duties are performed. It is not the job of the state, however, to perform functions properly belonging to a lesser society.

When the Christian Democrat applies this conception of a social order to the contemporary scene, he is led to contend that persons should enjoy greater equality of opportunity than they now have, and that income should be distributed more equitably than it now is. To bring about greater social and economic equality, the Christian Democrats urge that the government take certain specific actions. For example, they propose legislation for public housing, price control, land reform, family bonuses, labor standards, woman suffrage, and for expanded public responsibility in the fields of social security and health.

Almost as distinctive as the reform goals are the methods the Christian Democrat advocates to achieve them. Most impressive is the absence of any doctrinaire approach to the solution of social and economic problems. This is in contrast to most European political movements. European Socialists have traditionally urged "nationalization of industry" as the means, just as European Liberals have traditionally urged "free enterprise" as a cure-all for social and economic ills. Not so the Christian Democrats. They do not object in principle to either nationalization or free enterprise; whatever method does the job best is acceptable to them. But they generally favor a method which avoids the extremes of individual or state action—a method of collective *group* action. This conforms to their Democratic conviction that popular participation in public affairs should be increased. What they favor is greater participation by the members of social groups in the making of decisions which affect the social and economic welfare of these groups. In the postwar program of one Christian Democratic party, we find this passage: "A true democracy could be formed only if political decisions were taken through a full and conscious and free participation of the people. Through the method of freedom, the changing substance of political and economic freedoms could be realized gradually in a much more satisfying way."

It appears that what is distinctive about the Christian Democratic program, what sets it apart from the programs of other European parties, is the basic position that a Christian social order should be achieved by Democratic means.

II.

We have seen that the reform programs advanced by Catholic Corporativists and Social Actionists are not "pro-Democratic" by profession. But we have also seen that these programs appear not to be singularly "anti-Democratic."

With Christian Democracy, the situation is somewhat different. The program is assertedly founded on Democratic as well as Catholic principles. Consequently it is in relation to this new Christian Democratic movement where the issue of Catholicism and Democracy is most clearly drawn. The issue centers on two questions. First, do Christian Democratic goals or methods represent a departure from genuine Catholic teachings? Second, does Christian Democratic theory or practice violate Democratic beliefs or principles?

We have seen that doubts about the answers to these questions have been raised, because some programs clearly incompatible with Democracy have been promoted by Catholics. Spain is a Catholic country where the Church enjoys a position of favor, and the Franco regime is anything but Democratic. Is the Falangist movement a true expression of Catholic teachings? Argentina is a Catholic country, and the Peron regime was frankly anti-Democratic. Is the Peronista to be explained by Catholicism?

Closer to home, we have the case of Father Charles Coughlin, the Detroit priest. Back in the 1930s he roused the rabble in fine style from the pulpit of his Church of the Little Flower.

But the answer to this first question appears clear enough. The fact that some Catholics sponsor anti-Democratic movements has no bearing on the issue. The Franco regime has been roundly criticized by prominent Catholic leaders of many nationalities. The Peron regime was overthrown by devout Catholics; it was the Church hierarchy which openly defied Peron immediately prior to his fall from power. Father Coughlin's so-called "Social Justice" movement was repudiated by many outstanding American Catholics. He was finally silenced by his own bishop. For every Father Coughlin, there is a Father Ryan.

It is true that Catholic teachings do prescribe certain principles, but these principles lend themselves to variant applications and implementations. Catholicism in practice admits many different political viewpoints but requires none in particular. Among others, Catholicism admits a Christian Democratic viewpoint. Christian Democracy is quite compatible with teachings expounded by recent Popes of the Church of Rome. In fact, those teachings inspired the Christian Democratic movement, as well as the Corporative and Social Action movements.

The answer to the other question—do Christian Democratic beliefs or principles violate Democratic theory or practice?— appears less clear at this point. To answer it satisfactorily, we must inspect the complicated relations between Christian Democratic beliefs and principles and those espoused by the American Democrat.

Perhaps there are many Democratic doctrines which we could consider, but we shall limit our discussion to three central tenets of Democratic theory—popular sovereignty, political equality, and majority rule. These are sufficiently crucial to American Democratic beliefs and principles that we can, in terms of them, determine what the actual relation is between Democracy and Catholicism.

Chapter Five

POPULAR SOVEREIGNTY

I.

The old wives' prescription for a bride's wedding out-
fit—"something old, something new, something borrowed, something blue"—describes, after a fashion, a political theory. Political
thinkers do not start afresh when they compound a theory. They
start where other thinkers have left off. Democratic theory certainly includes some old and some borrowed, and perhaps
some blue, notions. It rests on some assumptions familiar long
before Democratic beliefs were fully articulated or Democratic
principles were widely accepted. But of course what is significant about any political theory is what is new: that makes it
distinctive.

Democratic theory includes at least two distinctive principles.
One is that in the exercise of political authority, each member
of a group should count for one and no more than one. This is
called the "principle of political equality." The other is that
a decision about the exercise of a community's authority should
be determined by a vote of a majority of members. This is the
principle of majority rule.

These principles of political equality and majority rule, taken
together, every Democrat by definition does accept, and every

non-Democrat does not. These principles imply a third, which is logically prior to the others, that the Democrat likewise accepts. It is that the authority to make decisions binding on a community should be located in the membership. This is a formulation in Democratic terms of a venerable idea which many political thinkers have espoused in some form—the principle of popular sovereignty.

Not all thinkers who have accepted this principle are Democrats, however. What the principle of popular sovereignty supplies is an answer to the question: Where should political authority be located? The answer is: In the people over whom it is exercised. Thinkers of strikingly different hues have held that authority should be located in the people. Many have moved from a belief in popular sovereignty to argue in favor of some kind of elite rule, by one man or by a few, thus rejecting political equality and majority rule. Thomas Hobbes is an example. So is John Locke. In the *Leviathan* (1651) after accepting the principle of popular sovereignty, Hobbes advocated virtually absolute rule by a "sovereign monarch." In the *Second Treatise of Government* (1690) Locke, after contending that the people are the source of authority, argued in favor of a "mixed constitution" under which the authority of the royal executive is limited by a "sovereign parliament." For the principle of popular sovereignty says nothing about *who* should exercise political authority, or *how* it should be exercised. To these questions the principles of political equality and majority rule do provide Democratic answers.

But, at this point, the important thing for us is that American Democrats who accept the principles of political equality and majority rule also accept a principle of popular sovereignty. In fact today popular sovereignty is so widely taken for granted that few American thinkers even bother to discuss the question of where that authority which present-day rulers exercise should be located.

This is not to say that the question no longer presents unresolved problems. In fact it presents some serious problems which are not resolved by contemporary theorists. Unfortunately these problems have been concealed somewhat by the terms in which the question has traditionally been discussed.

Throughout the history of Western thought, political thinkers have entertained the question: What is the source of political authority? Virtually every political thinker starting with Plato has offered some sort of answer to this question. On this issue modern thinkers have held one of two general positions—either that political authority has a divine source or that it is of human origin. Religionists of course have adopted the former position. This is the case, we shall see, with Catholic thinkers, who hold that God is the source of all authority. Political thinkers of religious inspiration, Catholics included, then proceed to discuss the location of political authority in terms of God's will.

The Liberal, in contrast, adopts a position that political authority is of human origin. The source of authority, he holds, is the people. The people are sovereign; there is no higher authority. The Liberal then similarly proceeds to discuss the location of political authority, though not of course in religious terms, since Liberals are "enlightened" thinkers.

It might seem at first glance that on this issue any Christian would hold a quite different view from a Democrat. The Christian by definition believes in an omnipotent Creator of the entire universe; the Democrat, on the other hand, believes that the people are sovereign.

However, it is not the case that there is any conflict here between Catholic and Democratic beliefs. It is true, we shall see, that there is a conflict between Catholic and Liberal beliefs about authority, and also between Liberal and Democratic beliefs. Both the Catholic and the Liberal have an answer to this traditional question about the source of political authority, and their answers differ. But for the Democrat the question makes no sense. The question implies that persons who exercise authority are different from those over whom it is exercised. This the

Democrat denies. He starts with the assumption that Democratic authority should be located in the same persons over whom it is exercised. The question about the location of authority is important, then, for the Democrat. So are questions about who should exercise authority and how it should be exercised. But the question about the *source* of authority is meaningless because in Democratic terms authority has no source—only location. We shall see that Liberal beliefs depart radically from Catholic teachings about these important questions, and that Democratic beliefs depart radically from Liberal teachings. But the Democratic doctrine of popular sovereignty does not conflict with the Catholic theory of authority. Let us now see how this is the case.

2.

The Catholic view about the source of authority is a traditionalist one. Along with the Thomist theory of natural law, the Catholic has inherited a theory of authority likewise of medieval vintage. In fact it was a theory which St. Thomas Aquinas fully articulated. It has undergone some refinement and elaboration since then, notably during the periods of the Reformation and the Counter Reformation. But today the lineaments of the theory are substantially the same as they were in the thirteenth century. This is evident from Papal encyclicals promulgated within the past hundred years. Perhaps the fullest and clearest modern statement of the theory is contained in an encyclical by Pope Leo XIII, *Immortale Dei* ("The Christian Constitution of States," 1885).

The Catholic theory of authority is not at all a simple theory, but it is easily understandable if one bears in mind that it is founded on certain religious beliefs. It rests on the supposition that God the Creator is the sole source of authority, whatever its character; any authority in human hands is necessarily a grant from God to man. As part of the divine plan of the universe, authority is willed by God, and for a purpose. God has granted His authority so that men can do His bidding on earth. To fulfill his "nature," man must live in society and a society can hold together only if there is a "ruling part," directing all to strive for the common good. Hence authority must be located in every human society. It is because authority is essential for achieving the goal of human life that God has willed that every person be subject to a higher human authority, just as every person is ultimately subject to the highest authority of God.

The divine origin of authority sets the character for the Catholic theory. A novel feature is the contention that God is "the one true Sovereign." In this sense of the term, nothing human is sovereign because everything human is a creation of God. No human ruler can rightfully claim sovereignty (in the Austinian sense of absolute supremacy) because God has not vested authority in any one ruler. Instead, God has distributed His authority widely among men. One ruler is the equal of another in that he exercises authority granted by God. But if only because God's authority is vested in other rulers as well, the authority of any ruler is by necessity limited. The specific limits depend on the terms of God's grant. These limits are set forth in the natural law.

The key to this theory of plural distribution of authority among many rulers is the Catholic conception of society. A society is an association of persons for some common purpose. It is "natural" for persons to form themselves into societies. The needs of men, both spiritual and temporal, are numerous and varied. For each set of human needs there is a natural form of society with its peculiar purpose. A person is thus a member of a number of different societies; the number is set by the variety of his needs.

This conception of society has been given a distinctive twist by a contemporary French Thomist philosopher, Jacques Maritain, in his book *The Rights of Man and Natural Law* (1947).

Maritain's formulation adds nothing to the theory but it does state the ideas in an interesting way. What Maritain calls his "personalist" theory is, he says, "organically linked to religion":

"God, principle and end of the human person and prime source of natural law, is by the same token the prime source of political society and authority among men." Maritain's theory is, in his own words, "characterized by the following features; it is *personalist,* because it considers society to be a whole composed of persons whose dignity is anterior to society and who, however indigent they may be, contain within their very being a root of independence and aspire to even greater degrees of independence until they achieve the perfect spiritual liberty which no human society has within its gift.

"This conception is, in the second place, *communal,* because it recognizes the fact that the person tends naturally towards society and communion, in particular towards the political community, and because, in the specifically political sphere and to the extent that man is a part of political society, it considers the common good superior to that of individuals.

"In the third place this conception is *pluralist,* because it assumes that the development of the human person normally requires a plurality of autonomous communities which have their own rights, liberties and authority" (pp. 20–22).

This conception is really not so complicated as his statement suggests. We can readily illustrate it in terms of the most elemental form of human association, the "domestic society." For a Catholic, the family is the natural basis for social life because a Christian can satisfy his material and spiritual needs only as a member of a family. God has ordained that mankind shall "increase and multiply." This command can be obeyed without falling into mortal sin only by the institution of lawful marriage. Marriage is therefore a right and duty of mankind. Members of this natural form of society called the "family" have certain rights and duties. For example, the parents have a right and duty to instruct the child in Christian teachings. The father, as the head of the family, has a right and duty to provide for the material and spiritual needs of the members. The wife and the child, too, have rights and duties derived from the functions they perform in the life of the family.

The family is a natural form of human association but it is also an "imperfect" society. The purpose of the family is an essential one in the life of the members, but it is still a limited purpose. Not all human needs can be satisfied just as a member of a family. Another natural form of society is the functional association. So is the civil community, which is more inclusive than the family or the functional group. Membership in these societies and others as well is necessary in order for a person to satisfy all his needs. Two other natural societies, which we shall discuss in a moment, are the state and the church.

The Catholic theory of authority is inseparable from this conception of the person as a member of various societies. In Catholic teachings the right to rule and the duty to obey depend on the purpose of the group over which authority is exercised. A basic distinction is drawn by the Catholic between "power" (or force) and "authority"—a distinction between the *ability* and the *right* to rule. A ruler may have much power but no authority. Authority is the "rightful" power which one person exercises over another, in conformance with God's will. Thus in contrast to mere power, authority implies a moral relation fixed in law. Because it is divinely ordained, authority entails moral rights and duties for both ruler and ruled. These rights and duties are prescribed by natural law. It is God's will that the authority of a society be exercised for the common good of the members. Therefore a ruler has a right to exercise the authority of the group but it is his duty to rule "justly"—for the welfare not of a part but of the whole society. In turn the ruled has a duty to obey the authority of a society. But no person has any duty to obey a ruler who rules without right or contrary to natural law. So as the member of society is bound to render dutiful obedience to the authority established over him, the ruler of a society is bound to exercise the authority with care and consideration for the common good.

What is significant for us about this theory is that authority is always related to membership in a society. God has vested in each society enough authority—no more or less—to fulfill the purpose of that society. Authority is dependent on the purpose of the society and the purpose of every human association is a limited one. The conclusion: every person is subject not to one authority, but to as many authorities as societies of which he is a member. It follows that no ruler has an absolute right to rule, and no person has an absolute duty to obey. This is the import of the Catholic teaching that God is the one true Sovereign.

3.

So far we have examined simply some basic ideas in the Catholic theory of authority. Another indispensable ingredient in this theory is the distinction between civil and ecclesiastical authority. At this point there appear to be some popular misconceptions about exactly what Catholics do and do not believe about authority. What we must bear in mind, in order to avoid any misconceptions, is that in Catholic theory the authority of a ruler is either civil or ecclesiastical but never both. This is most important to remember because the Catholic doctrine of ecclesiastical authority is not at all the same as the doctrine of civil authority. This distinction between civil and ecclesiastical authority rests on a religious belief. This belief, formulated as the doctrine of the "Two Cities," is historically linked to the name of St. Augustine, a fifth-century Latin Father, who propounded the doctrine in a famous early Christian treatise, *The City of God*.

Catholics of course accept the Christian dogma that man, the creature of God, has a dual nature, a mortal body and an immortal soul. For each nature, man has a corresponding God-given purpose in life, temporal and spiritual. For each purpose there is an appropriate realm of authority. God has provided civil authority for the care of man's bodily needs, ecclesiastical authority for the care of his immortal soul.

This suggests a problem as old as the Christian religion. The authority vested by God in human societies is divided into two realms, corresponding to the twofold spiritual and temporal purposes in human life. The civil realm is concerned with the material aspects of human existence, the ecclesiastical with the spiritual aspects. This means that every person is subject to two realms of authority. The problem immediately presented is: What is the proper relation between them?

Very early in the development of the Roman Church, a Pope, Gelasius I, propounded a doctrine in an effort to resolve this problem. It is called the doctrine of the "Two Swords." It was accepted by medieval churchmen and became incorporated into Thomist thought and therefore into Catholic teachings.

According to this doctrine, the two realms of authority are independent and coequal. Every ruler is an agent of God, but the functions of rulers differ. The function of the civil ruler is to take care of the worldly needs of the members of the society. The function of the ecclesiastical ruler is to take care of man's spiritual needs. For each realm of authority, there is a suitable "sword," or means for enforcing the rule. The civil ruler can use physical force and lawful punishment, taking action against "the body and goods of men." The ecclesiastical ruler can use exhortation and prayer, with the ultimate sanction being excommunication—ostracism of the offender from the religious group. Pope Gelasius taught that the rulers of the two realms should cooperate with one another, with each supplementing the efforts of the other. But the important point to notice in this doctrine is that both rulers are accountable to God and neither is superior to the other within his appropriate realm. The civil ruler does not depend for his authority on the ecclesiastical ruler, or conversely.

At this point in the Catholic theory of authority, it is easy to become confused. The Catholic holds (1) that authority is distributed among the many different societies of which men are members and (2) that authority is divided between the civil and ecclesiastical realms. To avoid confusion, let us return to the Catholic notion of society which, we said, is the key to understanding the Catholic theory of authority.

Strictly speaking, the realm of neither ecclesiastical nor civil authority coincides precisely with any human society. However, two societies do play exceptional roles in the exercise of authority within the respective spiritual and temporal realms. The two societies are the religious community of the church and the civil community of the state. The human institutions of church and state do not entirely occupy the respective realms. But in Scholastic terms both the church and state are "perfect" societies. A perfect society is endowed with the essential means for achieving the purpose of its members. That is: man's spiritual needs can be fully realized as a communicant of the church, and his temporal needs can be fully satisfied as a citizen of the state. Not simply that: as a churchman and a citizen, man's highest purposes in life can be realized—his ultimate needs in this world can be adequately satisfied through membership in the two societies of the church and the state.

Perhaps what is confusing here is the rather distinctive Catholic conception of the Church and state. This conception involves a notion of hierarchy of authority, or rather, authorities, since there are as many authorities as there are societies. In medieval times it was accepted that the head of the ecclesiastical hierarchy was the Pope, while the head of the civil hierarchy, then a feudal system, was the Holy Roman Emperor. At the present time the Catholic still maintains that the Holy See is the highest authority in the ecclesiastical realm. What this means is that on questions of faith and morals (which concern salvation of the soul) the Papacy, as the head of the Church hierarchy, is the court of last resort, so to speak. The Pope is a sort of constitutional monarch elected for life. While in office, he is the supreme ecclesiastical official of the Church.

Throughout the modern period the Catholic has, of course, recognized the nation state as the highest civil authority. The monarchical form of rule accepted for the ecclesiastical realm is not prescribed for the civil realm, but the same notion of the role of the head of the hierarchy—essentially a medieval notion —does apply. That is, just as the primary responsibility for the spiritual welfare of man is in the hands of the Church hierarchy headed by the Papacy, so is the primary responsibility for the temporal welfare of man in the hands of the head of the civil hierarchy, the rulers of the state. This does not mean that the state has a monopoly of civil authority or that it is "sovereign." For the Catholic, the state is one of a number of societies, but it is exceptional because it is a "society of societies." As any other society, the state is vested with authority to fulfill its purpose, but that is all. Its purpose is to promote the common good of the citizens. Hence, the peculiar role of the state is to foster the proper functioning of the various lesser societies which are parts of the whole political community. Its responsibility is to regulate and coordinate the activities of other groups but not to perform their functions for them. For the state's authority is strictly circumscribed by the authority vested in these lesser societies. For example: "The family possesses a sphere and function that, as it existed before the state, must be preserved against the state; never can the state substitute itself for the family, without destroying the human values nursed by the family" (H. Rommen, *The State in Catholic Thought*, 1945, p. 14). In other words, it would be contrary to the nature of the state for it to undertake any function, or to exercise any authority, of a lesser society, such as the family.

142

To sum up: The Church and state are the highest authorities, ecclesiastical and civil, but neither is a "sovereign" authority. The Church and state play primary roles in the realms of ecclesiastical and civil authority respectively, but they do not play *all* the roles. Other essential roles are played by "imperfect" lesser societies. The distinctive roles of the Church and state stem from their ultimate responsibility for the proper exercise of authority by the rulers of lesser societies within the respective realms.

With this theory a complication arises because certain aspects of human life simultaneously involve the welfare of the body and the soul. That the two realms to some extent overlap is contemplated in Catholic teachings. Marriage is an example. Marriage in its spiritual aspect is a union of souls symbolized by a religious sacrament. In its temporal aspect marriage is a civil contract which entails legal privileges and obligations for the parties to the contract. But for the Catholic this is no particular problem, at least in theory. All authority is derived from God and the purposes of the two realms are set by God. Ecclesiastical and civil authority do not conflict; they complement one another in promoting the common spiritual and temporal good of mankind as willed by God. What the complication consists in is a question of overlapping jurisdiction—dual responsibilities. In Catholic teachings where both realms of authority are concerned, the rights and duties of all rulers must be recognized and respected. To avoid undue conflict, the exact responsibilities of the ecclesiastical and the civil rulers in such instances should be clearly defined. It is the special task of the Church and state to see that a definition is worked out to the satisfaction of everyone concerned. The Church and state should negotiate an agreement setting forth precisely the relation between the ecclesiastical and civil authorities on such matters as marriage. This agreement is called a "concordat"; it is a kind of treaty negotiated and signed by the heads of the Church and state. By a concordat, relations within the whole community can and should be ordered so that all societies function harmoniously for the common good of all members.

We have examined in some detail this Catholic theory which holds that God is the source of all authority. But the important points for us to notice about this theory, since these points do bear on the Democratic doctrine of popular sovereignty, are the following: (1) Authority is widely dispersed, located in numerous "societies" (or, as I shall subsequently refer to them, "communities"—associations of persons for a common purpose), some religious and some secular in character. (2) Authority located in any community is circumscribed by the limited purpose of that association of persons. (3) Authority entails moral rights and duties both for those who exercise it and for those over whom it is exercised.

4.

This Catholic theory of authority is, we shall see, quite compatible with the Democratic doctrine of popular sovereignty, even though the Catholic does assume that God is the source of authority, whereas for the Democrat this assumption is superfluous. However, the Catholic theory of authority is clearly at odds with a doctrine of popular sovereignty espoused by the Liberal. He tries to justify his doctrine by a most ingenious theory of authority. But this is a theory no Catholic or Democrat can accept. To avoid any possible misunderstandings about the relation between the Catholic theory of authority and the Democratic doctrine of popular sovereignty, we should be clear about how the Liberal theory differs from both the Catholic and the Democratic beliefs about the location of authority.

In contrast to the Catholic, the Liberal holds that the source of authority is strictly human. It is the "people." They are supreme. The Liberal therefore says that sovereign authority should be located in the people who are ruled. But in contrast to the Democrat, the Liberal does *not* believe that the people should rule themselves. So he draws a distinction between *sovereign* and *governmental* authority. Governmental authority, he says, should be located in the constitution. What the Liberal in effect does by this principle is to interpose an impersonal "supreme law" between the people who are "sovereign" but do not rule and the government which is not "sovereign" but does rule—under the constitution of the "sovereign state."

The doctrine of popular sovereignty, locating the authority to rule in a constitution, is part and parcel of the Liberal theory of authority. This theory is supposed to provide principles for guiding political conduct. The Liberal insists on discussing a fundamental moral issue: What should be the relation between the rights of individuals and the authority of government? When is the citizen obliged to obey the government? When is the government obliged not to interfere with the citizen? The Liberal insists on discussing this issue because he wants to justify certain political conduct; he wants to show that in certain cases the citizen has a right to resist the government; in other cases, he has a duty to obey. Unfortunately for the Liberal, no resolution of this moral issue is actually supplied by his theory.

The Liberal theorizes about authority as follows: The sovereign people who compose the civil state enact the supreme law. In the constitution the rights of citizens are defined and government is authorized to make and enforce the laws necessary to preserve them. The government is granted constitutional authority and the citizens are guaranteed constitutional rights. So long as the government acts to protect the rights of citizens, well and good; it acts as the constitution prescribes. If the government infringes the rights of citizens, it acts "unconstitutionally"— without authority. Just as the government has constitutional authority to make and enforce ordinary laws required to protect constitutional rights, the people have sovereign authority to make and enforce the supreme law of the constitution.

In this theory the Liberal assumes that rights and authority are separable. A line can be drawn separating individual rights from governmental authority, and it should be drawn in the constitution. When the government acts to prevent one individual from violating the rights of another, it acts constitutionally; the citizen has a duty to obey. But if the government acts to infringe individual rights, it acts without authority; the citizen has a right to resist. Resistance can take the form of revolution if necessary.

What does this Liberal theory mean in practice? What principles does it actually provide to guide political conduct? The answer is that this theory of authority makes no sense whatsoever in practice. It provides no practical principles. The most it does is to conceal a difficulty fatal for any theory of authority. The difficulty is that any grounds for establishing the authority of government to protect the rights of citizens are undermined by Liberal principles. They can be used with equal warrant to justify resistance or to compel obedience to government. For this Liberal theory is a bundle of logical inconsistencies which cannot be concealed in practice.

Whenever the government acts, the practical question is not about the relation between rights and authority. Instead, it is about the proper relation between the different rights of different persons. The question is: Which rights of which persons should the government use its authority to protect? Somehow this question must be answered for the government ever to act. But it is never an easy question to answer, because to protect certain rights of certain persons the government must infringe other rights of other persons. So the way a person in fact answers the question is likely to depend on how he is affected by the exercise of governmental authority.

To illustrate this difficulty, let us assume that we attend a meeting of the Westside Civic Improvement League. I decide to exercise my right of free speech by exhorting the membership to burn you at the nearest stake because you practice a religion

I do not like. I charge that you are a menace to the community, that you are corrupting the youth, that you are inhabited by the spirit of the devil, and that everyone who associates with you is risking eternal damnation. The constable of the peace hears the commotion, enters the meeting, decides enough is enough, and off he hustles me to jail. But being a good Liberal who believes in individual rights, I protest the constable's high-handed action. I withdraw my consent to his authority. I declare before mankind and nature's God and the membership of the Westside Civic Improvement League my right to resist on the grounds that the government constituted to protect my right of free speech is now trying to infringe it. The constable and I find ourselves back in a state of nature. I resort to my natural right of self-help by clipping the constable on the chin. He clubs me with his nightstick. What he lacks in authority over me, he makes up for in superior force. In fact, the rest of the police force soon appears to assist the constable in restoring law and order.

Now: Has my right to speak freely been denied by governmental action in favor of your right to practice the devilish religion of your choice? When the constable takes me off to jail, he is answering the question about which rights of which individuals should be protected, and in your favor. You believe that the government should protect your freedom of religion, and the constable concurs. But I believe that the government should protect my right of free speech. Notice that in Liberal terms, we both have rights. The government has authority to protect rights but not to infringe them. But actually my right of free speech conflicts with your right of religious freedom. When the government acts to protect your right, it violates mine. We are both sound Liberals: You believe that it has authority to protect your right, but I believe that it has no authority to infringe my right.

What about the constable's authority in this case? Here is a real dilemma for the Liberal. If you have a right of religious freedom, the government has authority to protect it. But if

I have a right of free speech, the government has no authority to infringe it. You may recognize the government's authority over me, but I do not consent to the government's action. In Liberal terms, the government therefore has no authority over me and I have a right to resist the government's action. So no matter what action the government takes in this case, the right of one of us is violated in favor of the right of the other. For one of us, the government is acting without authority.

Notice too the broader aspect of this difficulty. If, as an American citizen, I have no right to resist the government's action when my rights are infringed, then the authority of the American government is not legitimate, because that government was constituted as a result of revolution. At the same time, if the government's authority under the Constitution is legitimate, then I have a right to resist. Why? Because Liberal theory says so.

How does the Liberal resolve this dilemma, where for one individual or another the government acts without authority? To say that the difficulty is overcome by drawing a line between rights and authority in a constitution is to ignore the problem. Liberals have actually tried to ignore it in this way, but unsuccessfully. Constitutions do not exercise authority; only people who make decisions are capable of doing that. In a question about rights and authority, the people involved are those who exercise authority (the government) and those over whom it is exercised (the citizens). In a given case, then, who is to decide where the line is drawn in the supreme law of the constitution? It would seem that the sovereign people should. But they are only the *source* of the authority; it is not located in them. So should the citizen whose rights are at stake decide? Or should the government whose authority is challenged?

As logical possibilities there are, of course, these two ways a Liberal could answer the question. He could say: Each individual should decide for himself when his rights are violated and when the government acts with authority. Or he could say:

Government should make these decisions for everyone. But neither possibility is in practice tolerable for the Liberal.

If he holds that each individual has a right to decide for himself whether his rights or the government's authority take precedence, then authority over the individual could be justified only when there is no occasion for the government to act. What is tacitly assumed here is that there is no real distinction between the state of nature, where the individual is sovereign, and the civil state. To argue this view consistently is to endorse an anarchist position—that no governmental authority over the individual is legitimate. To put the same point somewhat differently: the government's authority is legitimate only so long as it's not exercised against me.

On the other hand, if the Liberal holds that the government should decide which rights of which individuals should be protected, then any action of government can be justified in Liberal terms, no matter the consequences for individual rights. If it is legitimate for the government to infringe any individual right it chooses, it is legitimate for it to infringe all rights. This is in effect a totalitarian position—that all governmental authority is legitimate, regardless of the consent of the citizen.

The Liberal never satisfactorily resolves this dilemma in theory or avoids it in practice. In trying to answer the question the Liberal gets hopelessly bogged down in contradictions within his own theory. For any attempt to draw a line in Liberal terms between rights and authority in practice requires the Liberal to assign superiority either to rights at the exclusion of authority or to authority at the exclusion of rights. So we find that even though every time the government acts, some sort of answer is in practice asserted, no answer is satisfactory for Liberals. About when and why a citizen has a right to resist or a duty to obey the government, they disagree widely among themselves. They continually jump from one horn of the dilemma to the other. One Liberal argues that a citizen is entitled to resist a govern-

149

ment action because his constitutional rights are being violated. Another Liberal argues that the citizen is obliged to obey the government because it has constitutional authority to act. Both are correct and both are wrong in Liberal terms. The fact is that for this question about the proper relation between rights and authority Liberal theory supplies no satisfactory answer.

5.

We find in this Liberal theory, then, no clear-cut answer to a question which cannot be dodged in any theory of authority. Where should political authority be located? The Liberal is clear about where it should *not* be located. It should not be located in a government of a dynastic king the Liberal hates. Nor should it be located in a government of a majority of the people the Liberal fears. But where should it be located? Political authority, he says, should be located in the constitution. Not in a government at all, but in the constitution enacted by the sovereign people. But in practice, who should decide what is and is not constitutional? Who should exercise the authority for which the sovereign people are the source? The Liberal's reply to this question is an epic in equivocation. To put it mildly, the Liberal theory of authority fails to do with success the job it was fashioned to do.

Or perhaps it does it too well. We have seen that Liberalism is a sort of halfway house between dynastic and Democratic rule. In America the Federalists once lived in this house; now they haunt it. Liberalism played a role in the development of modern political thought. It was no doubt an important role, historically. But the Liberal movement outlived its usefulness long ago. Yet the hold that Liberalism still has on the thought and practice of present generations of Americans is remarkable. It is so remarkable because Liberal theory is a surprisingly inadequate formula for masking the content of Liberal beliefs.

Let us not underestimate the difficulty facing the Liberal when he tries to clothe his naked beliefs in the reputable garb of a theory of political authority. The form of Liberal theory was set by historical necessity, the mother of political inventions. But the content of Liberal beliefs was shaped by the ambitions of a prosperous and talented middle class, a class now extinct in this country. What the Liberal believes is that authority should be exercised by a special few who regard themselves as exceptionally endowed with wisdom and talent. What he needs is a theory which sanctions conduct by this self-chosen elite in a political way to which no one else is privileged. He must justify resistance by the middle class to a government it does not like, but also condemn resistance by everyone else to a government run by middle-class gentlemen. By what legerdemain can a theory assure that the middle class can eat their political cake yet keep it too? Not at all an easy question to answer. In fact what the Liberal really needs is a theory which works a miracle, because he has cut out for himself a task as difficult as squaring a circle. But the Liberal theory of authority works no miracle. The best it does is to provide an elaborate formula for advancing covertly the ambitions of a middle-class elite to rule.

Historical circumstances conspired to place the Liberal in this predicament. Remember that the forerunners of Liberalism were enthusiastic royalists. The early modern thinkers opposed ancient rulers like bishops and barons exercising authority. They wanted to justify the supremacy of the dynastic king over the petty medieval rulers within the kingdom, and also to justify the independence of the king from the "international" overlordship of the Pope and the Holy Roman Emperor. To this end the early modern thinkers coined the concept of a sovereign in whom is located all authority, ecclesiastical and civil, within the estate of the realm. This concept, we have already noted, is unintelligible in medieval terms. They also invented the doctrine of the divine right of kings to rule. So, they said, the dynastic king is the sovereign ruler of the state. Louis XIV of

France believed them when he proclaimed: *"L'état, c'est moi."*

Dynastic rule was for Liberals like John Locke odious. They were of course no lovers of bishops and barons, so they accepted the ready-made concept of the sovereign state. But they wanted to transfer authority to rule the state from the king to an elite of wealth and talent. To make a persuasive case they had to resolve a problem of political morals. If the king had a right to rule and the subjects a duty to obey, resistance to royal authority would be wrong. How to prove the immorality of such rule? How to show that dynastic beliefs and principles were "wrong" while Liberal beliefs and principles were "right"? We have seen that the Liberals worked this out to the satisfaction of their Protestant conscience. They rejected the divine-right-of-kings doctrine and contended that the king exercises authority by convention but without right. By the laws of nature, each individual has a right to rule himself. When the individual in a state of nature is supplanted by the citizen in a civil state, the sovereign authority is located in the people—they are the one true sovereign. In its earliest formulation the Liberal doctrine of popular sovereignty meant simply that the king does *not* have a right to rule. Then civil resistance to royal authority could be justified as a natural right of individuals.

Once the dynastic kings were disposed of, the middle class had its own way—until the people the Liberals claimed were sovereign began to act as if they believed it. This is what so disturbed the American Federalist after the Revolution. The citizens began to demand a voice in the government. It was then that the Federalist discovered that some people are more sovereign than others and nothing is more sacred than a constitution.

Notice the problem circumstances presented for them. If a dynastic king should not rule, who should? Where should authority be located in the state? An obvious answer is that the people should rule themselves. But this would not serve the ambitions of the middle class. It was with the formula of a constitution enacted by the sovereign people that the Federalists tried to justify rule by an elite of wealth. When the question about where authority should be located was raised, the Federalist would declaim about the supreme law. Of course the people have a sovereign right to constitute the government of the state. But only as the constitution prescribes should governmental authority be exercised.

This formula breaks down because it answers no important question. It explains where authority comes from, but the source of authority makes no difference in practice. The important question is: Where is it located—when it is exercised? This the Liberal theory does not satisfactorily explain. Or perhaps it explains it too well, for the Liberal, regardless of his principles, always ends up with the conclusion that authority should be exercised, not by one man or the many, but by a superior few. The argument he relies on is that the common people should not rule themselves because they do not really understand what the constitution provides. Fortunately, a few exceptional people do. They should rule the state. The conclusion: governmental authority should not be exercised by a majority of the people but should be exercised by a superior few—who just happen to be prosperous middle-class gentlemen.

This elitist argument we shall examine in some detail later. Now our main concern is the doctrine of popular sovereignty, the joker in the Liberal house of cards. For many years the Liberal has played in the political game with his loaded deck. When he wants to justify resistance to government, the Liberal becomes lyric about the rights of the sovereign individual which no government can constitutionally violate. When he wants to justify obedience to government, he pontificates about the authority of the sovereign state which no citizen can constitutionally defy. The sovereign individual and the sovereign state exist only in the Liberal imagination, but he finds them handy notions for warding off demands that authority should be exercised by the many rather than a few.

Let us not allow the form of this theory to distract us from the content of Liberalism. The political morals of the Liberal are tied to his elitist beliefs. The governing principle for his conduct is that authority should be obeyed when it serves his interests and ignored when it does not. The principle is summed up in the saying: "Heads I win, tails you lose." Henry David Thoreau of Walden Pond fame, a darling of American Liberals, was quite frank in asserting this position. The Liberal principle of political conduct can be properly described as the ethics of unmitigated gall—all for the Liberal and the Liberal for himself. Most devotees of the Liberal ethic have preferred to be less outspoken than Thoreau in entertaining such an untenable position. It does make a mockery of political morals, and without beliefs about the morality of political conduct—cherished by the rabble, that is—the Liberal can neither keep his political cake nor eat it. A dire prospect indeed for a person with a ravenous appetite for ruling others.

6.

The intellectual bankruptcy of Liberal theory is not news to the Catholic political thinker. All along he has contended that Liberalism suffers a poverty of morals. The Liberal belief that authority should be exercised to advance the interests of the middle class violates the principle of the common good. The doctrine by which the Liberal tries to justify elite rule, that authority should be located in a constitution enacted by the sovereign people, is a false doctrine. It is incompatible with the teachings of the Christian religion. In fact, the whole body of Liberal theory is founded on "naturalistic error."

Of course the Catholic, like the Liberal, has relied on natural-law assumptions to provide a foundation for his theory of authority. But the Catholic and the Liberal have not relied on the same natural-law assumptions, or, indeed, the same conception of natural law. In his "enlightened" theory the Liberal depends on "secular" natural-law assumptions. Because of them he becomes entrapped in a serious theoretical difficulty. The difficulty is so serious that even the most imaginative and resourceful Liberal thinkers have been unable to overcome it. The Catholic has never hesitated to point out in the Liberal theory of authority this difficulty, which is easily avoided with a Thomist conception of natural law.

Take the case of the American Revolution. The Colonists wanted to justify their resistance to British authority. They could not justify their conduct by citing British law or custom. So they appealed to a "higher" moral law—"the law of nature." In these terms they proceeded, to their satisfaction and the discomfort of the British, to portray their revolutionary conduct as morally valid.

To provide leverage for criticizing the regime, the Revolutionists relied on the Liberal distinction between "nature" and "convention." Convention describes what actually exists; it is the accretions of prejudice and ignorance. In contrast, nature reveals what ought to exist. It is what reason dictates; it is the source of moral truth. The rational principles of nature any rational man can recognize as self-evidently true. Hence, as the conventional laws are by definition "bad," so are the laws of nature "good." A most convenient distinction.

Remember what the American Revolutionists contended: By the laws of nature, the source of supreme authority is the people over whom it is exercised. By convention the Colonists consented to obey the authority of the British government. They agreed to abandon their right of "self-help" and obey the British government, so long as it protected their precious natural rights to life, liberty, and the pursuit of happiness. But the British government in fact failed to protect those rights; indeed it violated them. In infringing the rights of the Colonists, the British government acted without authority, since no rational man could consent to violation of his natural rights. Therefore British rule rested on force, not consent. The Colonists had a natural right to use force themselves in defending their rights, to revolt against British rule. The sovereign people of the American Colonies had a right to abolish the imperial government and to establish a new one. In this new government they could vest the authority to rule the American people.

What the Revolutionist is assuming here is that "rights" are an attribute of man's "nature," while authority is a product of convention. Authority results from an agreement among rational men. Government, then, is merely a convenient means to the end of preserving individual rights. In the event of conflict between a right derived from nature and authority resting on convention, the Revolutionist inferred that the end should take precedence. When the government violates the individual rights it should protect, it ceases to be a suitable means to the end. So the citizen is no longer obliged to obey the government—according to the Liberal theory.

Of course, the Catholic cannot concur at all with this conception of natural law which allows individuals the "right" to defy "authority" at will. Instead of resting his final case for political morals on an appeal to religious faith, as the Catholic does, the Liberal appeals to "natural reason." Reason is in the Liberal theory of natural law what God is in the Catholic theory. For the Liberal, natural-law principles are what men "reason" to accept rather than what God commands to be obeyed. So the Liberal finds himself, whether he likes it or not, holding that questions of political morals should be answered by each person. But the Liberal can never divorce "natural reason" from actual men—in whom the light of reason is but a flickering candle. Different men "reason" to make different choices about the principles which should govern political conduct. One man's reason may be another man's poison. Natural law becomes nothing more than an impossibly flexible formula by which each and every person can decide that whatever he pleases to do is "right."

This difficulty in Liberal theory, founded as it is on assumptions about a "secular" natural law, the Catholic avoids in his theory of authority. Instead of relying on the slender reed of human reason to discern moral truth about man and society, the acceptance of natural law is for the Catholic an article of religious faith. He postulates a realm of supernatural truth which serves as the touchstone for moral truth about this world. For him truth is revealed to man through the grace of God, not concocted by fallible men who employ reason as a servant of their passions. For the Catholic, reason is a valued instrument that man can use to discern God's law and choose to obey it, not a convenient tool for enacting a "higher" law to suit an individual's desires.

Hence we find that the Catholic does not postulate a state of nature wherein an individual is free to recognize whatever rights or duties he may find convenient. Instead he holds that the only "natural" state is for man to live as a member of society in which rights and duties are God's dictates rather than man's choices. Men are endowed with natural rights, but duties are natural as well. Both are the will of God for which natural law is evidence. Authority, too, is natural to man; it is prescribed by God, not conventional in origins. The idea of a "sovereign" individual who stands in direct relation to a "sovereign" state cannot be reconciled with Catholic teachings about society. No matter man's desires, God has vested authority to rule in the many societies of which men are members. So for the Catholic, the authority of societies as well as the rights and duties of their members is set by natural law. The laws of nature define the moral principles all men should observe, as the Creator wills. The obligation to do so is not merely a requirement of human reason: it is the command of the one true Sovereign. Failure to obey invites divine retribution, perhaps not in this world, but certainly in the next.

7.

No doubt some members of the Westside Civic Improvement League share the popular notion that Liberalism and Democracy are closely related, perhaps even blood brothers. Since Democracy has become in our day a term of approbation, elitists of all descriptions, including the Liberal, have tried to get under the Democratic tent. The claim that Democracy and Liberalism are related has some validity, but the relation is merely historical. It is true, we have seen, that Democracy emerged out of a Liberal tradition. But remember that it was in reaction *against* Liberalism that Democratic theory and practice developed. What is distinctive about the Democrat is his rejection of Liberal beliefs and principles.

However, because of the historical accident of association, Democratic thinkers have displayed some trouble in emancipating themselves from Liberal preconceptions which have no bearing on Democratic theory or practice. Many Democrats are still so confused that at times they argue a Democratic position, while at other times they give sanction to a Liberal position on the same issue. In part, this is simply because they become entangled in Liberal terminology. Liberal ideas are especially familiar to Americans; for that reason, when the American Democrat discusses a political question he is likely to draw on them. For example, Democrats have been particularly inclined to discuss the relation between rights and authority in Liberal terms. When they do, they come up with answers as unsatisfactory as those the Liberals have made so famous. But they are not Democratic answers.

In time Democrats will probably divest themselves of the intellectual baggage of the Liberal heritage. This will be for the good. It is a quite unfortunate, as well as a quite unnecessary, tendency among Democrats to talk like Liberals. It is unnecessary because the important political questions which disturb the people of our day can be meaningfully posed and discussed in Democratic terms. It is unfortunate because the Democrat finds no difficulty in resolving controversial political questions when the answers are worked out in Democratic terms. Of course, the Liberal does not accept the Democratic answers to these questions, but this certainly is nothing for anyone to regret. He doesn't even accept Liberal answers with any consistency.

The Democrat appreciates the important historical role that

Liberalism played in destroying the dynastic system. But unlike the Liberal, the Democrat refuses to stop midway along the road from dictatorial to popular rule. The Democrat rejects the Liberal belief that authority should be exercised by a few for the benefit of a middle class. He rejects the Liberal doctrine that authority should be located in a constitution enacted by the sovereign people. The Democrat rejects Liberal beliefs, along with the theory used in an effort to make them intellectually respectable, but for somewhat different reasons than the Catholic does. Where the Catholic says that Liberal beliefs are morally wrong because they conflict with Christian teachings, the Democrat says simply that they are impractical in present-day political society. Where the Catholic says that Liberal theory is false because it is contrary to natural law, the Democrat says that the theory is hopelessly unrealistic. It is neither meaningful nor workable in the political experience of our time. The Catholic and Democrat follow different courses to arrive at the same point: that Liberal theory and practice are unacceptable.

For the Democrat the natural-law approach to problems of political conduct is fruitless. The moral validity of a principle of conduct can be neither proved nor disapproved by an appeal to so-called "laws of nature." No alleged demonstration of the existence, within human experience, of objective moral principles embedded in the nature of things stands up. One can accept, as an act of religious faith, a belief in a higher moral law evidencing the will of the Divine Creator. But then one actually determines the morality of a principle by an appeal to a supernatural, not natural, truth. This can be a satisfactory method for resolving questions of political conduct, provided a procedure for maintaining the orthodoxy of religious interpretation is established, as it is with the Catholic Church. But a painfully obvious lesson of modern history is that not everyone shares the same religious beliefs or accepts the Roman Church as the custodian of Christian orthodoxy. Does this mean that persons cannot agree on the principles of conduct that should be observed in politics? No, it does not.

There is another method, we shall see, for resolving questions of political conduct. This method has nothing to do with natural law. So the Democrat rejects any assumptions of natural law as simply irrelevant to the serious political business at hand.

Hence the Democrat regards the Liberal postulate about the natural rights of individuals as an unrealistic metaphysical construct. The notion of a "sovereign individual" in a "state of nature" jibes with nothing in our political experience. The Democrat denies that the Liberal notion of "rights" derived from "nature" is meaningful. He denies that a person has a "natural right" to rule himself. He also denies—this is most significant—that any person has a "natural right" to rule another. Any claimed "right" to exercise authority depending on natural-law assumptions he rejects for lack of convincing evidence. In the absence of any suprahuman "right" to rule, the Democrat declines to draw any significant distinction between those who exercise authority and those over whom it is exercised. The authority exercised over a person depends in practice on his choice to accept it and obey. So the Democrat concludes that there is no evidence for either "rights" or "authority" prescribed "by nature" for men.

Perhaps at first glance this conclusion of the Democrat, at least about authority, looks like a position a Liberal would entertain. The Democrat holds that authority is in practice, when exercised, conventional. It depends on agreement between ruler and ruled. But first glances can be misleading. The Democrat's approach to questions about authority is radically different from that of the Liberal. Consequently, we shall find little in common between the Liberal theory and the Democratic doctrine of popular sovereignty.

8.

The Democrat's approach to questions about authority is to start with the evidence of our political experience. This no more includes a sovereign state in a civil society than it does a sovereign individual in a state of nature. In practice we do not find authority concentrated in any person or group. We do not find any absolute right to rule or duty to obey recognized by anyone. However, the evidence of our political experience does include members of such organizations as the Westside Civic Improvement League. Let's start with them.

The members of the League, we find, have certain desires they seek to satisfy through political activity. The League is one way they try to obtain political satisfaction. They agree that a person who belongs to the League has certain privileges and certain obligations of membership. He is privileged to participate in League activities, and he is obliged to abide by the actions of the organization. The members claim privileges and fulfill their obligations with varying enthusiasm. As League members they do observe certain principles to guide their conduct. But not all members observe the exact same principles, nor does any one member always follow the same principles. However, some principles they choose to follow work out in practice better than others. To the extent that the members observe these rather than alternative principles, they obtain the greater satisfaction from their political activity. Which principles of political conduct these are and why they work out better in practice is a matter of interest to the members of the Westside Civic Improvement League.

In these terms the Democrat proceeds to discuss questions about authority. Any question about the "source" of authority he regards as nonsense. The answer makes no difference in practice anyway. What is important is where authority is located. The Democrat assumes that in practice authority is in some sense located in the numerous decision-making groups of which persons are members. The question is where within a group it should be located when it is exercised. In one person who rules the entire community? Or in a few who rule the rest? Or in the many members—a majority? Or in the entire membership? The Democrat recognizes that in the practice of different communities authority is exercised in many different ways. Many communities are ruled by some sort of elite. Many communities are ruled by force. But the Democrat maintains that authority *should* be located in the same persons over whom it is exercised—*all* the members of a community. So the principle: the authority to make decisions binding on a community should be located in the membership.

The Democrat's case for accepting this principle is his doctrine of popular sovereignty. The argument is rather difficult to follow in the abstract. In understanding it, perhaps it would be helpful to keep in mind our friends who belong to the Westside Civic Improvement League. The argument runs as follows: Authority implies a relation between a ruler and a person who authorizes the ruler to make decisions binding on him. This political relation between ruler and ruled is a reciprocal one. For the ruler to rule, the ruled must obey. The political problem is how to assure that the ruled will accept the authority of the ruler. This problem cannot be resolved simply by declaring that the parties have certain legal or moral "rights" and "duties." What is required is not only that the parties agree to recognize certain principles of rule, but also that in practice they conduct themselves accordingly. The problem can actually be resolved only to the extent that conflict between ruler and ruled, which results in either the abuse or the defiance of authority, is removed in political conduct. So the practical question is: By which principles of political conduct can such conflict most effectively be removed? To the extent that persons desire that authority be exercised, these principles, whatever they are, should be recognized and followed in practice.

Now, as a practical matter, authority is contingent on membership in a political community. A person who is not a member of such a community has no recognized political privileges, but neither does he have any obligation to obey the authority of the community. But as a member of a political community, a person agrees to recognize certain privileges and obligations. A member of a political community may have, in the eyes of the ruler, certain privileges; definitely he has certain obligations—at the least that of obeying the ruler's authority. But there is no assurance that the ruled will recognize the obligation simply because the ruler does. However, the ruler can exercise authority only to the extent that the ruled actually obeys. As a practical matter, persons cannot be successfully ruled against their consent; they must agree to accept decisions about exercising authority over them. Force may be effective in exceptional cases, but it does not work as a general rule. In any case, to the extent that force is required, it is not authority that is exercised, since consent is lacking. Authority can be exercised in practice, then, only to the extent that conflict between ruler and ruled is actually removed. Conflict between ruler and ruled can be removed to the extent that the members of a political community share an agreement to recognize certain privileges and obligations of membership and everyone conducts himself accordingly. The problem is one of correlating the privileges and obligations recognized by ruler and ruled. How can this problem be solved?

As a practical matter, a person is more likely to fulfill his obligations of membership if he is entitled to enjoy his privileges. He is less likely to obey authority exercised for the benefit of someone else than he is to obey authority which benefits him too. The most practicable way to assure that each member benefits from the exercise of authority is to allow him to participate in its exercise. A person who does not participate in the exercise of authority may still obey it, but then again he may not. There is no assurance that he will and the ruler may have to use force. But a person who does participate in the exercise of authority performs a dual role: part ruler and part ruled. This reduces to the minimum the practical possibility of conflict between ruler and ruled.

So the Democrat concludes: Any significant distinction between ruler and ruled is not warranted. Where authority should be located is a question persons answer for themselves as they choose. In practice they answer it every time they decide to obey, or to defy, the authority exercised over a group of which they are

163

members. In a Democratic political community the same person functions as both ruler and ruled. As a member of the Democratic decision-making group, he is privileged to participate in exercising authority over the membership. He has a reciprocal obligation to abide by the group's decision. These privileges and obligations are contingent on his membership in the community. To the extent that he participates in exercising authority, he can be expected to obey it. The most practicable principle to follow in locating authority to make decisions binding on a community, therefore, is to locate it in the membership.

9.

We have already seen that the notion of a social contract constituting the authority of a sovereign state is a meaningless fiction for a Democrat. But as Thomas Hobbes once remarked, error can be helpful in disclosing truth. The germ of truth in this Liberal notion is the principle of consent. The Democrat accepts this principle that the Liberal is wont to talk about but reluctant to act on, that authority depends on consent. The Democrat believes that authority requires the consent of the person over whom it is exercised.

Implicit in the principle of consent is a concept of unanimity: that persons who differ about answers to political questions unanimously agree on how to resolve their differences. This underlying agreement is about norms of conduct—the principles which should be observed in political conduct. Liberals like to describe these underlying agreements by the term "value consensus."

For the Liberal, the problem of value consensus centers on the constitution which prescribes rights and authority. He assumes that the citizens must accept the established "values" in order for the political system to work properly. The problem is resolved to the extent that the citizens abide by the principles of the constitution. So the Liberal discusses the problem in terms of individuals who do or do not "value" the constitutional principles. For example, let us say that the constitution guarantees certain rights of private property. Most members of the political society agree, say, that production for profit is a more desirable principle than production for use. A person who owns property has a right to make a profit from its employment. Now a Socialist who does not believe in production for profit does not share the consensus on the value of private property rights. He does not really consent to the constituted authority to protect such rights. His presence in the society, so the Liberal argues, threatens the satisfactory working of the system because unanimity on underlying principles is lacking.

The Democrat cannot accept this problem of consensus as a genuine one. Consensus on principles is a serious and ever-present problem in political practice, but the actual problem is not this one the Liberal worries about. It was invented by Liberals anxious to impose curbs on governmental action. Nor does the Democrat regard the Liberal notion of consent as meaningful. In practice consent is not formally declared once and for all; it is affirmed by a person every time he obeys authority exercised over him.

But for the Democrat, the concept of unanimity is meaningful. He recognizes consensus on principles as a sort of prerequisite for any political community. Group activity depends in practice on the membership abiding by the established rules. These rules prescribe norms for guiding conduct. Members are recognized as having certain privileges and obligations; they can and cannot do certain things in principle. To the extent that members observe the rules, they can successfully engage in their group activity. Unanimous agreement, then, is required for the effective functioning of a political community.

But in Democratic terms a consensus on principles does not involve an agreement about "right" and "wrong" values. The agreement is simply about how members should conduct themselves. Take the case of the sport of football. Football is a game played by teams according to recognized rules. To play football a person must join a team. He also must accept the rules for playing the game. If he fails to observe the rules for membership on the team or for playing the game, he cannot play football. To play together in a game, the members of a football team must agree that the game should be played according to rules. They must agree about the norms of conduct to which members should conform in running offensive and defensive plays. But it is not necessary for every player on the team to believe in the sanctity of private property or the nobility of holy matrimony or the divinity of Jesus Christ. Nor is it necessary for the members of any political community to agree on such questions. They must merely agree about the principles they should observe in practice while conducting their group activities.

The Democrat appreciates that in practice to achieve a consensus among the members of a political community on the principles for guiding their conduct is a very real problem. In practice the members of political communities are confronted with questions about their conduct which are difficult to answer. But in Democratic terms the conflict over values is not between some odd "individual" and the constituted "authority." The conflict is within the personality of the member of a political community.

For the Democrat, the problem of consensus is a psychological problem which confronts every member of every political community. The conflict is between the different desires a person entertains. A person can, by membership in a political community, satisfy some of his desires. Others he cannot. In fact some he must forego and leave unsatisfied, since as a member of a political community he has obligations as well as privileges. Perhaps he would like to eat his political cake, yet keep it too; to enjoy his privileges, but shirk his obligations. But as a practical matter, he cannot do this because both his privileges and obligations—including the obligation to abide by the rules—

are contingent on his membership in the community. So, whether he likes it or not, he must make a choice: either go along with the group or go it alone. He must make this choice whenever, in order to satisfy certain desires as a member of the political community, he must leave others unsatisfied. In making this choice he must appraise the relative advantages and disadvantages of membership. He must decide whether his most vital desires are best satisfied by membership in the political community.

Often in practice this is a difficult decision for a person to make. On the other hand, it may be a very simple decision. If the obligations are great and the privileges are few, a person is not likely to prize highly his membership in a political community. To the extent that a discrepancy between privileges and obligations is removed, a person is likely to decide that his affiliation with the political community is important enough to warrant bearing the burdens of membership.

The key to the Democrat's resolution for this problem is the concept of participation. In a Democratic community the problem is to achieve a consensus on how decisions about the exercise of authority over the membership should be arrived at. A Democratic decision is one made according to rules set by Democratic principles. Unanimity on the procedures which should be observed psychologically precedes, so to speak, the process of decision-making. To the extent that the members of a Democratic community accept these rules, the process works properly.

Hence, the Democrat insists on what might be called "the principle of mandatory disaffiliation": Either fulfill the obligations of membership, or get out of the community. A person who decides to continue his membership consents to the exercise of the community's authority over him.

But the Democrat recognizes that, as a practical matter, the decision-making process can work only to the extent that the member would rather go along with the community for the sake of participating in the decision-making process, even when he dislikes a decision, than withdraw his membership. He must believe that his affiliation with the community is more important to him than the adverse effect on his personal desires which some decision entails. He must believe that the persistence of the community is more important to him than any single decision. He must believe that his privilege of participating in the decision-making process is at least equal in importance to his obligation to abide by a decision he does not like.

So the question for the Democrat is: How can the greatest possible assurance that the members of the community consent in practice to the authority exercised over them be achieved? The Democratic answer is that participation by the membership in the activities of the community should be maximized. Privileges should be commensurate with obligations, for participation is the other side of the coin of consent.

The Democrat does not claim that these Democratic principles provide a sure-fire solution to every problem of consensus. That problem could be thoroughly solved only by breeding a new type of political personality with human traits left out. However, the Democrat does contend that Democratic principles are better attuned to the circumstances of present-day political life than the alternative principles endorsed by the Liberal. Democratic principles provide a more practicable guide for political conduct. They give recognition to the enriched meaning and enhanced significance our lives acquire from community affiliations. We are not in fact lone and rugged "individuals" adrift in a sea of open-ended political relations. Whether we like it or not, we are members of communities. The inveterate individualist who clings to the canons of the Liberal ethic, who refuses affiliation with (or is refused affiliation by) Democratic communities—such a person finds himself today politically helpless. The person who wants to exercise authority over others but does not want authority exercised over him is of an obsolete political breed, fast disappearing from the American scene. The only choice in practice is between ignoring political communities and being ruled against one's consent, and participating in the life of political communities and trying to exert influence in the shaping of group decisions. To recognize this and to accept the responsibilities of membership in political communities is a mark of political maturity.

IO.

Now we are in a position to answer the question posed earlier in this chapter: What is the relation between Catholic teachings about authority and the Democratic doctrine of popular sovereignty? We have seen that the Catholic and the Democrat express some rather different views about authority. The Democrat does not even consider the question of the source of authority, a question the Catholic insists on discussing since he holds that the source of all authority is God. But the significant issue about authority—where should it be located?—both the Catholic and the Democrat do discuss. A doctrine of popular sovereignty is the Democrat's answer to it. Is this doctrine compatible with the Catholic theory of authority?

At the outset we should notice that both the Catholic and the Democratic theories of authority are "pluralistic." Neither the Democrat nor the Catholic accepts the notion of a "sovereign state." The Democratic doctrine is that the authority to make decisions binding on a group of persons should be located in the membership of a political community. The persons who are members of any community which makes decisions about exercising authority, that authority—no more or less—should be located in the membership. This doctrine is predicated on an assumption that authority is widely dispersed among many groups and concentrated in none. It is assumed that authority emanates from the bottom up—from the members to the community— rather than from the top down, so to speak.

This is a quite different conception, we have seen, from that entertained by the Liberal. It is for sound reasons that Democratic thinkers have habitually eschewed any theory of a "state." Instead they have focused their attention on the small, local organized group—the "community." For Democracy is a theory about exercising authority within a community. Democratic theory concerns the relations among persons who are members of a decision-making group. Democratic principles prescribe rules for governing the process by which members of a group exercise authority over themselves.

Hence the Democrat rejects any notion of a "sovereign" individual in a state of nature, or a "sovereign" state in a civil society. He rejects the notion that "supreme" authority is located in a sovereign people who are the source of constitutional authority. The Democrat believes that people as we know them are not "individuals" who are citizens of an omnipotent "state." They are members of many and varied groups: from such membership they acquire their political significance. They are members of organizations like the Westside Civic Improvement League— a church, a labor union, a professional association, a political party, a social or service club, a sports organization, or perhaps a school district or a councilmanic district. Whatever their group affiliations, these set their political character. They are more or less subject to the authority of the communities to which they belong—by choice. They more or less consent to the authority exercised over them as members of communities. And they more or less participate in the decision-making process by which authority is exercised. They would participate more rather than less—if the Democrat had his way.

So on the question of whether authority should be located in a sovereign individual or a sovereign state or a sovereign people, the Democrat answers that it should not be located in any of these sources. Political authority should be located in the persons over whom it is exercised. But it should be located in the membership of each and every decision-making group that exercises authority. This is the Democratic doctrine of popular sovereignty.

The Catholic agrees with the Democrat about where political authority should be located, but for different reasons. He arrives at the same conclusion by an evidently different route. The Catholic relies on natural-law assumptions which are founded on his religious beliefs. According to the teachings of his Church, persons are "by nature" members of "natural" societies, some religious and some secular in character. God has vested in every human society authority sufficient to achieve the purpose of that association. The Catholic doctrine of ecclesiastical rule does not, of course, conform to Democratic principles. But this is no difficulty. The Democrat has no theory about ecclesiastical rule: his theory is about the exercise of political authority. As far as "civil" societies are concerned, the Catholic teaching about ecclesiastical rule does not apply. Each civil society has divinely sanctioned authority over its members, but over its members only. The members of the civil society can exercise this authority by any means they choose. They can exercise it, as the Christian Democrat urges they should, by Democratic means.

So we conclude: A Catholic cannot accept the Liberal theory of authority, but neither can a Democrat. A Catholic can accept the doctrine of popular sovereignty espoused by the Democrat, even though Catholic teachings do not require him to do so. Most important for us: The Catholic theory of political authority is quite compatible with the Democratic doctrine of popular sovereignty.

Chapter Six

POLITICAL EQUALITY

I.

The Athenian Plato—one of the first and best-known of all political philosophers—started the fashion of classifying forms of government. He used as one criterion the number of persons who participate in exercising authority. Logically, there are three possibilities—one person, a few, and many people. Thus Plato's basic classification of the three "pure" forms of rule were monarchy, aristocracy, and democracy. Since Plato's time, many philosophers have in some respects altered his system of classification by introducing additional criteria. Plato himself distinguished between "lawful" and "corrupt" forms of government. For example, he classified oligarchy as the corrupt form of rule by a few. Using such a system of classification, thinkers have described governments in terms of who actually rules.

But far more important in this connection than any question of fact about who *does* rule has been a question of value about the "best" form of government. Here the issue is who *should* rule. Should one person only, or a few, or many people participate in exercising political authority?

It was also Plato who set the custom of discussing this issue in terms of a "superior right" to rule. Plato posed the question: Do a few have a superior right to rule the many? In propounding his famous answer he postulated, as part of his idealist metaphysics, that an order of eternal truth "objectively" exists, completely independent of human minds. But it is possible, he assumed, for certain persons, by proper use of reason, to deduce moral truth from the principles of this rational order. These rational principles "show" that some people are entitled to claim a moral right to rule while others have no such right. For Plato, only the philosopher-kings should rule because no one else has any "rational" claim to a right to exercise authority. For him it followed, in these terms, that aristocracy—rule by a superior few—is the best form of government.

Since then many other philosophers, who did not necessarily accept Plato's system of metaphysics, have from time to time discussed the question about who should rule in terms of some "superior right." They, too, have assumed that some men are politically superior to others, and that those who are superior have a right to rule the rest. Some have argued this way to justify rule by one man—a king perhaps, or a dictator or an emperor; others, to justify some form of rule by an elite class or group. At the same time, some thinkers have contended that the right to rule is founded on divine law, while others have founded it on a distinct natural law. But in all cases they have assumed that there are principles above and beyond human control from which a moral right to rule can be derived. We mortals have no choice but to accept the "fact" that God (or nature) has decreed that some people should rule and others should not.

For many, many centuries, theories of government concocted in these terms were the stock in trade of political philosophers. Modern thinkers, too, have discussed the issue of who should rule in traditional terms. We find that Liberal thinkers have characteristically contended that an exceptional few have a superior right to exercise authority. They have not always agreed on who the "best men" are or in what their superiority consists, but they have never deviated from the contention that rule should be by an elite.

Strictly speaking, the formulation of this question about who should exercise authority in terms of a superior right to rule makes no sense to a Democrat. The Democrat, we have said, refuses to draw any significant distinction between those who exercise authority and those over whom it is exercised. He sees no valid warrant for any such distinction. His position is that no one has a "special right" to rule anyone else. In the absence of any such right, the members of a community have an equal claim to participate in exercising authority. So the Democratic principle is that in the exercise of political authority each member should count for one and no more than one. The Democrat's argument in behalf of this principle is called "the doctrine of political equality."

In this chapter, then, our question is whether this distinctive Democratic doctrine of political equality is compatible with Catholic teachings about authority. Let us proceed with the business at hand.

2.

Religionists have claimed that the concept of human equality orginated with the Christian belief in the brotherhood of man and the fatherhood of God. It is true that ancient pagan philosophers, including the Greeks Plato and Aristotle, assumed that men are not equal. Plato believed that inequality is a distinctive attribute of human nature; Aristotle believed that some men are "by nature" slaves. But it is also true that before the Christian era Roman philosophers had developed theories of human equality independent of what we ordinarily regard as religious belief. The Stoic philosophers Cicero and Seneca both started their theorizing about politics from an assumption of human equality. In fact a case can be made for the view that it was from these pagans that the early Christians acquired the idea of human equality. But whether or not the claim of a peculiar affinity between Christianity and the concept of human equality is warranted is not really pertinent to our inquiry. It is clear that the Christian belief in the brotherhood of man is certainly equalitarian in character.

We find in the teachings of the Catholic Church, as part of the Thomist conception of a rational man in a moral universe governed by natural law, that each person is equal in the sight of God. As a creature of God, every man is endowed with rights so essential to the purpose of human life that they are inseparable from him. Of course, no right-thinking person would want to surrender these precious natural rights. But then a person could not yield them up even if he wanted to, for that man possess them is God's will, not man's choice. So too, man has God-given duties essential to his nature. Indeed, in Catholic teachings men are endowed with rights so that they can fulfill their duties to God. Both rights and duties are prescribed by moral law, which evidences the divine will in the nature of things.

Up to this point, no complication appears about the relation between Catholic teachings and the Democratic doctrine of political equality. The Catholic holds that men are equal in possessing God-given rights and duties. In regard to other Catholic teachings, complications do appear, however.

We have already noted that the Catholic derives from the Thomist natural-law teachings a theory of justice. Justice, in Catholic terms, is the proper ordering of relations among persons; the principles of justice indicate what relations should prevail. The principles, in other words, prescribe the rights and duties of persons. Rights and duties depend on relations which "naturally" obtain among persons. The key to these relations is, of course, natural law. That the rights and duties of persons, according to natural law, be recognized and observed is required by justice.

This theory includes, you recall, a doctrine of social justice. It also includes two other doctrines: of "commutative" and of "distributive" justice. Commutative justice pertains to relations between persons "equal in dignity." The object, as set by natural law, is the good of both parties. Commutative justice, then, calls for equality of treatment. This doctrine suggests no difficulty.

However, the doctrine of distributive justice appears, at least at first glance, not to jibe with the Democratic doctrine of political equality. Distributive justice pertains to relations among persons "unequal by nature." Natural law requires that the burdens and benefits of membership in society be assigned ("distributed") in proportion to the functions performed by persons. The more important the function, the greater a person's rights, and also his duties. The principle is that the rights and duties of persons should be correlated. From this the Catholic argues that society should be ordered as a hierarchy of human relations. So that the many different functions required to satisfy human needs can be adequately performed, a person's rights and duties should be appropriate to his rank in the social hierarchy. Incidentally, this doctrine was first expounded by the Greek philosopher Aristotle, who, we have already observed, assumed that men are by nature unequal.

These doctrines of justice, taken together, rest on two assumptions: (1) that persons are equal in certain respects, and (2) that they are unequal in other respects—naturally so. It is assumed that God has endowed persons unequally with talents and abilities, hence with rights and duties. An assumption of human inequality is clearly evident.

It is therefore plausible that the doctrine of distributive justice conflicts with the Democratic principle. Whether this is actually the case we can determine only after we have carefully inspected the Democratic doctrine of political equality. Before we do that, let us first make clear what appears to be another point of conflict between this Democratic principle and Catholic teachings about authority.

We have already considered, in connection with the question of popular sovereignty, the Catholic teaching that God is the source of authority. A ruler, then, must exercise divinely ordained authority. Its exercise is governed by natural law. By definition, a ruler who exercises authority bears a special relation to God that those subject to the authority do not. This suggests a possible conflict.

Moreover, there is an affinity between Catholic teachings and monarchical rule. Catholic political thought is mainly medieval in origin and character. During the Middle Ages, the prevailing form of government was monarchy. In fact, it was the only familiar form of government for many centuries. We find in the writings of St. Thomas Aquinas and his followers elaborate doctrines of kingship. It is a medieval conception of kingship, to be sure. The king is regarded as a servant of the community; he receives his office by a ceremony of coronation; he takes an oath to uphold the law of the realm; and so on. But it is still a conception of rule by one man.

St. Thomas applied the principle of monarchy to the government of the Church Universal. This doctrine, along with other accepted Catholic teachings about the exercise of authority over spiritual affairs, certainly makes monarchy a plausible form of rule over the membership of the Catholic Church. Control within the Church officialdom is exerted from the top down. The Roman Church is ruled by a hierarchy headed by a monarch elected for life tenure. The Pope is a royal ruler of sorts, selected and assisted by the princes of the Church, the cardinals. This system of Church government, which is clearly justified by Catholic teachings, no one supposes to be Democratic in character. Is there a conflict here with the Democratic doctrine of political equality?

3.

In Catholic teachings we actually find no doctrine that monarchy is the best form of civil government and no doctrine that anyone has a divine right to exercise civil authority.

Just why this is the case becomes clear when we understand the origins of doctrines of divine right and what such doctrines entail by way of a claim to rule.

The idea of a divine right to rule is distinctly modern. The doctrines were originally propounded by Reformation thinkers who were opposed to the Church's teachings about civil authority. The doctrines have taken two general forms: the divine right of kings, and the divine right of "the elect of God." The divine right of kings is historically the older doctrine. It was in a sense a logical imperative of the Protestant Reformation.

During the Middle Ages, it was taken for granted that a Christian ruler occupies his royal office with the sanction of ecclesiastical authority. The ceremony of the coronation was a religious sacrament whereby the king became the anointed of the Lord. Of course, Protestant kings could no longer rely on this religious sanction to justify their claim to occupy the throne, after they had repudiated Papal authority. Nor could they rely on the sanction of the established church of the realm, since dynastic rulers claimed that the royal authority was sovereign—superior to the ecclesiastical authority.

Without religious sanction, the claim of a dynastic king to rule lacked a firm moral foundation. Moreover, the dynastic king claimed not only a right to occupy the throne; he also claimed an absolute right to rule—free of the control of Pope or emperor, bishop or baron—and an absolute duty of subjects to obey. What was needed then was a doctrine which justified, in religious terms, such a royal claim to sovereign authority. This need was supposedly met by the divine-right doctrine.

A classic statement of the doctrine was made by King James I of England in a tract, *The Trew Law of Free Monarchy* (1598). James felt obliged in this tract to discredit two familiar views which jeopardized the legitimacy of dynastic rule: (1) the authority to rule is not vested directly in the king but rather indirectly, through, say, a Pope or the community; and (2) the *de facto* occupancy of a throne confers a *de jure* right to rule.

James of course assumed that civil authority is divine in origin and that monarchy is the only divinely prescribed form of rule. So did most everyone else in his day. But then he contended that a *legitimate* king receives his authority directly from God and is accountable only to God. Such a king has a God-given right to rule his realm which no human power can rightfully set aside. The argument James advanced runs as follows: The essential quality of a claim to rule is "legitimacy"—lawful descent from a lawful monarch. A legitimate monarch is God's agent on earth. He receives his authority by a mysterious transmission directly from God. The original grant of authority to a dynasty must be accepted as an act of religious faith. Subsequently the right to rule is transmitted by hereditary succession, according to the principle of primogeniture, a principle of natural law. The legitimate monarch's hereditary right to rule is indefeasible. It cannot be annulled by deposition, by usurpation, by force of arms, or even by the incapacity of the heir. No human power (or lack of it) can invalidate the divine right of a legitimate king to rule. The monarch's authority, moreover, is not limited by any human law. The authority granted by God to the monarch is ample for him to rule the realm as God's agent. The king is the one and only recipient of civil authority in the realm. Subjects therefore have a Christian duty to obey the commands of the sovereign monarch. Resistance to his authority is not only an offense against the state but also a sin against God. A legitimate monarch, then, has an absolute right to rule, and his subjects have an absolute duty to obey—according to these "reformed" Christian teachings.

Strange as it may seem, this was a famous and popular doctrine for many centuries in Europe. Today in this country no one could take seriously such a claim to rule. In fact this form of divine-right doctrine was never widely accepted by American thinkers. Even during the early Colonial period, Americans were antiroyalist in sentiment, just as they were nonconformist in their religion. Perhaps they admitted a notion of kingship, but it was a conception of constitutional monarchy, which incidentally bears an affinity for the medieval notion of kingship.

With the doctrine of the divine right of the elect of God to rule, it is another story entirely. Historically, this doctrine is closely linked to the Protestant reformer of Geneva, John Calvin. The American Puritans were mainly Calvinist in their theology. Their movement began with an attempt to reform ("purify") the established Church of England and ended as a separatist Protestant sect. The Puritans, who represented a Liberal revolt in religion against the dynastic system, rejected the divine-right-of-kings doctrine. But following Calvin, they espoused a doctrine of the divine right of the elect of God to rule. The doctrine was part of the Puritan theory of theocracy. This is evident in the writings of John Winthrop, Nathaniel Ward, Jonathan Mitchell, and other seventeenth-century American Puritan "divines."

The Puritans believed that it was their divinely inspired mission to establish in New England "Christ's kingdom on earth." In a sermon entitled "The Great End and Interest of New England" (1662), Jonathan Mitchell declared: "The erecting of Christ's kingdom in whole societies was our design and is our interest in this country." The Puritans assumed that, to achieve this mission, "true religion" should pervade the lives of Christians; every facet of human existence should be ordered in accord with God's will, the universal and immutable supreme moral law.

In their theory, the Puritan theocrats distinguished between ecclesiastical and civil rule. The church, the congregation of true believers, is the instrument of religion. A true believer is a person who understands the word of God, is endowed with "grace," and performs good works—"walks in the way of the Lord." The church is composed of the "brotherhood of true believers" and the "elders." The elders are the preachers, teachers, and "lay divines." They govern the religious affairs of the community; they define the dogma, establish qualifications for church membership, settle disputes, and impose religious discipline. They can punish errant members by requiring repentance, by public

180

censure, by trial, even by excommunication. The church government is entirely in the hands of the ruling elders.

Every church member is at the same time a citizen of the "commonwealth." The task of civil government is to promote the welfare of the community—the spiritual as well as the temporal welfare. This requires that civil affairs be ordered to conform to the principles of the true religion. In the Hartford Convention (1649) it was proclaimed that the commonwealth was founded "to maintain and preserve the liberty and purity of the Gospel of our Lord Jesus Christ which we now profess, as also the disciplining of the churches, which according to the truth of said Gospel is now practiced amongst us." Thus the civil magistrates are allies of the church elders in promoting the true religion.

However, a distinctive position of the theocrat is the contention that the spiritual welfare of a Christian is superior to his temporal welfare. Church authority, accordingly, takes precedence over civil authority. The Puritans in fact made church membership the basis for civil status, such as citizenship, voting, property ownership, office holding, and the like. So Jonathan Mitchell tells us (in a sermon, "Nehemiah on the Wall in Troublesome Times," 1669): "In the Commonwealth, Christ's kingdom is set up, when all things therein are so ordered (laws and all civil adminstration) as doth most fitly and effectually tend to advance, promote, and maintain religion and reformation."

The Puritans proceeded, in terms of this theory, to argue their case for rule by a religious elite: A Christian ruler, an agent of God, must possess exceptional qualifications. He exercises divinely sanctioned authority, and he must exercise it according to God's will. A ruler does not "make laws"; he merely administers God's law in human affairs. This law is contained in the Scriptures. They provide a complete guide for ruling the affairs of men, public and private, secular and religious. A ruler of a Christian commonwealth, then, must understand fully and correctly the Scriptures. But to interpret the Scriptures "truly," he must possess "grace" as well as learning. Few people are so qualified. Those who are constitute "the elect of God." Who are the members of this elect? That is easy to determine. Obviously the ruling elders of the church are; for that matter, they are the only persons competent to decide whether a person is qualified to rule. The elders, who are directly accountable to God, are entitled to exercise authority. The conclusion: the elect of God have a divine right to rule the civil community.

4.

We have said that the Catholic does not derive from his belief that God is the source of authority any inference about a divine right to rule. Both forms of the divine-right doctrine are contrary to Catholic teachings. Indeed the doctrines were devised by Protestants who repudiated the teachings of the Church of Rome.

But why is it that in Catholic theory no one can have a divine right to exercise civil authority? Why is it that monarchy is not the best form of civil rule? To answer these questions we must bear in mind two crucially important distinctions drawn with clarity in Catholic thought.

One is the distinction between civil and ecclesiastical authority. We said before that Catholic thought in a sense includes two theories—one a theory of ecclesiastical authority; the other, of civil authority. In discussing government the Catholic always carefully observes this distinction between ecclesiastical and civil rule. The Catholic theory of church government is certainly not a Democratic theory. But then there is no Democratic theory about the realm of spiritual affairs. The Democrat is concerned solely about what a Catholic would term "civil rule." Nothing in Catholic teachings requires—or even suggests—that the system of rule used in the Church has any application for civil rule. Remember the doctrine of the two swords. So when the question about who should rule is posed, it is necessary, in Catholic terms, to determine whether the question pertains to the Church or to civil government. It is the Catholic answer to the question about who should exercise civil authority that concerns the Democrat.

The other distinction in Catholic thought important to remember is between a public office and a person who may occupy it. This is a familiar distinction in the political tradition of the West. It dates back actually to the Roman Stoics, who devised one of the earliest theories of constitutional rule. The idea is that authority is vested in public offices, not private persons. A person is not, in his private capacity, entitled to exercise authority. What he exercises is the authority of the office he occupies. This authority is circumscribed by moral principles. We have seen that in Catholic teachings the authority of a constituted office is divinely sanctioned and that authority should always be obeyed. However, a person who rules may not have a right to rule. He may exercise power, not authority. The Christian duty is to obey only authority. There is no duty to obey a ruler who commands what is contrary to natural law. In fact, if obedience requires acting contrary to God's will, there is a Christian duty to disobey the ruler.

The import of this distinction in Catholic thought is that no answer to the question of who should occupy a civil office is in any way provided by natural law. No person can have, in Catholic terms, a God-given right to occupy a public office. Recall the Catholic teaching that enough civil authority is located in a "natural society" to achieve the purpose of that society. It is up to the members of a civil society—the community—to decide who should exercise the authority.

This means that in Catholic teachings no form of civil rule is prescribed as the "best." It is true that some Catholics (as well as many non-Catholics) have advocated monarchical or aristocratic forms of government. Some Catholics have favored a "mixed" system of government, where the democratic principle is combined with the monarchical and aristocratic in the same constitution. However, Catholic teachings do not require a Catholic to accept as necessary any particular form of government. Nor do they even specify that one form is preferable to another. There are no natural-law prescriptions, according to Catholic teachings, about who should exercise authority or how they should acquire their office. There is no authoritative Catholic answer to the question: What is the best form of civil rule? Any form of government, by itself, is acceptable.

Since Catholicism neither favors nor opposes any form of government as such, the policy of the Roman Church has traditionally been one of "neutralism"—a policy of tolerating any legitimate regime. Because of this policy, the Church has sometimes been unwarrantedly accused of supporting certain regimes, since it did not openly oppose them. But the Church's opposition to or favor for a regime does not depend at all on the *form* of government. It depends on other considerations entirely. We shall later see, when we consider the principle of majority rule, that Catholic theory contains strict imperatives about *how* authority should be exercised. But on the question of *who* should exercise civil authority—who has a "right" to rule—on this question Catholic theory is silent.

Not so with Liberal theory. It is true that both forms of divine-right doctrine were severely attacked by Liberal thinkers. In his *Two Treatises of Government* (1690) John Locke elaborated what proved to be a definitive Liberal critique of the doctrine of the divine right of kings to rule. The doctrine of the divine right of the elect of God to rule, Roger Williams attacked. From the standpoint of the early American Puritans, Williams was a dangerous radical, a renegade to be ostracized. But Williams's beliefs, it turned out, reflected the growing tendencies of the times. We have seen that theocratic views were gradually abandoned in the American Colonies. Church government was "Liberalized"; so was civil government. By the eighteenth century, when John Wise was writing, most Americans had come to reject the native form of divine-right doctrine. Instead they accepted the views which had been strange and novel a century before when Williams first expressed them.

We emphasized above that the Liberals attacked divine-right doctrines by appealing to natural-law assumptions. The historic alternative was a doctrine of popular sovereignty, an ingredient in the natural rights–social contract theory of authority advanced by Liberal thinkers. By this theory, church government was rigidly separated from civil government. However the Liberals did not abandon their belief in elite rule. They addressed themselves directly to the question about who should exercise political authority, and they propounded a definite answer to it. In fact they reformulated and elaborated the doctrine of civil rule by an elite. But we shall see that for them it was nature, not God, that prescribed that a few have a right to rule the many. It was relying on nature, too, that they concocted their doctrine about the "best" form of rule.

5.

It was those indigenous American Liberals, the Federalists, who were first confronted with the task of justifying rule by an elite of wealth and talent. Their skill in performing this task has ever since inspired the ardent praise of Liberals, foreign and domestic. The Federalists did perform this task most ingeniously. The ingenuity consists in the remarkable way their theory camouflages their elitist beliefs.

Let us be quite clear about the character of this task the Federalist thinkers performed so well. We have already noted that the Federalists, whether they liked it or not, were committed by the American Revolution to the principle of popular sovereignty. To avoid serious trouble, they first shaped this doctrine so as to locate governmental authority in a constitution, safe from the sovereign people. Who should exercise this authority? Only a superior few should, the Federalists were firmly convinced. But no case for such rule could be made if men have an equal right to exercise authority. To justify elite rule, it was necessary to show that men are not equal in political wisdom. If it could be shown that a few are politically wiser than the many, then those few have a superior right to rule.

The Federalists were fully enlightened and emancipated Americans. They were not at all receptive to any idea of political superiority by virtue of blood and birth. For generations Americans had denounced the pretensions of the titled nobility of Europe. Nor were the Federalists inclined to argue their case in religious terms. On the question of divine right, the late eighteenth-century Americans had been completely reformed. The Federalists wanted no "artificial" distinction drawn among citizens. What the Federalists did believe in was an "aristocracy of merit." They advanced their cause in the familiar terms of the principles of nature. In this behalf they invented a doctrine of "natural aristocracy." In the *Federalist Papers,* authored in the main by Alexander Hamilton and James Madison, this doctrine was explained with skill and cogency as well as enthusiasm.

In any elitist doctrine it is necessary to provide some criterion for dividing the superior few from the rest of the people. The Federalists never questioned the criterion of "merit." Only men of merit are entitled to rule, certainly. But the Federalists did not entirely agree among themselves about how to measure "natural" abilities. They assumed that the wise should be wealthy and the wealthy should be wise. But the extent to which wealth is a proper yardstick for measuring merit was a matter of some difference of opinion, among the talented if not among the wealthy. Sometimes cruel fates conspired to upset the true nature of things by preventing wealth and talent from going hand in hand. Fortune may allow a talented man to suffer a menial condition in life while elevating a fool to affluence. But no person should acquire political privilege by accident of birth or fortune. He must earn it by his own abilities. So the Federalists maintained that merit must be measured in terms of intellectual ability of a special order.

Politics, the Federalists declared, is a rational science. There exist "true principles of politics." These principles are implicit in the nature of things. They are, of course, knowable, since they are rational principles; a rational man can perceive them. These principles supply a true guide for governing. If political affairs are conducted according to these rational principles of politics, all is well. The best interests of everyone—the public good—are promoted by government.

To understand these true principles and to apply them in political affairs requires exceptional qualifications. Only a few persons are so qualified. They make up the "natural aristocracy." The natural aristocrat, in contrast to the untutored mass, understands the true nature of politics. He possesses superior political wisdom. What is denied the common man but possessed by the natural aristocrat is knowledge about how to promote the public good.

This concept of the public good has a very special meaning in Federalist thought. When the Federalist proceeds to explain the concept in terms of his class analysis of society, the meaning becomes clear. Strictly speaking, the public good is "the best interests of all" in contrast to the special interest of some part. Of course government should serve only the public good. The public good requires that the rights of every individual be duly protected. The good of any society is the sum of individual contributions. The greater the industry and ability displayed by individuals, the greater the wealth and accomplishments of the society. In every society the individuals of outstanding wealth and talent who make the greatest contribution to the good of the society are few in number. The many are poor and lacking in ability. But the good of society requires that the rights of every individual be protected, so that each individual is allowed to make the greatest contribution he is capable of to the public good.

In a popular system of government, there is no danger that the rights of the many will be infringed by government, at the expense of the public good. But there is a danger that a majority of the people may try to use government to promote their special interests. They may try to profit from the bounty of the rich and the achievements of the able. They may infringe the rights of the wealthy and talented minority to the detriment of the good of the whole society. So it is imperative, the Federalist concluded, that only those who understand the true nature of the public good—the natural aristocrats—exercise governmental authority.

6.

By the doctrine of natural aristocracy, the Federalists made a case for the political superiority of a few over the many. But a difficulty remained. What is to prevent the common people from usurping the offices of government from the natural aristocrats and ruling themselves? To discourage such an eventuality, the Federalists had to draw a sharp distinction in the political system between those who should exercise authority and those who should not. Somehow they had to make a public office a monopoly of the natural aristocrats. So included in the Federalist formula for reconciling elite rule and popular sovereignty was the principle of representative government. James Madison, one of the more articulate and temperate Federalist thinkers, as well as the chief architect of the constitutional structure built at the Philadelphia Convention, explained this formula with striking candor in the *Federalist Papers,* notably numbers 10, 14, and 39.

Madison launches his argument by defining a "republic." In contrast to a monarchy, a republic is founded on the principle of popular sovereignty: the government "derives all its powers directly or indirectly from the great body of people." But, says Madison, we must distinguish between "small" and "large" republics. In a small republic no distinction is drawn between those who govern and those who are governed. The people meet together and directly exercise the governing authority. In a large republic, the responsibility for administering the people's affairs is placed in the hands of a few outstanding citizens. They are elected to represent the people in conducting the government. In other words, a small republic is a Democracy; a large republic has a system of representative government.

Madison next proceeds to sing the praises of large republics. If a vast and populous country is to be blessed with popular rule, it must be based on the principle of representation. On such a scale self-government is impossible. Besides, representative government has some definite advantages over Democratic rule. In any country the number of natural aristocrats is relatively small in proportion to the population; the larger the population, the more men of exceptional merit there are available for public service. So in a large republic more "good men," who understand the nature of the public good, can participate in public affairs.

Further: in a small community "factionalism" tends to prevail. The community is divided into groups, each attempting to promote the special interests of its members. The ensuing conflict is disruptive of public peace and order. Especially serious always is the conflict between the few wealthy and the many poor. Now, in a large and populous country, interest groups are many and varied and dispersed. Thus the influence of factions is lessened. Opposing factions tend to cancel out one another. The result is that no special interest becomes predominant and agitation to advance special interest is discouraged. This is desirable, since then there is less likelihood that the public good will become confused with the special interests of any part of the population.

The third advantage Madison imputes to representative government is most significant. In a large republic where representatives are elected to govern the people, the public good is best secured.

The government does not bow to expediency or cater to special interests. As public opinion passes through able representatives, a selected body of citizens, it is "refined" and "enlarged." The representatives, better than the people themselves, exercise the authority of government for the public good.

This advantage of the large republic is predicated on a distinct doctrine of representation. This doctrine has never been assigned a label, so let's call it the "safety-valve" doctrine of representation. This label, we shall see, aptly describes the character of the doctrine.

In any doctrine of representation, the question to be answered is: What is the function of the representative? How can it be decided whether or not a representative is doing a good job? What criterion can be used to judge his record? Quite different answers to this question have been worked out by American thinkers. None has ever received overwhelming acceptance. But the Federalists regarded Madison's answer as the ripe fruit of pure reason. It was that the function of the representative is to promote the public good. Why the Federalists were so enthusiastic about Madison's doctrine of representation is not hard to understand.

The representative, says Madison, should be a man of outstanding merit. He should possess exceptional intelligence and training. He should be experienced in public affairs and imbued with public spirit. When he assembles with his colleagues, the representative of the people should deliberate the affairs of the commonwealth with dignity and detachment. He should distill out of public opinion the passions and follies which so grievously afflict the common people. He should not allow the transient desires of the untutored masses to deter him in his quest for the right decision. He should always be guided by the principles of politics which reason reveals to be true. For it is the function of the representative, says Madison, to promote the public good—"the best interests of all."

Of course the stinger in this doctrine is that only the natural aristocrats are qualified to serve as representatives. In effect Madison is saying that the common people should not try to govern themselves. They are easily swayed by emotions and they fail to understand the nature of the public good. Governing is a task for the specially qualified. Representatives "whose patriotism, and love of justice will be least likely to sacrifice it to temporary or partial considerations" can discern the public good. Madison once remarked that "the public voice, pronounced by the representatives of the people, will be more consonant with the public good, than if pronounced by the people themselves, convened for that purpose." So the common people should select their rulers from among the natural aristocrats. The role of the representative, in this safety-valve doctrine, is actually to save the people from themselves: to serve as a check on popular influence in government.

This Federalist scheme for reconciling elite rule and popular sovereignty by the formula of representative government run by natural aristocrats entails certain theoretical difficulties. The Federalist tacitly assumes that the sovereign people know what they want if you don't ask them, and don't know what they want if you do. He draws a distinction between what the people *say* they want and what they *really* want. The people should get, the Federalist believes, not what they say they want but what they really want—what they should want. Only an elite of natural aristocrats knows what the people *should* want, namely, "the public good."

But if this is the case, then the expression "the sovereign people" is a contradiction in terms. The people should not possess the supreme authority. They should be ruled by the "best men," who know what the public good is. Not by the representatives of the people, notice, but by the natural aristocrats. Otherwise the principle of representative government is merely a guise behind which the best men, who should rule, do rule. They rule not because they are representatives of the people. They rule in spite of the people, because they are the best men.

The Federalists were practical politicians. They were not easily dismayed by such a thing as logical inconsistency. They eagerly grasped one horn of the dilemma—the one that served their interests. They knew exactly what *they* wanted. Their underlying conviction was that a few who possess great wealth and talent have a natural right to exercise authority. For the Federalists, the principle of representative government was merely a convenient screen for their distinctive principle of elite rule, that a superior few should rule the many. Accordingly the Federalists promoted the institution of political practices which would curb popular influence in government. They advocated the indirect election of government officials. The original provisions of the Constitution for selecting the President and the Vice President and United States Senators evidence the Federalist aim to make public office a monopoly of natural aristocrats. The Federalists advocated a restricted franchise and high property and age qualifications for voting to keep the electorate as exclusive as possible and to prevent the common people from participating in important elections. The Federalists advocated that these and many other practices be encased within our constitutional system—practices which have been the target for generations of American Democratic reformers.

7.

The chances are that the members of the Westside Civic Improvement League would take no stock in this Federalist theory of representative government. It is their practice when making a decision for the League members to assemble and discuss the question at issue and resolve it to their satisfaction. No one supposes that the elected officers are different from the other members of the League. They have no right, natural or otherwise, to tell the membership what to do. They have no special pipeline to a fountain of political truth. They know no better than anyone else what the League membership really wants to do about a question.

If an officer should suddenly acquire delusions of grandeur, the membership would probably relieve him of the pressing burdens of his office at the first convenient opportunity. In fact, if he should persist in his strange behavior, they might even arrange to make an opportunity remarkably convenient.

The members of the League would take this attitude because they do not believe in elite rule. They accept instead Democratic principles about the exercise of authority, including the principle of political equality. So did the anti-Federalists who, under Thomas Jefferson's leadership, fostered the reform movement which achieved the "Democratic franchise." We said that this reform movement as well as later movements for Democratic reform was inspired by a belief that men should equally share in exercising political authority.

The Federalists' theory of representative government was, we have seen, part of an effort to justify elite rule. Elite rule is not, of course, sanctioned by a Democrat. Neither is the principle of representative government. The making of political decisions by an agent vested with authority to act for the group is precisely the way of exercising authority that the Democrat objects to. The Democratic process is a way of making decisions about the exercise of authority on a group basis, directly by the membership affected by the decisions. In fact in Democratic theory there is no provision for a principle of representation as the Liberal thinks of it.

At the same time, American Democrats have of course recognized a principle of representation in government above the level of the local community. In this country such a principle is incorporated into the constitutional system and pervades much American government, local as well as state and national. But this recognition by the Democrat is predicated on a conviction that above the level of the local community authority cannot be Democratically exercised over people. Of course any group of persons, regardless of the level of organization, can use a Democratic process for making decisions. But the exercise of authority by a representative is not, by definition, a Democratic method of rule.

This is not to say that Democratic theory inadequately takes into account the need for making political decisions above the level of a community organization. There is a counterpart in Democratic theory of the Liberal principle of representative government. It is the principle of a convention of delegates.

Most Americans are familiar with the institution of the convention for the simple reason that they have attended conventions. The convention is most extensively used, and significantly so, by voluntary organizations like political parties, labor unions, and trade and professional associations. Every year thousands of local, state, and national conventions are held by organizations as different as the Rotary International and the National Association for the Advancement of Colored People. Conventions have taken on a social function for those who attend, but the serious business of most conventions is still to make decisions which affect the members of the organizations. Convention practices vary widely but conventions have a common character which differs in important respects from an assembly of legislative representatives.

A convention is a temporary rather than a continuing body. It is called for a purpose, and when its business is transacted it is adjourned. A convention can decide any question—whether legislative, administrative, or judicial in character—which concerns its membership. It can pass on the credentials for seating delegates, instruct the officers on their duties, set the agenda for conducting business, and take final action on matters before it.

A delegate to a convention performs a function much different from that of a legislative representative. The delegate is not a free agent. He is selected by a group and sent to a convention to speak for the organization. He has a mandate to act only in regard to matters properly before the convention. He is expected to express the attitudes and promote the desires of his organization as best he can. He may be instructed by his organization specifically to oppose or support certain proposals before the convention. And when the business is finished and the convention is adjourned, the delegate automatically goes out of office.

Yet a delegate does not exercise authority in the sense that a representative does. As a member a delegate of course participates in exercising the authority of the convention. But strictly speaking, convention delegates do not make decisions binding on anyone else. In fact, it is common practice for convention actions to require ratification by the affiliated local groups before a decision becomes binding on the full membership. To this extent, what the convention does is to propose that an action be taken. Then the full membership passes on the proposal by a kind of plebiscite.

The need for a method of decision-making above the level of the community organization can be met without sanctioning elite rule and without violating the principle of political equality. It is thus met by the principle of a convention of delegates—a Democratic method.

8.

The members of the Westside Civic Improvement League may reject the Federalist principle of elite rule and accept the Democratic principle of political equality, but so far we have not given any reasons why they should. Let us correct this omission now.

We said that the general question at issue is: Who should rule? The Liberal believes that men are not equal in political wisdom. The few who are wiser than the many have a superior right to rule. His conclusion: an elite of "merit" should exercise authority. This the Democrat denies. He believes that persons should equally share in exercising authority.

It might appear that the Democrat has a difficult case to sustain. Actually this is not so. The Democrat's belief, that in a political community the members should equally share the privileges and obligations of membership, remains undisturbed even by the most resourceful elitist dialectics. In fact, the Democrat's case for political equality logically falls into two parts: one is the rebuttal of elitist claims; the other is the affirmative argument that men are equal in political wisdom.

First we shall consider the elitist claim that a few have a superior right to rule and why the Democrat finds this claim without warrant.

The elitist claim depends on two assumptions which the Democrat charges are untenable. One is the assumption that from the fact that persons are different, a superior right can be derived. The other is that superiority in respect to certain qualities is evidence of superior political wisdom. Neither of these assumptions on which the elitist claim rests stands up under close inspection.

The Democrat's case for political equality does not include a pretension that persons are in fact equal. The Democrat recognizes that persons actually differ in many respects. They differ as to age, sex, physique, intelligence, education, experience, income, and so on. In respect to any quality, some persons are no doubt "superior" to others, depending on the criterion somewhat arbitrarily applied. Some men are more intelligent, better informed, wealthier than others. Some men are more skilled, more industrious, more courageous than others. There is no doubt that people are different, but this fact is beside the point. The Democrat insists that actual "superiority" in respect to any quality, or any combination of qualities, does not furnish support for claiming a superior right to exercise political authority.

Notice that what is at stake is a question of value, not of fact. The Democrat contends that the members of a political community *should* equally share privileges and obligations. The elitist claims they *should not*. Both are judgments of value. The Democrat denies that the elitist can in any way substantiate his value judgment that a few should have rights superior to the many. From the fact that one person is older, or wealthier, or better educated than others, no inference can be warrantedly drawn that he should rule the rest.

Now, on what can the elitist rest his claim that a few have a superior right to rule? We have seen that many years ago elitists attempted to uphold their claim by appealing to supernatural truth. The Puritan held that the elect of God are morally superior to plain Christians. But religious dogma proved to be a slender reed indeed for supporting claims of a divine right to rule. Such attempts were abandoned by elitists in favor of a more promising appeal to some sort of principles of "nature." The Federalist, we said, believed that an elite of "merit" should rule. The wealthy and talented few were alleged to be better qualified than the common people to decide questions about exercising authority. Because the natural aristocrats better understood the nature of the public good, they were, the Federalist contended, morally superior.

In recent times the totalitarian ideologists have likewise claimed a moral superiority for their elite. The Fascist said that the *Duce* best understood the *real* will of the Italian nation. The Nazi said that the *Führer* best understood the *real* will of the German *Volk*. The Communists still say that the party elite, intimates with dialectical materialism, alone understand the *real* course of history. The Communist knows better what the proletariat want than the proletarians themselves, at least until they become class-conscious by understanding the eternal truths of Marxist dialectical materialism. These totalitarian ideologists are the intellectual progeny of the German philosopher Hegel. What they mean by "real" is what Hegel meant by "real"—right. In Hegelian terms, what is real is morally right. We find that in all cases the totalitarian elites are alleged to possess a moral superiority denied to the common people.

Apparently the lovers of their own liberty are no longer comfortable talking about the moral superiority of a few over the many. Such talk certainly got out of hand in recent decades. Anyway, the contemporary Liberals rely on a claim of what is supposed to be the intellectual superiority of a few. The most plausible form in which this Liberal claim has been advanced is that of a "scientific elite." The "masses," so it is contended, are not qualified by training, intelligence, or whatnot to make political decisions. Those who possess exceptional intellectual qualifications are. These few specially qualified "experts" have a superior right to rule the masses. This form of the elitist claim, to which present-day Liberals cling as the very last straw, is at least worth consideration.

What about these experts? No doubt a well-trained and talented expert is better qualified than a layman to decide certain technical questions. A practicing attorney's judgment about the outcome of a case at law is more reliable than the judgment of a person without legal training or experience. A competent medical doctor's diagnosis of a patient's ailment is a more reliable judgment than a bricklayer's. This is not to say that lawyers and doctors don't make mistakes. Prisons and cemeteries are full of evidence to the contrary. But it is clear that there are numerous areas of human experience where the decision of a trained and skilled expert in the field is more highly regarded, and properly so, than that of someone who is not specially qualified.

But because a person has special legal or medical skill, it does not follow that he is politically wiser than others. If we want to build a brick wall, we don't call in a heart specialist or a corporation lawyer for advice. Nor do we call in a bricklayer when we want to make a political decision. The fact that a person is an expert in one field is testimony that he is not a specialist in another. Intellectual superiority in any field is not evidence of superior political wisdom.

With one possible exception, of course. What about the "political expert"? Some persons, so the elitist claims, are particularly expert in making political decisions. They are trained and experienced scientists. They know the answers to political questions. Let's do away with political shenanigans and let the experts make the decisions.

Since Plato's time, political thinkers sympathetic to elitist rule have entertained in some form this notion of the political expert. Interestingly enough, they have never agreed about the exact character of political *expertise*. Even more interesting, no thinker has ever made a case to substantiate a claim that political experts should rule. Nor will a convincing case ever be made for this claim.

The difficulty arises from an assumption that because there are persons like legal or medical experts, there must be political experts too. There must be persons who are as qualified to make political decisions as the lawyer and doctor are to make decisions within their specialty. Experience fails to bear this assumption out. Plato, as well as others who have assumed this, was much given to analogical reasoning. His doctrine of elite rule by philosopher kings depends on the analogy that politics is like medicine. This analogy simply does not hold up in practice.

This is not to deny that on any given political question some persons may have at their command information more useful and relevant than others have. What is useful and relevant information, however, depends on the particular question to be decided. It varies from question to question. The specialists who are expert about political matters are concerned with a host of different fields, not one. None is a *political* expert. For example, a government attorney who is a tax expert is less qualified than a public-health administrator to decide whether a community should be placed under quarantine. A government inspector who is an expert on postal regulations is less qualified than a foreign-service officer to decide whether trade relations with Spain should be curtailed. The trouble is not simply that no expert is specially qualified outside his field and no specialist is better informed about other specialties than the experts in those fields. The difficulty is that politics is not a special field at all. It is a congeries of many different fields in which many different persons, by reason of training and experience, have acquired information of a specialist order. Each expert may be specially qualified to decide technical questions within his field. But from this it cannot be inferred that he is qualified to decide questions outside his field—political questions that bear on the specialties of many experts.

It is significant that those who claim to be political experts seldom carry the same credentials. The political experts are always self-chosen for that august status; never are they elevated by their peers. For the fact is that there is no such thing as an expert who is better qualified than the rest of us to make *political* decisions.

Why is it, then, that the Democrat finds elitist claims that a few should rule the many without warrant? Because the elitist is unable to show that "nature" is a source for superior political rights or superior political wisdom. The elitist rests his claim on alleged "evidence" of human inequality. Experience does reveal that persons are unequal. In fact, no two persons are exactly the same. From this the elitist tries to infer that a few should have a superior right to exercise authority. But for this inference he has no warrant. He cannot demonstrate that because some persons are in fact exceptional they have superior political rights. He cannot demonstrate that because some persons are exceptional in respect to certain qualities they have superior political wisdom. The elitist case fails for want of evidence.

But does not the Democrat's value judgment—that in a political community the members should equally share privileges and obligations—suffer from the same lack of evidence? On the contrary, it benefits. The crucial difference is that the Democrat makes no special claims. He rests his argument on the absence of demonstrable grounds for elitist claims. The Democrat says merely that if persons are not politically unequal, they should equally share political privileges and obligations.

9.

But the Democratic case for political equality includes an affirmative argument too, we said. The Democrat believes not only that the elitist claim for political inequality is unfounded, but also that the Democratic claim that men are equal in political wisdom is securely founded. The Democrat therefore holds that the members of a community are in practice equal in wisdom when deciding a question about the exercise of authority. Why does the Democrat believe this?

It was perhaps apparent, when considering the Democratic critique of the elitist claim, that the Democrat's conception of a political decision is rather distinctive. A political decision is unlike a technical decision which an expert is competent to make. The distinction between the character of a political decision and that of a technical decision we should now make clearly explicit.

In making a technical decision, an expert relies on a body of technical information. This information about a narrow area of experience has been acquired by special study. Through careful analysis, reliable principles have been abstracted out and formulated to describe that certain kind of experience. These principles an expert specially understands. His skill consists in an exceptional ability to apply these reliable principles in answering questions about that narrow area of experience. Relying on his *expertise,* he can make a more accurate decision about how to solve a technical problem than a nonexpert can. A lawyer can decide how to present a case in court; a doctor can decide how to cure an ailing patient. Even though the doctor and lawyer make mistakes, the bricklayer can certainly decide how to build a solid, straight brick wall. Bricks are much easier to handle than judges or sick people. But how do technical decisions of this sort differ from political decisions?

Let us consult again the experience of the Westside Civic Improvement League. The membership is meeting to decide, say, how to raise $100,000 for the new community hospital. They need the money within ninety days in order to get the project under way. A proposal is made that the League's finance committee be instructed to solicit Westside businessmen for subscriptions to the hospital fund. Another proposal is offered that the League sponsor a fund-raising carnival at the Youth Center. A third proposal is introduced to require each member to pledge $1,000 to the fund, either to pay the money himself or raise it from personal solicitations. Other proposals are made, and after much discussion about the problem the membership decides to act. They vote to set an initial goal of $50,000 within sixty days and to raise the fund by a program incorporating features of several proposals. The membership is bound by the decision about exercising the League's authority. The meeting breaks up with the members feeling that they have made the best decision under the circumstances. Everyone hopes it is a wise one.

The League members have made a political decision. What is the distinctive character of it?

The decision was made for a definite purpose. The League members were confronted by a common problem. To resolve it, they had to agree on actions to be taken. It was a collective decision. It affected in some way the daily lives of every one of the League's members. It was a decision about exercising the authority of the League over the membership. As a result of the decision, members were expected to take certain actions, and not to take others, regardless of personal desires. It was a complicated decision. The members answered not a single question but a cluster. They determined that a certain goal should be set for the group. They determined that certain means should be taken to attain it. It was a unique decision. They had not been confronted with the exact same problem before. To resolve the problem confronting them required creative judgment. They had to invent a solution for a novel problem.

Several points deserve special emphasis. One is about what we can call the "synthetic" character of a political decision. We said that in making their decision the League members answered a cluster of questions. Consider what the process by which they arrived at their decision therefore involves. It involves combining a number of different ingredients.

An important ingredient is information. Any and all information relevant to the problem under discussion can be useful. Information about past experiences can be helpful, if not relied on too heavily. It is said that the generals who lost the war were the ones who were fighting the battles of the last war. So it is in politics. A political decision is a resolution to act in regard to a different problem in a different way at a different time and in a different place than ever before experienced. Information of technical sorts also can be useful—the technical information that many different experts can supply, not one. So far as questions of fact must be answered in the decision-making process, experts with suitable experience and training can provide valuable assistance.

But a political decision involves much more than answering questions of fact. It involves questions of value too. Choices must be made which no expert, singly or in a group, is competent to make. In arriving at a political decision, choices must be made about the desirability of ends of action and about the desirability of means—about what is wanted as well as how to get it. So far as determining means is concerned, again experts can be useful. No one expert is qualified by his specialist skill to make a determination of means; no group of experts, alone, is competent to make the determination either. However the advice and opinion of numerous experts are ingredients in the decision-making process. Experts can appraise the possible means to an end. They can tell the League members how to raise funds for a hospital project and how to construct hospital buildings. Financial experts and architects can do this. But they cannot tell the League members that they *should* build a community hospital. These questions of ends—what is wanted—are as vital ingredients in the decision-making process as questions about how to attain them. In practice the choices about ends and means of action are inseparable. The desirability of an end depends on the desirability of the possible means, and conversely. Choosing a set of suitable means implies a desirable end; choosing a desirable end implies a set of suitable means, as a practical matter. So in arriving at a political decision, choices about what is wanted and how to get it must be made. Questions of value must be answered.

Another point about the character of a political decision that bears emphasis concerns the inconclusiveness of human action. When the League members broke up their meeting they felt, we said, that they had made the best decision and they hoped it was a wise one. We often remark that a political decision, in our opinion, is wise or unwise. We may believe or feel that it is or is not wise, but we cannot know in advance whether it is. There are no practicable criteria for appraising the "rightness" of a political decision.

The reason for this is that the effects of a political decision are determined by the actions of people. To the extent that people act in accord with a decision, it works out in practice. To the extent that it works out in practice the way it was intended and expected to when made, a political decision is, we say, "wise." For example, the passage of the Eighteenth Amendment to the Constitution has frequently been pointed to as an unwise decision. The American people continued to manufacture, sell, buy, and drink alcoholic beverages, despite the prohibition of the Federal laws. As a practical matter, then, we can say that a political decision is wise to the extent that a desired end is actually achieved by desirable means.

It is, of course, people who decide that ends and means are desirable. They decide to what extent a political decision satisfactorily resolves a political problem. Yet there are no final and conclusive solutions to political problems. They exist because a group of people want something they do not have. People never have everything they want and they never stop wanting things. They always have problems of greater or lesser import to them. Resolution of any such problem consists in working out a more satisfactory adjustment between what people want and what they have. For example, the League members may want the finest hospital in the world for their community. This they cannot have in Westside. What they can have is a modest facility which would fairly well serve the hospital needs of their community. Their problem is resolved by determining what they can, as a practical matter, have by way of a community hospital facility. The decision the League members took at their meeting was a step in that direction. They decided what they should have and how they should go about getting it.

Was their decision wise? That depends on the extent to which the actions of League members in practice conform to their resolution to act. If the decision passes muster as a wise one, the choices made in the decision-making process must prove to be acceptable, in practice, to the League members affected by the decision.

Now let us sum up the Democratic case for political equality. The Democrat believes that no member of a community is politically wiser than the rest. It is the part of political wisdom to know how authority should be exercised. No man knows this better than the next. As a practical matter, no one knows better than a person himself how he wants authority over him exercised. He knows best what he wants and how he wants to get it. It is in this sense that men are equal in political wisdom: the many members of a community know better than a few how authority over the membership should be exercised. A decision by the many members of a political community about exercising authority is wiser than an opinion of a few, regardless of their special qualifications. For in practice a political decision works out no better or worse than the persons over whom the authority is exercised choose to make it work out.

The Democrat concludes: In a political community the members should equally share the privileges and obligations of membership. No member should have a superior right to exercise authority over the rest. Authority should be exercised the way the members want it exercised. Each member should have an equal stake and an equal responsibility in the affairs of the community. Each member should have an equal voice and vote. In making political decisions affecting the membership, each member of a community should count for one and no more than one. That is the Democratic principle of political equality.

So: Who should rule? The many, the Democrat replies. Why? Because any alternative principle is impractical in a political community.

10.

Let us now return to the question posed earlier in this chapter: What is the relation between the Democratic principle of political equality and Catholic teachings?

We have seen that as far as the issue of who should rule is concerned, Catholic teachings are compatible with Democratic principles. In Catholic terms, rights and duties are divinely prescribed, but there is no claim that anyone has a divine (or "natural") right to rule another. Catholic principles simply do not ordain that any form of rule is best.

But what about Democratic principles and the Catholic doctrine of distributive justice? It is clear that no disagreement about questions of fact divides the Catholic and the Democrat. Both recognize that persons actually differ in many respects. What is involved is a question of value. The Democrat holds that privileges and obligations should be equally shared in a political community. The Catholic holds that rights and duties should be distributed proportionate to the capacity of persons to contribute to the common good. But do these views indicate contrary positions on the same issue, or compatible positions on different issues?

The Catholic view provides an answer to this question: So far as persons actually differ in their abilities to contribute to the common good, should these differences be ignored in assigning rights and duties? The Catholic replies: No. A person's rights and duties should correspond. Persons of exceptional wealth, for example, have special obligations in contributing to the material good of a society. But to say that rights and duties of persons should be unequal does not necessarily deny that members of a political community should equally share privileges and obligations.

This Catholic doctrine is most significant in regard to inequality among groups of persons rather than among individuals. Remember the assumption that persons are "by nature" members of societies. But the principle of social hierarchy does no violence to Democratic beliefs. From the view that members of different groups have different rights and duties appropriate to their rank and station, it does not necessarily follow that the members of the same group should have unequal privileges and obligations. In other words the Catholic assumption of value most pertinent to the question about who should rule is that underlying the doctrine of commutative justice—persons equal in dignity should have equal rights and duties. Members of a political community equal in political wisdom should have equal privileges and obligations.

At the same time, the Democrat does not necessarily deny that obligations should correspond to privileges or that great privileges impose great obligations. Take for example the principle of ability to pay in levying income taxes. The graduated, or progressive, income tax puts a proportionately heavier burden on persons of high income. The tax rate increases as the amount of income increases. This the Catholic justifies by an appeal to the doctrine of distributive justice. This principle of taxation was actually promoted in this country by Democratic reformers. No

Democrat claims that a progressive income tax is contrary to Democratic principles. Democratic principles do not prescribe *what* the members of a political community should decide about any question of policy. They merely prescribe *how* the members of the community should decide any question about exercising authority. The Democrat's position, then, is that the levying of such a tax on the members of a political community is a question for the membership to decide. But in the process of arriving at any decision about tax policy, each member of the political community should count for one and no more than one.

We conclude: So far as the Democratic principle of political equality is concerned, the crucial question is whether the members of a political community should equally share the privileges and obligations of membership. Catholic teachings about authority and justice do answer questions related to this one. These answers are compatible with Democratic principles. To the question of concern to the Democrat, the Catholic Church has no set answer. Catholic teachings prescribe no principles contrary to the Democratic principle of political equality. Nothing in Catholic teachings forbids a Catholic to accept this Democratic principle. Nothing in Catholic teachings requires him to do so. When a Catholic accepts this principle, or any alternative, it is not his religious faith that guides him. It is his political beliefs.

Chapter Seven

MAJORITY RULE

I.

Let's assume that we attend a meeting of the Westside Civic Improvement League. By now we're members in good standing. A problem about a proposed zoning change is brought before the meeting. The planning commission has been petitioned by a mortician to make a "spot" rezoning of a parcel of land which is zoned for residential use only in the master city plan. The League members feel that locating a mortuary in the area would hurt the Westside residents. The planning commision has approved the petition despite protests from some Westside property owners. The problem is what the League should do now to stop the proposed change in the planning code.

You suggest that the League send a delegation to see our city councilman. In our town the planning commission recommends but the city council takes final action. I object to your suggestion on the grounds that it would be ineffective. Our councilman has already publicly announced his support for the petition. Anyway, the fellow who wants to open the mortuary is his brother-in-law. I argue that we must so arouse public opinion about zoning matters that the city council will refuse to approve the planning commission's recommendation. But the councilman is a member of your church, his wife is a friend of your wife, you don't want to stir up trouble, so you hold out for a direct appeal by the League to our councilman.

After the membership has deliberated the matter for some time, you introduce a motion that the League send a delegation of three members to our councilman to urge that he oppose the petition. I offer a substitute motion that the League sponsor a mass protest meeting of Westside residents to which the mayor, all the councilmen, and the press should be invited, and that we censure our city councilman for his stand on the petition. My motion is amended to strike the censure action. The question is put to a vote, and my substitute motion as amended carries by a narrow margin. Everyone assumes that you will go along with the decision and cooperate in sponsoring the public rally, while I will not try to commit the League publicly to a censure of our councilman.

This hypothetical account no doubt suggests a type of experience familiar to most Americans. Decisions are voted by members of organizations to which we belong and we abide by them, regardless of our personal desires. We go along because we accept a distinctive Democratic principle. It is that a decision about exercising a community's authority should be determined by a vote of a majority of the members.

This principle of majority rule is a practical imperative if we also accept the principles of popular sovereignty and political equality. If the authority to make decisions is located in the membership of a political community, and if in making decisions each member counts for one and no more than one, then action is impossible unless the principle of majority rule is adopted. This is the case at least unless it is assumed that authority should be exercised only by unanimous consent. But this assumption is untenable in any political theory. There is no need to exercise authority when there is unanimity among the members of a community about the action to be taken. In fact, there is no political situation. In political practice, persons disagree about questions

210

of common concern. The members of communities feel a need for concerted action, yet they differ in their opinions about the action that should be taken. They can resolve their differences and agree on a common action by the method of voting. Abraham Lincoln framed the issue thus: "Unanimity is impossible; the rule of a minority, as a permanent arrangement, is wholly inadmissible; so that, rejecting the majority principle, anarchy or despotism in some form is all that is left." Unless the principle of majority rule is accepted by the membership, the authority of a Democratic community cannot, as a practical matter, be exercised.

So the Democrat believes that authority should be exercised as determined by a vote of a majority of the members. The membership should regard a decision voted by a majority as the decision of the entire community. Acceptance of this principle is the acid test for separating from the Democratic fold those who entertain elitist convictions—Liberals, for example.

This principle of majority rule is the Democrat's answer to an important issue in modern political thought. It is: How should authority be exercised? The question at stake here has traditionally been discussed by political thinkers in terms of the "legitimacy" of authority. It is assumed that a ruler has a right to exercise, and the ruled has a duty to obey, legitimate authority. Presumably some decisions about exercising authority are legitimate and some are not. The question then becomes: What makes authority legitimate, so that political rights and duties are clearly recognized? Does the ruler have a right to exercise authority? Does the ruled have a duty to obey? To answer such questions a criterion for differentiating between legitimate and nonlegitimate rule is needed. A test is required for determining whether authority is exercised as it should be.

About the proper way to resolve this issue, political thinkers have of course differed widely. The doctrine of majority rule is the way the Democrat resolves it. When posed in these traditional terms the question of concern to the Democrat is about the "right" of a majority to rule. Does a minority have a duty to obey authority exercised as a majority decides? What is the proper relation between majority rule and minority rights? We shall later see that the issue about how authority should be exercised, when posed in these terms, makes no sense for the Democrat. For him the test for determining the "legitimacy" of authority is exclusively a procedural one. Decisions should be made by a decision-making process governed by Democratic principles. A decision about exercising authority voted by a majority of the community is legitimate and should be obeyed by the members. The case for accepting this principle takes the form of the Democratic doctrine of majority rule, which we shall later consider in detail.

But, at least initially, we must consider in traditional terms this issue about how authority should be exercised. In this chapter the question we are to answer is about the relation between the Democratic principle of majority rule and Catholic teachings. The Catholic has customarily discussed the exercise of authority in terms of the rights and duties of persons regarding legitimate authority. So has the Liberal. In determining the legitimacy of authority both rely on a criterion which tests the "validity" of a decision, rather than on the procedure used in making the decision. Decisions are valid depending on their conformity to the criterion invoked. The Catholic doctrines about how authority should be exercised must be examined in order to determine whether they conflict in any way with the Democratic principle. So let us next examine those Catholic teachings about how authority—legitimate authority—should be exercised.

2.

So far we have seen that for the Catholic the legitimacy of authority does not depend on who exercises it or how he acquires his office. There are no natural-law prescriptions, as far as the Catholic is concerned, about who should rule. However, in Catholic teachings there are definite injunctions about *how* civil authority should be exercised. Regardless of the form of government, political authority must be exercised "justly" to be legitimate. The main Catholic principle is that the ruler is morally obliged to exercise authority justly, while the ruled is morally obliged to obey authority justly exercised.

The Catholic doctrine of just rule is, of course, part of the Catholic theory of authority, and like the rest it is derived from Thomist natural-law assumptions. In the Catholic theory, God instituted authority among men for a purpose. The purpose of civil authority is to take care of the material needs of the members of societies. Authority must be exercised in conformity with the laws of nature. It is contrary to natural law for authority to be exercised for the benefit of the ruler or for any part of a society at the expense of the rest. Such rule is, by definition, unjust. Unjust rule is an exercise of power rather than authority. The ruler has no right to rule unjustly, and the ruled have no moral duty to obey such rule. So the question about how authority should be exercised, the Catholic answers: It should be exercised for the common good of those subject to it. Authority exercised this way is legitimate; such rule is just. "To despise legitimate authority, in whomever vested, is unlawful, as a rebellion against Divine Will." A person who defies legitimate authority is subject to punishment in God's name.

The doctrine of just rule is the key to another doctrine which further clarifies Catholic teachings about the exercise of civil authority. We have already mentioned this doctrine in passing, but we have not yet examined it. The doctrine answers a question of much practical import.

The Catholic believes, we have said, that authority exercised for the benefit of the common good is legitimate and such rule is just. The Catholic also believes, as part of his religious faith, that men are stained by original sin. Rulers as well as the ruled are subject to human imperfections. It is to be expected, therefore, that in practice rulers may abuse their offices, as the ruled may lapse into disobedience, contrary to natural law. So the question arises: What is the duty of the ruled when a ruler governs unjustly? Such a situation is fully contemplated in Catholic teachings.

On several occasions during the late nineteenth century, the Vatican took pains to explain the Catholic answer to this question of political morals. In that period anticlericalist movements in several European countries—notably France—launched bitter attacks against the Church. These movements gained control of the governments and passed anticlericalist legislation and implemented policies hostile to the Church. Thus, the Catholic citizen was presented with practical questions about obedience to civil rulers. So Pope Leo XIII set forth the basic Catholic teachings in two significant encyclicals: *Diuturnum Illud* ("On Civil Government," 1881) and *Sapientiae Christianae* ("The Chief Duties of Christians as Citizens," 1890). Perhaps the fullest formulation of the teachings by a Vatican spokesman in recent times was made by Pope Pius XI. During his pontificate—the period between the two World Wars—the question of Christian obedience to civil rulers was frequently posed by the ugly course of events. Especially in the encyclical *Firmissimam Constantiam* ("On the Religious Situation in Mexico," 1937) the Pope defined the Catholic doctrine of resistance.

The Catholic doctrine of right of resistance to civil rulers is founded on a religious conviction that the Christian's highest duty is to obey God, not man; men are obeyed only because God so commands. A Christian is bound to obey human law, but he must do so only in so far as it accords with God's will. Human "law" which is contrary to reason, faith, or morals is not "true law." To partake of the quality of true law, human law must conform to the universal principles of natural law. Since "an immoral and unjust law carries no obligation," a

214

Christian citizen has a right to resist an unjust ruler who commands what is contrary to God's will.

But civil resistance is always a means to an end. Violent resistance to civil rulers, no matter how unjust, is a drastic measure and must never be undertaken unless the evil of submission is worse than that of resistance. The means should be used, in the words of Don Sturzo, "only in so far as is necessary to obtain the end or make it possible to attain it either entirely or in part, and in such a way as not to cause greater harm to the community than that which it attempts to remedy." If the spiritual welfare of the citizen is endangered by obedience, the presumption is that resistance is a lesser evil than submission. If the material welfare is impaired, the contrary assumption obtains. Yet even the material welfare of the citizen can be so endangered that resistance may be justified, since "the Christian life requires for its development the support of external and tangible means." When obedience is a greater evil, it is a crime against God for a Christian citizen *not* to resist: resistance then is a duty.

These Catholic teachings have been most cogently elaborated by Don Luigi Sturzo in several articles, particularly in the *Dublin Review* (July, 1937) and the *Contemporary Review* (September, 1928). Sturzo makes a double distinction between (1) the right and duty to resist, and (2) individual resistance to an unjust law and collective rebellion against an unjust regime. A Christian has a *right* to resist any unjust law. He does not have a *duty,* however, unless obedience would "violate conscience," that is, compel an immoral act. Then he is obliged to resist. In either instance the question is one of private morality. On the other hand, collective resistance against an unjust regime (such as the Spanish Republic during the 1930s) is a question of "public morality," for it concerns the common good of society. Rebellion is an extreme measure of popular action by which the "collective conscience" of society may be asserted. Such a measure should not be taken against a truly "free" regime, where lawful means are available for redressing grievances; nor should it be used by a minority unable to form a "collective conscience" in opposition to the regime. But even when the right of collective resistance against a regime is clear, the question of the duty to resist still remains. The answer to this question turns on the consequences of rebellion for the common good. If the exigencies of the common good require that support for an unjust regime cease, then rebellion is warranted. Even so, those who undertake violent resistance to civil rule must bear the moral responsibility for the awful consequences such action occasions for the many members of society.

This doctrine of resistance underscores the criterion the Catholic uses in determining the legitimacy of authority. Regardless of the form of government, when the common good is served, authority is legitimate. Similarly, regardless of the form of government, rule for the benefit of a part of a community at the expense of the rest violates natural law. The Catholic insists that authority entails moral relations between ruler and ruled. These relations are ordered by natural law. Authority exercised in conformity with natural law is legitimate. But to be legitimate, authority must be exercised for the common good of those subject to it.

3.

Both the Catholic and the Liberal, we said, discuss the issue of how authority should be exercised in terms of "legitimacy." They say that rulers have a right to exercise legitimate authority and the ruled have a duty to obey it. We have seen that for the Catholic the test of legitimacy is always the common good. Authority should be exercised so that the consequences of a decision benefit everyone subject to the authority.

These Catholic teachings about what constitutes the legitimacy of authority differ radically from Liberal beliefs. For the Liberal, legitimacy depends less on a decision's consequences for the people over whom authority is exercised than it does on the ruler's credentials to make a decision about exercising authority. The effects of a ruler's decision are not important. To be legitimate, for the Liberal, the authority of a ruler to make a decision must be properly derived from its source.

To understand why the Liberal is more concerned about the source of authority than the effects of a decision, we must bear in mind Liberalism's peculiar institution, elite rule. In order to institute elite rule, it was necessary for the Liberal to discredit dynastic rule. Then American Liberals—the Federalists—found it also necessary to discredit popular rule. In the interest of maintaining the institution of elite rule, the Federalists concocted, we have seen, a most ingenious formula. This formula includes the Federalist principle about the legitimacy of authority. Let us see how this is the case.

The Federalist formula depends on the distinction mentioned before between the "constituent authority" of the sovereign people and the "constitutional authority" of government officials. The supreme law enacted by the sovereign people is the Constitution. By the Constitution, authority is vested in government offices, like the office of President of the United States. The purpose of this authority is to protect the rights of citizens. For preserving the rights of citizens, the best form of government is a "mixed" system, where the monarchical, aristocratic, and democratic principles of rule are combined in the Constitution. The powers of government are separated among the legislative, executive, and judicial branches. Each branch is empowered by the Constitution to check and balance the other two. Only that authority vested in his constituted office can a government official exercise. That authority is by definition "constitutional." So according to this doctrine of constitutionality, the people are supreme but they speak only through the Constitution, which imposes curbs on the exercise of governmental authority.

We saw earlier how the Federalists tried to monopolize officeholding by an elite of wealth and talent. The principle of constitutionality goes even farther than that of representation in trying to maintain elite rule. The principle of constitutionality is a scheme for denying the citizens any constitutional right to use governmental authority for serving popular desires.

The trick in this elitist scheme is to equate "constitutionality" with "legitimate authority," and then to substitute the principle of constitutionality for the principle of majority rule in exercising authority. Notice how this works out. In Federalist terms, "constitutionality" is the test for determining the legitimacy of governmental authority. A government official has a right to exercise the constitutional authority of his office, and a citizen has a duty to obey the duly constituted authority—legitimate authority—of the government official. But an official has no right (constitutional, that is) to decide any exercise of authority not vested in his office by the supreme law of the sovereign people. The government official is bound by the higher law of the Constitution, rather than by a mandate from a majority of the people. Only if exercised as the Constitution provides is governmental authority legitimate. Governmental authority exercised as a majority of the people desire is not legitimate—unless, perchance, it is "constitutional" too.

This principle of constitutionality suggests a practical problem. The exact meaning of a constitution may not always be clear to everyone. There may be differences of opinion about what a certain provision means. Any ambiguity in a constitution presumably indicates an inadequate expression of the "will" of the sovereign people. Also the "will" of the people no doubt changes from time to time, as circumstances, needs, and attitudes change. So in case of doubt about construing a provision of the supreme law, how can the "will" of the sovereign be accurately determined?

Thomas Jefferson assumed that the only practicable way to find out what the people mean by a constitutional provision is to ask them. This assumption really does no violence to common sense. Jefferson believed that to determine the "will" of the

American people, an adequate opportunity should be provided for them to express themselves. They express themselves directly and bluntly when they revolt. But in a constituted society, there is a peaceable equivalent for expressing popular desires. That is by changing the constitution. Jefferson accordingly advocated frequent use of the amending process of the Constitution. This process is suitable for minor and piecemeal changes. As a method for general revision of the "people's law," he advocated periodic constitutional conventions, at least every generation.

But Jefferson's views about determining the "will" of the people were not accepted by the Federalists. The amending process written into the Federal Constitution was not a simple and easy method of constitutional change, as Jefferson urged, but rather an awkward and cumbersome one. It has seldom been used to amend the Constitution. Most states did hold constitutional conventions fairly often in Jefferson's day, and a number of state constitutional conventions have been held since. On the whole, the state constitutions are much easier to amend than the Federal Constitution. The Federal government, as we have said before, is the last stronghold of elitist rule in this country. The Philadelphia Convention was the first and last general assemblage for deliberating the principles of the United States Constitution.

Of course, this was as the Federalists wanted it. They did not want to provide the people with an opportunity to express themselves about the supreme law. They wanted to prevent any such expression. The Federalist doctrine about the legitimacy of authority was instrumental to this end. But in practice, the principle of constitutionality not only prevented popular influence in the exercise of governmental authority. It also served to discourage the people from exercising their constituent authority. It curbed popular control over the supreme "people's law." But to achieve this remarkable result, the principle of constitutionality had to be coupled with another Federalist scheme for perpetuating elite rule. This scheme, we shall see, has proved to be one of the most notorious features of the American political system. But before we consider it, let us first make clear what it was the Federalists were trying to accomplish by their elaborate formula.

4.

The Federalists' overriding fear was that the people would actually rule themselves. Popular rule had to be curbed to allow elite rule. The problem was how to keep authority out of the hands of the people and in the hands of an elite. The formula was worked out in terms of constitutional principles. These principles the Federalists used to justify restraint on rule by a majority of the people.

As a result, we find that in this country the issue of majority rule, set by Liberals, has taken the form of the relation between the right of a majority to rule and the "constitutional rights" of a minority. In these terms the present-day Liberal discusses it. According to him, a majority has a right to exercise legitimate authority but has no right to exercise authority contrary to constitutional provisions. Hence, majority rule should be restrained to prevent the exercise of any but legitimate authority, that is, to protect minority rights guaranteed in the Constitution.

When the Liberal talks about "restraint" on the right of a majority to exercise authority, what he means is something other than self-restraint. If the members of a majority restrain themselves, so to speak, they can in practice make any decision they choose. Even though they may act with "restraint," they can still decide how to exercise authority. So what the Liberal means is some kind of external restriction, imposed from outside the majority. He means restraint over which a majority have no control.

What kinds of restraint could be imposed on majority rule? One kind we can call "substantive" restraint—an absolute prohibition defining what cannot be decided by a vote of a majority. An example in the United States Constitution is the provision

(Article V) "that no State, without its consent, should be deprived of equal suffrage in the Senate." Applied literally, this means that representation in the Senate cannot be altered at all, even by the same procedure originally used to adopt a basis for Senate representation. The purpose of such restraint is to remove the substance of a matter from further consideration by a majority vote.

Another kind of restraint we can call "procedural." Such restraint consists in rules specifying how proposals shall be introduced, deliberated, voted on, and the like. Manuals of parliamentary procedure, like the familiar *Roberts' Rules of Order,* are devoted to procedural rules for guiding the conduct of members of decision-making groups.

As a practical matter, procedural restraints do not necessarily impose any restraint on what a majority can decide. Rather, they fix the rules that the entire membership of the community should observe when participating in the decision-making process. Such rules may have the effect of temporarily delaying final action on a proposal. They may impose a time restriction. But they do not necessarily prevent action from being taken later by a majority vote. Generally speaking, then, rules of parliamentary procedure allow a majority to decide any question as it may determine, provided the specified procedures are followed in arriving at the determination.

At the same time, what may appear to be a procedural restraint on majority rule may actually be a substantive restraint. A common rule contained in manuals of parliamentary procedure is the requirement for an abnormal vote, say two-thirds or three-fourths the membership, rather than a simple majority (50 per cent plus one). Such a rule may be merely a procedural restraint, if applied only to postpone temporarily a final vote on a proposal. So applied, to avoid hasty action, a two-thirds rule, say, does not prevent a majority from determining any decision. It only controls the time when a majority vote can be taken. However, strict application of a two-thirds rule can prevent any majority from making certain decisions about how authority should be exercised. An example is the provision in Article V for amending the Federal Constitution. To initiate any constitutional amendment requires a two-thirds vote; to ratify any amendment requires a three-fourths vote. These requirements for abnormal votes are in effect substantive restraints, tantamount to minority vetoes. A minority can block the initiation or the ratification of any proposal to amend the Constitution. The result is that any action by majority vote on a constitutional amendment is prohibited.

The Federalists of course favored substantive as well as procedural restraints on majority rule. They designed the constitutional system to facilitate imposing such restraints. Present-day American Liberals likewise favor substantive restraints because they are indispensable for elite rule. But it is not an easy task for an American who maintains an outward profession of faith in popular government to defend such restraints. To justify any restraint on majority rule, it is necessary to repudiate either the principle of political equality or the principle of popular sovereignty. It is also necessary to reject the principle of majority rule itself. Notice why this is the case.

In practice this question must be answered: If the right of a majority to rule should be restrained, who should impose the restraint? Now, if a majority are held to be unfit to restrain themselves, as the Liberal believes, then the restraint must be imposed either by a minority of the community or by an "authority" outside and independent of the community. Either choice invites trouble. To say that the restraint should be imposed by a minority is to give implicit recognition to political inequality. It is implied that a minority's right to prevent action is superior to a majority's right to take action. This is, of course, contrary to the principle of political equality, which denies superior rights to any part of a community.

On the other hand, to say that the restraint should be imposed by an "authority" external to the community is to deny by implication the principle of popular sovereignty. The practical effect of a substantive restraint on majority rule is to restrict the jurisdiction of the community. A majority cannot decide how authority it does not have should be exercised; nor can a minority. In fact, even if the members of a community were in unanimous agreement, restraint imposed from the outside would prevent a decision. Such restraint on majority rule, then, in effect denies that a community has any authority to decide certain questions; they must be decided by an "authority" independent of the community. This position is unacceptable to anyone who takes seriously the principle of popular sovereignty.

Not only that: any restraint on majority rule is a tacit denial that the principle itself is valid. This point Thomas Jefferson made amply clear in his doctrine of continuing majorities. By this doctrine, Jefferson answered a contention advanced by Chief Justice Marshall that a constitution is a solemn contract which cannot be altered by the action of a mere majority. Jefferson's position was that one majority cannot irrevocably bind another, later majority without contradicting the principle of majority rule. His argument ran as follows—the formulation is in my terms, but it is faithful, I believe, to Jefferson's meaning:

A constitution depends for its original acceptance on the action by which it was adopted. The contention that a constitution adopted by a decision voted by a majority is immune to change by a vote of a later majority is untenable. (The states, in fact, adopted the Federal Constitution by resolutions passed by a simple majority vote.) A substantive restraint on majority rule contained in such a constitution can have no validity. If the original (or "ground floor") majority had no authority to act, the constitution itself is not binding on the members of the community. If the original majority did have authority to adopt the constitution in the first place, it had authority to impose a substantive restraint on majority rule by a majority vote. But then a later majority must have the same authority to decide the question differently. That is, if it is legitimate to adopt restraints by majority vote, it is legitimate to abolish them in the same way. To claim otherwise is to assume that the authority of the original majority was superior to that of a later majority. This assumption violates the principle of popular sovereignty; it implies that the authority to make a decision affecting a political community is not located in the membership. If so, the original majority itself lacked authority to act. The assumption also violates the principle of political equality, for it implies that the original members of the political community counted for more than one. Again if this is so, the vote by the original majority was not a legitimate exercise of authority.

Furthermore, the right of continuing majorities to rule, each the equal of others, must be recognized in practice. Any action by a previous majority vote depends for its actual acceptance on the consent of present members. The decision is effective to the extent that they abide by it; it has no practical effect, as an exercise of authority, if consent is lacking. Then rule according to the action of the original majority would depend on force, not consent; it would not be an exercise of authority at all. There is no feasible way to find out whether consent is present, unless the right of continuing majorities is recognized. Therefore, if the principle that a decision about exercising authority should be determined by a vote of a majority was valid for an original majority, it must also be valid for continuing, later majorities.

We have seen that the Federalists never took seriously the principles of popular rule. Nor does the occasional profession of some attachment for popular government hinder the present-day Liberal from advocating substantive restraints on majority rule, regardless of the consequences. He believes that restraints should be provided for in a constitution which cannot be amended by majority vote. He believes that a minority should have a right to impose a veto on majority rule and that an "outside" authority should enforce constitutional restraints on majority rule. It is easy to understand why the Liberal regards the United States Constitution rewritten by the Federalist politician John Marshall as one of the finest products of the political art. This is even easier to understand in the light of Marshall's unique contribution to the cause of elite rule.

5.

By saying that restraint should be imposed on majority rule to protect minority rights, the Federalists did not solve the practical problem of who should enforce the restraints. In Federalist terms, the problem remained: How to construe the provisions of the Constitution so that the legitimacy of governmental authority can be properly determined? Who should decide whether the government has exceeded its authority under the Constitution? The Federalist solution to this problem proved to be a notorious feature of the American political system—"judicial review."

Judicial review is the practice of a court of law to pass on the "constitutionality" of actions by other branches of government. This practice is not general throughout the world. In fact it was originally peculiar to the United States. For the ordinary function of a court is to settle controversies between parties, each of whom claims some legal right. The judicial function is to rule on the principle of law which applies in the case before the court. In this way a court decides which claim to enforce. British courts perform this function. But they do not review acts of Parliament as to their "constitutionality." However American courts have assumed the function of reviewing the constitutionality of legislative and executive actions, thanks to the Federalists.

The principle of judicial review was well known to the delegates at the Philadelphia Convention. For some time a British imperial court (the Judicial Committee of the Privy Council) had reviewed Colonial legislation to determine compatibility with British law. In fact, the question of writing a provision for judicial review into the draft constitution was considered several times by the Convention. James Madison urged that the judiciary be granted that power. A number of delegates voiced strong objections to the principle that (in the words of John Mercer of

Maryland) "the Judges as the expositors of the Constitution should have authority to declare a law void." On three different days, proposals to adopt the principle were voted down. No provision was written in then and none exists there now. Judicial review is a so-called "implied" power of the Federal judiciary, headed by the Supreme Court of the United States. By an interesting coincidence, the constitutional principle of implied powers was invented by a Chief Justice of the Supreme Court.

Judicial review was first declared as a "constitutional principle" by Chief Justice John Marshall in the famous case of *Marbury v. Madison* (1803). Marshall, a faithful Federalist politician, had served as Secretary of State in President Adams's cabinet. After Jefferson was elected President, but before the Federalist administration went out of office, Marshall was appointed Chief Justice. Even though the Federalists lost the election and later became extinct as a political movement, through Marshall they won the Supreme Court. The victory was symbolized by Marshall's politically astute opinion in the Marbury case.

The facts in the case were these: The outgoing Federalists, anxious to reward their friends, made a number of appointments to government jobs just before leaving office. A Federalist politician by the name of Marbury was commissioned a justice of the peace. His commission was prepared and signed but had not actually been delivered when the new Secretary of State, Madison, took office. Madison refused to give Marbury the commission. So Marbury sued with an original action in the Supreme Court for a writ requiring the Secretary of State to do his duty as the Federalists saw it. The issue in the case turned on a provision of the original Judiciary Act of 1789. This act established the Federal courts and among many other things provided that they could issue common judicial writs, such as the one in question, called a "writ of mandamus."

In his opinion for the Court, Marshall discussed the merits of the case and resolved them in favor of his Federalist colleagues. After settling the issues, Marshall then said that unfortunately the

Court lacked authority to hear the case. So he dismissed the suit, on the grounds that the relevant provisions of the Judiciary Act could not enlarge the original jurisdiction of the Supreme Court as set by Article III of the Constitution. In other words, the Congress did not have legitimate authority to enact that provision of the act; the provision was unconstitutional. In the course of his opinion, after lecturing the Jeffersonian Republicans about truth, justice, and the American way, Marshall gave the doctrine of judicial review a definitive statement.

The Federal judiciary, said Marshall, has a right and duty under the Constitution to review the actions of government as to their constitutionality. As the supreme law of the land, the Constitution is binding on all government officials. It is a duty of the judges, by their oath of office, to uphold the Constitution in cases coming before their courts. It is a function of the judiciary to declare what the ruling law is in a case. This includes the function of declaring what the supreme law is.

Now, the Constitution limits the authority of the Congress and the President to enact statutes. Certain powers are delegated, others are prohibited, some are reserved to the States, and the rights of citizens are declared. An ordinary statute cannot alter a provision of the Constitution. An act of Congress repugnant to the Constitution must be null and void; it cannot be law because Congress has legitimate authority only to legislate as the Constitution provides. It is the duty of the courts to uphold the Constitution and the laws made pursuant to it. An unconstitutional act of Congress cannot be enforced by the courts. In cases coming before them, the judges must therefore declare that such an act is "unconstitutional." In this classic statement of the doctrine, Marshall claimed that the Federal judiciary had an implied power to review legislative enactments as to their constitutionality and to refuse to enforce those the courts regard as unconstitutional.

Notice what this practice of judicial review involves. It becomes the function of the judiciary to decide whether the other branches of government are exercising legitimate authority. The question that a court, say the Supreme Court, ostensibly decides is whether the authority claimed by government officials has actually been granted by the Constitution. If in the judgment of the Court it has, the authority is legitimate. If it hasn't, the action of the government official is unconstitutional. Then the supposition is that the official acted in excess of the legitimate authority of his office. He acted as a private person rather than a government official. He may, therefore, be personally liable for the consequences of his action. Of course, such an illegitimate action a citizen has no constitutional obligation to obey. In theory, he may actually have a constitutional right not to obey because no constitutional authority is exercised.

The "constitutional principle" of judicial review embodies three striking Federalist claims. Two are rather odd, and the third is truly incredible.

One odd claim is that the judicial branch should determine the constitutionality of actions by legislative and executive officials in a system where the powers of government are separated, checked, and balanced. As one branch of the government, the judiciary is vested only with "constitutional" authority. Yet according to this Federalist claim, the court decides not only about the legitimacy of legislative and executive authority but also about the legitimacy of its own authority. Judicial actions are not subject to review by the legislative and executive branches while the actions of those officials are subject to check by the judiciary. This results in more check than balance.

Another odd claim is that one branch of government is the custodian of the people's law. The branches of government receive their legitimate authority from a grant in the Constitution. The people authorize government officials to exercise certain authority. According to the doctrine of judicial review, a branch of government created by the people has a right to determine its own credentials as well as the credentials of the other branches. This is like a beneficiary under a will claiming a right to decide for the maker what he bequeathed in his will.

Rather odd indeed, for an agent to claim to specify his commission from a principal.

The truly incredible claim judicial review involves is that a few members of the nonelected judiciary know better than the elected legislative and executive officials, who quite possibly have acted in concert, what the "will" of the American people is. That is, when a law is passed by the two houses of Congress and signed by the President, the officials of both elective branches have gone on record that, in their collective judgment, they have legitimate authority to take the action provided by the law. But then the Court, according to the Federalist claim, can rule the law unconstitutional. The judicial judgment takes precedence in determining the content of the people's law. By what mystical process the Supreme Court is supposed to divine the "real will" of the people of the United States has never been adequately explained. However judicial review does jibe neatly with a Federalist belief we encountered before: the people know what they want if you don't ask them, and they don't know what they want if you do. So, ask the Supreme Court instead.

Why the Liberal praises the judiciary, representing in our "mixed" system of Federal government the aristocratic principle of rule, is not difficult to comprehend. Judicial review is an integral part of the Federalist formula for curbing popular influence in governmental affairs. It is essential for imposing restraints on majority rule. In practice, it has well served the cause of perpetuating rule by an elite minority in this country.

6.

Of course, the Democrat sharply disagrees with the Liberal about majority rule. The Democrat does not accept the principle of constitutionality used to justify restraints on majority rule. For him a constitution is not a legalistic device for muffling the expression of popular desires. It does not prescribe rights for some and duties for others, or restraints on majority rule to protect "minority rights." For the Democrat, a constitution is merely convenient evidence of agreements shared by the members of a constituted political community. The constitution declares the privileges and obligations which members of the community share and sets forth rules which the members agree should be observed in exercising authority.

Nor does the Democrat accept the principle of judicial review which Marshall smuggled into the Federal Constitution. For the Democrat, the legitimacy of authority does not depend on a ruling by the judiciary or any other elite about whether the authority exercised was properly derived. What is crucial in determining the legitimacy of authority for the Democrat is how the authority is exercised. His concern is about procedures. He believes that authority should be exercised according to a decision-making process prescribed by Democratic principles. A decision about exercising authority voted by a majority should be obeyed by the members of a political community, whatever the decision. For the Democrat, then, authority exercised as determined by majority vote is legitimate.

Unfortunately, this principle of majority rule is probably the most thoroughly misunderstood, as well as the most bitterly controverted, Democratic principle. In fact it seems that between the amount of confusion and the amount of controversy there is a significant connection. Much of the confusion is attributable to the Liberal who considers majority rule only to condemn it. He insists on discussing the issue in flagrantly misleading terms. The Liberal trick is to pose the issue of majority rule in terms which are not meaningful, and then to contend that the principle is unacceptable. What is unacceptable is the unrealistic conception of majority rule the Liberal entertains.

Let us now try, therefore, to clear up the gross misconceptions about majority rule instigated by the Liberal. Let us clarify the issue from the standpoint of a Democrat. Then we can proceed with our inquiry into the relation between the Democratic principle and Catholic teachings.

1. The issue of majority rule is meaningful in terms of authority, but not in terms of power. Power, we said, is the ability to do something affecting others, while authority is the right to do something. It makes sense to talk about a recognized right of a majority to rule and to consider whether this *right* should be restrained to protect a right of a minority. But it makes no sense to talk about restraining the *power* of a majority. If it is a question of power, any consideration of restraint is irrelevant. Whoever has the power, whether a minority or a majority, can do what he wants. The issue is not whether a majority *can* exercise power. Instead, it is: *should* they exercise authority without restraint?

2. The issue is meaningful in terms of a majority of votes, but not in terms of a majority of people. A majority of votes (50 per cent plus one) means simply the larger number cast in balloting on some proposal. It is at least intelligible to consider restraining majority rule in the sense of excluding certain questions from resolution by a simple majority vote.

The term "majority" is often used, however, to describe the larger part of a group of people. It is assumed that some common quality or attribute, such as class, religion, race, occupation, income, intelligence, or the like, is shared within that part. Old-time Marxists, for example, talk about "the working-class majority" and the "owning minority." Liberals frequently talk in similar class terms. But the question of restraining the "will" of such a majority is nonsense. Unless a vote is taken there is no way of finding out what their "will" is. Someone may claim to express the "will" of a majority of people. Hitler, for example, claimed to represent the "will" of the German people. But what such a self-appointed spokesman expresses is some "real will"—what the people should want rather than what they say they want. So if no vote is taken, the "will" is unknown and there is nothing to be restrained.

231

If a vote is taken, it is a majority of votes rather than a majority of people that is at issue. Imposing restraints on a voting majority at least is intelligible.

3. The issue is meaningful in terms of a process of decision-making, but not in terms of an abstract situation wherein no functioning community is contemplated. If majority rule is regarded simply as a device for arriving at a single decision, certain ridiculous consequences follow. One would be that a "majority" of a moment could foreclose for all time the consideration of a question. This would, as Thomas Jefferson once pointed out, be contrary to the principle of majority rule itself. Another consequence would be that such a "majority" could destroy any opportunity for subsequent decisions to be made on other questions—again an absurd inference. In addition, when majority rule is abstracted out of a decision-making process and only a single decision is contemplated, there is no provision for any relation between the "minority" (which presumably has rights) and the "majority" (which presumably should be restrained). A member of a minority who accepts a majority's decision compromises a private interest for the sake of a public interest—not the interest of a majority, but the general interest of the community. In the absence of a functioning community with a continuing decision-making process, no basis for such compromise exists.

More important, it is plainly unrealistic to regard majority rule except in the context of a decision-making process. Our only experience with majority rule is where a procedure of casting votes is used as an operating rule for resolving differences among the members of a community. In practice, a decision voted by a majority is one of many the community determines in a continuing process. Thus majority rule implies a decision-making process whereby a member may sometimes vote with a majority, at other times with a minority, of the community. In these terms it is at least intelligible to talk about restraint on majority rule.

4. Finally, the issue is meaningful in terms of relations among the members of a political community, but not in terms of

relations among persons who are not members of such a community. In Democratic terms, a person who is not a member of a political community cannot be subject to its authority. A Democratic community cannot have authority over a nonmember; its jurisdiction is, by definition, limited to its membership. If an effort is made to bind by a majority decision a person who is not a member and who does not consent to the authority, the community is obviously exceeding its jurisdiction. The action would be in violation of the principles of popular sovereignty and political equality. A Democratic community could not take such an action. But in any event, the issue of restraint on majority rule would not be involved by the action. That issue pertains only to relations among the members of a community, some of whom vote in a minority and others in a majority. So it makes no sense to consider restraints on the right of a majority to make decisions which the community has no authority to exercise. It is, on the other hand, at least intelligible to consider restraining the right of a majority to make decisions about exercising authority over the membership of a community.

Let us now, with more precision and in meaningful terms, reformulate the issue of majority rule as the Democrat sees it, stripped of extraneous and irrelevant considerations. Should the right of a majority to decide questions about exercising the community's authority be restrained in the process of making decisions to protect the rights of members voting in a minority?

When posed in these terms, the issue of majority rule is at least understandable. It has nothing to do with power or classes or metaphysics or the jurisdiction of rulers. Nor does it have anything to do with those privileges and obligations equally shared by the members of a political community. The question at stake is whether the members voting with a majority have special obligations while those voting with a minority have special privileges.

The Democrat believes that the minority members of a political community have exactly the same privileges and obligations—no more, no less—as the majority members. Members of a political community should have equal privileges in exercising authority and equal obligations in obeying it. The Democratic principle is that a vote of a majority should determine how the authority of a community is exercised over the members.

7.

The members of the Westside Civic Improvement League understand this principle of majority rule. They have often seen it applied as a working rule in their own organization. They accept it as the method by which differences of opinion among their members can be composed so that the League can take action. The League members do not worry about the principles of constitutionality or judicial review. They assume that, as a practical matter, when a majority of members vote for a proposal, that determines the League's action.

At the same time perhaps the more reflective League members have sometimes wondered about the consent of a minority to a majority's decision. What prevents a majority from abusing its authority? Why should a minority consent to a majority's decision? What should a minority do if they do not consent to a majority's exercise of authority? Should the right of a majority be restrained? If any League members have pondered questions such as these, they are in distinguished company. The problem of minority consent is the central problem in Democratic theory. Starting with Thomas Jefferson, virtually every American Democratic thinker has addressed himself to this problem of political conduct.

The problem of minority consent is implicit in Democratic beliefs. The Democrat believes that authority should not be exercised over a person without his consent. He also believes that after a vote has been taken on a proposal, those who voted in a minority should nevertheless abide by a majority's decision. They should consent to a majority's decision about exercising the community's authority. What the Democrat assumes here is that two things which are not the same should still be regarded as if they were. A *majority's* decision should be regarded as the *community's* decision. But why should the members of a minority compromise their desires to accept a decision contrary to their desires, as if it were the decision of the entire community?

Thomas Jefferson did not regard this as a particularly troublesome problem. He believed that he had a solution for it. In a sense he did, but Jefferson's resolution of the problem of minority consent is something less than adequate.

A minority, said Jefferson, should always accept a majority's decision. Restraint should not be imposed on majority rule, but a majority has no right to do anything it pleases. A majority should restrain itself; it should always act "right and reasonable." Then it is right and reasonable for a minority to accept the decision. This is well and good. But what assurance is there that in practice the members of a majority and minority can recognize what is "right and reasonable"? Political decisions, Jefferson assumed, are objectively right or wrong. There are self-evident principles in the nature of things. Any intelligent, informed, public-spirited citizen can readily perceive these principles and thus tell political right from wrong. Everyone, members of a minority and a majority, should observe these principles in his political conduct and act "right and reasonable."

Jefferson's introduction of a moral standard external to the community into his discussion of this problem serves no useful purpose. In fact, it unduly complicates the problem. If there is an "objective" standard of political right to which members of a community can properly appeal, it is possible for there to be some discrepancy between a majority's decision and these moral principles. A majority's decision may appear to a minority to be contrary to moral law and therefore "wrong." Then, on the grounds that the majority's decision conflicts with the higher law, it would be plausible for a minority to refuse their consent to the decision.

On this possibility of conflict Liberals have seized, in their effort to build a case against majority rule. In his essay *On Civil Disobedience*, Thoreau pounced on the likelihood of a majority's decision violating the moral principles of Christianity. He summed up his case in the famous remark: "A man more right than his neighbors constitutes already a majority of one." A majority has no *right* to rule, Thoreau concludes; minority consent is simply a matter of expediency. Other Liberals have argued in the same vein.

On this point, Jefferson actually gives a Liberal no comfort. Conflict between a majority decision and a higher moral law he admits as an abstract possibility, but denies as a practical problem. No one knows for certain, Jefferson says, what the higher moral law provides. Everyone is fallible; we are equal in our ignorance as well as our wisdom. Since no member of a community knows with certainty what is right, in trying to determine the right decision two heads are better than one and many heads are better than a few. When the members disagree about the right action to take, a majority is more likely than a minority to make the right decision. In other words, it is better for a majority to make mistakes than for a minority to make decisions, because a majority is likely to make fewer and less serious mistakes.

When coupled with this view that no man knows better than the next what is right, Jefferson's assumption about objective principles of political right affords no grounds for imposing restraints on the right of a majority to rule. But his assumption also adds nothing to Democratic theory, except an artificial difficulty. If no one knows better than another what these principles actually are, they can be of no practical use in determining the moral quality of a political decision. Despite his assumption, Jefferson still concludes that in practice the moral content of a political decision should be determined by a quantitative means—a majority vote.

But the point by Jefferson that a majority decision must possess a moral quality in order for a minority to consent to it is most significant. For Jefferson, the problem of minority consent centers on a moral relation which binds together the members of a community. If a decision is morally right, it would be wrong for a minority to disobey it. But the decision must possess this moral quality. What Jefferson apparently means is that a majority should not act to promote its special desires. If in making a decision the choice is between the private desires of a majority and the private desires of a minority, there is no moral basis for minority consent. Minority consent implies a moral standard common to the members of the community. That standard, for Jefferson, is the general welfare. It is right and reasonable for both the majority and minority members to restrain themselves and compromise. The moral problem confronts every one of them. They desire to promote the general welfare, as well as their private desires. They should compromise their special desires for sake of their common desire. The majority's responsibility, then, is to determine how the general welfare can be best advanced. It is right and reasonable for a majority to make a decision that promotes the general welfare of the community. It is right and reasonable for the minority to consent to a decision that possesses this moral quality. Jefferson's point, that a majority decision should represent a compromise of desires in which everyone gives and takes a little and no one gives or takes all, is a real contribution to the Democratic doctrine of majority rule.

8.

The problem of minority consent to majority rule was most searchingly and cogently probed by a famous nineteenth-century American statesman, John C. Calhoun (1782–1850) of South Carolina. Calhoun was a distinguished political leader of his day. His long career in public life included service in the South Carolina legislature, the House of Representatives, the Senate, several Cabinets, and as Vice President of the United

States. But Calhoun is perhaps most noted for his pleading of the Southern cause during the great controversy which ended in the violence of the Civil War. Because he was a champion of a lost cause, Calhoun is sometimes dismissed as just another wrong-headed propagandist. This is most unfortunate. No matter how we feel about his defense of slavery and states' rights, we should recognize that Calhoun was one of the ablest political thinkers this country has produced. His analysis of the problem of minority consent, though part of an apologia for the Southern states, is still one of the most constructive we can find in Democratic literature. This problem he tried to resolve by his doctrine of concurrent majorities. It was after many years' experience as a member of Democratic communities that Calhoun propounded this doctrine in his treatise *A Disquisition on Government* (1851).

Calhoun's underlying concern in this treatise was the practical operation of the Democratic decision-making process. For historical reasons, he discussed Democratic practice in the setting of the Federal system, where, by the Constitution, the powers of government are divided between one central government and the several state governments. The question he tried to answer is: How, in such a system, can minority consent for decisions voted by a majority be in practice assured?

Calhoun began his analysis by drawing a distinction between "absolute" and "constitutional" government. Absolute government is where authority is exercised for the benefit of a part of the community. Constitutional government is where authority is exercised for the benefit of the entire community. The shortcoming of absolute government is that it works poorly in practice. The purpose of government is to protect the common interest in peace and order. If the actions of government benefit a part of the community at the expense of the rest, citizens resist the authority. To obtain obedience, the government must use force. Force and violence disrupt the society. The public interest in which everyone has a stake suffers because the purpose of government is not actually achieved.

Constitutional government works much better in practice, but at the same time it is much more complicated and difficult to operate. To assure that the actions of government do benefit the public interest, it is necessary that exclusive control of the government by any part of the community be prevented. This can be done by placing in the hands of every special interest with a vital stake in community's affairs the power of a "negative" over governmental actions. A special interest by exercising a veto can block an action by government. By withholding the veto, it consents to an action. This means, in practice, that all parts of the community must compromise their special interests in order for authority to be exercised. It means, too, that any action taken by government does benefit the public interest. The difficulties of operating a constitutional system are more than offset, said Calhoun, by the advantage that the common interest is, in practice, promoted. To enforce an action of a constitutional government, the use of force is never required because the citizens consent to the exercise of the government's authority.

This analysis Calhoun then applied to popular government. In a Democracy the problem of the abuse of governmental authority, he said (as had Madison before him), is not especially serious for a majority of the community. They can use the suffrage to control public officials. They can vote out of office an official who endangers a majority's interests. So there is little danger that a Democratic government will exercise authority to infringe the interests of a majority. However, a minority cannot use the suffrage to protect its interests. A Democratic government can, if it chooses, oppress a minority. So the main problem in a Democracy is how to prevent the tyranny of a majority over a minority.

A system of government where decisions are made by a simple numerical vote, said Calhoun, is unsatisfactory in practice. The danger is that a majority in control of the government will improperly identify their special interest with the interest of the whole community. A system where a majority govern in their own interest has all the disadvantages of absolute government. Minorities refuse consent to the exercise of authority and the government must use force to compel obedience. Such government is unstable and poorly serves the public interest.

So Calhoun asked: How can we enjoy a system of government that is both constitutional and Democratic? His answer was: By incorporating into the decision-making process of government the principle of concurrent majorities. In making governmental decisions, interests as well as numbers should be organically represented. Representatives of important interests should have a concurrent voice in governmental affairs, and a concurrent veto over governmental actions. By this system, where a minority can prevent a government action, a majority cannot press its special interests at the expense of the rest of the community. A majority must compromise for sake of the public interest. So must a minority. Any action for the benefit of special interests can be blocked by the veto. But when no interest uses the veto, the government's action receives the consent of all. Force is not required to exercise governmental authority. The interests of the whole community are promoted, while the abuse of authority for the benefit of a part is avoided, by a system of concurrent majorities. So Calhoun concluded at least.

Calhoun's doctrine of concurrent majorities has been viewed by some as a veiled attack on majority rule. This view is not warranted. At no point did Calhoun advocate that decisions about the exercise of authority be made according to any principle other than majority rule. But he was concerned about the jurisdiction of majorities in a Federal system, where a majority within one state may be at odds with a majority of the nation. A decision voted by a majority of the nation could be contrary to a majority decision voted within a state. In fact, Calhoun was concerned that the national government may make a decision about exercising authority which, in the judgment of a majority within a state, the national government does not have under the Constitution. Here in a Federal system, the problem is not that of the relation between a majority and a minority. It is a problem of the relation between the jurisdiction of a smaller political community and a larger one which embraces it. As a solution to this problem he proposed that decisions of the national government be made, not by an absolute numerical vote, but on the basis of concurring majorities. The decision by the government would still be made by majority rule. Any exercise of governmental authority would be determined by a vote of a majority. But a minority could prevent a majority from exercising authority. The effect of Calhoun's solution would be to allow any important minority to clear from the agenda a question it preferred to fight about than vote on.

Our attitude toward Calhoun's solution to the problem of the jurisdiction of majorities in a Federal system should not deter us from appreciating his penetrating analysis of the problem of minority consent to majority rule. Calhoun identified the problem in terms no Democrat can afford to ignore. As a practical matter, majority rule works only to the extent that those participating in the decision-making process are willing to compromise. A Democratic majority cannot in practice exercise authority against the consent of a minority. A majority could use force to rule a recalcitrant minority, but this would not be Democratic rule; it would confess to a failure of the Democratic process. After all, a Democrat believes that no person should be ruled against his consent. Unless a minority consents to a majority's decision, authority cannot be exercised Democratically. If a minority refuses consent, the decision-making process itself breaks down.

So the problem is how to assure in the decision-making process that minority consent will be forthcoming to a majority's decision. It was Calhoun's contention that a majority must compromise its desires. Either it does compromise, or else it does not exercise authority. It becomes the majority's responsibility to secure minority consent, in the interest of maintaining the integrity of the community. To the extent that a majority fulfills its responsibility and no more, the Democratic decision-making process works satisfactorily in practice.

What Calhoun's analysis stresses is that, as a practical matter, certain questions cannot be decided by voting on them. It is a psychological fact that there is a point beyond which any person will refuse to compromise. Up to this point, he will accept a group decision as binding on his conduct. He will compromise a desire for some private end for sake of the desire he shares in common with others—that the community achieve its purpose. But on a question a person regards as so vital to his welfare that he would rather fight than agree, compromise is not possible. Such questions cannot in practice be settled by voting decisions about exercising authority, since persons will refuse to consent to the exercise of any authority over them.

9.

What does this all mean to our friends of the Westside Civic Improvement League? Thomas Jefferson has told us that a decision determined by a majority vote should contribute to the general welfare. A decision about exercising authority must represent a compromise by the members of their desires for their private welfare for the sake of their common desire for the welfare of the entire community to be an effective exercise of authority. John C. Calhoun has told us that it is dangerous as well as futile for a community to attempt to decide by majority vote questions about which members feel so strongly that they refuse to compromise their private desires. A community must keep such questions out of the decision-making process to be effective in exercising any authority. These requirements for the successful operation of a decision-making process are recognized by the members of the League, experienced as they are in political practice.

What the League members appreciate is the psychological basis on which political decision-making in practice depends for success. They realize that their organization is held together by the members' desires to achieve a common purpose: a better Westside community in which to live. When the League members concern themselves with questions which directly bear on this common purpose, they can make decisions about exercising authority which work out satisfactorily in practice. The members regard the integrity of the League as more important to them than any single decision about such questions.

At the same time, the League members realize that they cannot at their meetings satisfactorily resolve questions about the divinity of Jesus Christ or the sanctity of private property or the blessedness of the matrimonial state. On questions of such vital concern to a member that he would rather resign from the League than compromise his desires any effective League action is impossible, so far as that person is concerned. A choice is before the membership every time the League makes a decision: to accept the decision or abandon the League. Only to the extent that members choose to accept a decision can the League actually promote the common purpose of the membership. So, in effect, every member holds a potent check over the League's actions. Any member has what amounts to a "negative" over what the League can, as a practical matter, decide to do.

Accordingly, the League members recognize that each person with a stake in the community has what might be called a "public responsibility" as a member. He cannot satisfy his desire to promote the purpose of the League unless the common actions undertaken by the membership are effective in practice. So it is his responsibility to see that his actions and the actions of other members actually serve the League's purpose. He is therefore responsible for the members' observing the rules of the League in their conduct. He is responsible for the members' complying with the procedures prescribed for the decision-making process. He is responsible for the members' working out decisions about exercising authority which give due consideration to the different opinions expressed by the membership. He is responsible for the members' restraining their private desires in the interest of their common desire that the purpose of the League be achieved. In short, the member has a public responsibility to see that the integrity of the community is preserved. He has this responsibility, not as a member of a majority or a minority, but as a member of a political community engaged in exercising authority as effectively as possible. In practice, the League can exercise authority only to the extent that the members fulfill their responsibilities to the community.

So the Democrat asks: How can the member of a political community be encouraged to fulfill his public responsibilities in practice? Apparently it is necessary to maintain a balance between the private and the public desires of the member. In the conduct of community affairs, those private desires not satisfied by the community should be subjected to as little frustration as possible. The public desire served by the community should be satisfied to the greatest possible extent. In other words, the rules of the community should assure that the common purpose of the members is promoted as well as possible in the conduct of community affairs. How can this be achieved? The doctrine of majority rule is the Democrat's answer to this question.

The Democratic case for majority rule runs as follows: A decision about exercising authority must, if it is to be accepted, have a quite distinctive character. It must not specially benefit any part of the community at the expense of the rest. It must in a significant sense be a collective decision: one which no one personally desires but everyone accepts. It must synthesize the many conflicting desires of the members of the political community, who compromise their private desires in order to reach a collective decision. An effective political decision, then, is a bundle of compromises which in practice serves a common desire of the members of a community.

A decision arrived at by a Democratic process is more likely to have this distinctive character than a decision made according to any alternative principle of rule. A Democratic decision is, in practice, a determination by a majority vote about how authority should be exercised to promote the general welfare of the community. A Democratic decision does not express the private desires of a majority; it expresses the common desires of the community, as determined by a vote of a majority. The right of a majority to rule is, in practice, a responsibility to decide how to promote the general welfare. The members of a community consent to authority exercised Democratically, not because a majority has decided, but because a majority decision is more likely than any other to serve the common purpose of the membership. In this way a decision voted by a majority is identified with a decision of the entire community. The common denominator is the general welfare. So, the Democrat concludes, to the extent that a decision about exercising authority works out satisfactorily in practice, it has the character of a Democratic decision.

A Democratic decision has this definite moral quality not because it conforms to some standard of value external to the community, some sort of "higher law" prescribed by God or nature for mankind. This moral quality results from the procedures used by the members of a Democratic community in arriving at a decision. The general welfare as a standard of conduct is the moral sense shared by the members of a Democratic community. It is what the membership deliberately determines through a process of compromising private welfares for a common purpose. This moral standard is set by the membership each time a decision is made by a Democratic process. What is determined by a majority vote is "right" for the community. Authority exercised according to a decision arrived at by a

Democratic process is, then, legitimate. The legitimacy depends on how the authority is exercised. The test is, for the Democrat, entirely procedural. The procedures are those required for authority to be exercised successfully in practice—that is, for the benefit of the general welfare.

To sum up the Democratic doctrine of majority rule: The Democrat believes that authority should be exercised for the general welfare of a community. The members of a political community can, in practice, undertake collective action only to the extent that authority is effectively exercised over the membership. A decision about exercising authority determined by a majority vote is more likely to advance the general welfare of a community than a decision made according to any alternative principle of rule. So if it is desired that authority be exercised at all, the principle of majority rule should be accepted, simply because it works better in practice.

10.

Let us now return to the main question of this chapter. What is the relation between the Democratic principle of majority rule and Catholic teachings? Do Catholic teachings about the legitimacy of authority in any way conflict with this Democratic principle?

Catholic principles, we find, neither favor nor oppose Democratic or any other form of rule as such. They do require that Democratic authority, like any other, be exercised in conformity with moral standards set by natural law. It is because a higher moral law circumscribes how authority should be exercised that there is always a possibility of conflict between civil rule and Catholic principles. The Catholic approach to the question about how authority should be exercised is in terms of legitimacy. The criterion for determining the legitimacy of authority is the common good. That authority should be exercised for the common good of those subject to it is required by the Catholic principle of just rule.

The Democrat's approach to this question is, we find, much different. Both the Catholic and the Democrat determine the legitimacy of authority in terms of how it is exercised, and, for both, a political decision, to be legitimate, must have a certain moral quality. But where the Catholic relies on a moral standard derived from religious teachings to determine the legitimacy of a decision about exercising authority, the Democrat recognizes no such standard. He depends on compliance with certain procedural rules in decision-making. Decisions should be made by a process prescribed by Democratic principles. To be legitimate, a decision about exercising a community's authority should be determined by a vote of a majority of the members. A decision made in this way best advances the general welfare of the community. So the Democrat believes.

Now, the pertinent question is whether a decision made according to Democratic principles is in practice more or less likely than a decision made according to some alternative principles of rule to comply with Catholic principles about exercising authority. To what extent is Democratic rule more likely than some form of elite rule to benefit in practice the common good?

To ask this question is almost to answer it. The Catholic principle of just rule was, after all, originally formulated to curb the abuse of authority by elite rulers who bore no affinity for their subjects. The principle does not conflict with the exercise of authority in a Democratic community, where no distinction is drawn between ruler and ruled. Any conflict with Catholic principles is unlikely where authority is Democratically exercised. In fact, Democratic rule is actually more compatible with Catholic principles than is any form of elite rule. Let us see why this is so.

It is significant that in recent decades Catholic spokesmen who have condemned the actions of rulers have reserved their most vigorous protests for anti-Democratic regimes. The actions of totalitarian rulers have received the sharpest denunciations by far. Time and again, the Vatican has been moved by the course of events to denounce the actions of totalitarian elites, whether Fascist or Nazi or Communist. The actions of governments where Democratic rule is more widely practiced have not been the objects of such protests. In particular, the Vatican has had no occasion to denounce the actions of American governments, where elitist principles are strongly tempered by Democratic practice. There is no evidence whatsoever that Democratic communities have exercised authority contrary to Catholic principles.

The reason for this is plain to see. When a few rule the many, the legitimacy of authority does not depend on how it is exercised. It depends on who exercises it and how he acquires his office. An elitist ruler may act "constitutionally" and hence exercise "legitimate" authority. Yet his actions may violate the common good. He may act "legitimately" for the benefit of a part of a community. He may act "legitimately" in excess of the authority he has—from the standpoint of a Catholic, or a Democrat. For with any elitist form of rule, no security against the abuse of authority is incorporated into the decision-making process. There is no procedural requirement which secures from the persons over whom authority is exercised consent to a decision about how it should be exercised. In fact there is no assurance that an elite ruler will exercise authority rather than wield force.

Not so, where authority is exercised Democratically. Of course, there is a logical possibility that the general welfare as determined by a vote of a majority may not jibe with the common good as the Catholic understands it. But this is an unlikely possibility in practice. If a Democratic community includes no Catholic member, there is no actual problem of conflict between Democratic practice and Catholic principles. But if, as is more likely, the membership of a Democratic community does include a Catholic, he is a participant in the process by which any decision about exercising authority over him is worked out—a decision about how to advance the general welfare of the community. As a practical matter, then, Democratic rule conforms nicely to the requirements set by Catholic teachings for exercising authority. Indeed, it is a more satisfactory form of rule in practice, for a Catholic, than any alternative form of elite rule.

Chapter Eight

CATHOLICISM AND DEMOCRACY TODAY

I.

The reader is perhaps familiar—if a parent, certainly so—with the old nursery rhyme:

For every evil under the sun,
There is a cure, or there is none;
If there be one, go and find it,
If there be none, never mind it.

That jingle captures in a striking way a belief of the Roman Stoic philosophers. Certain matters are within the ability of men to control, they believed, while others are beyond human control. The proper use of intelligence is to mind the matters we can do something about. As far as I know, I am not a Stoic in my philosophy. But that nursery rhyme does sum up my attitude in writing this book.

We live in a country and a world where Democracy is, in David Lilienthal's words, "on the march." Every American has at least a bit of the Democrat in him. Some have much more than others, but most everyone in this country to some extent accepts the tenets of what has become our national ideology. We live in a country and a world where Catholicism is an expanding movement of vast political and social dimensions. While many Americans are communicants of the Church of Rome, many others suffer in some degree from a social malady we can call "anti-Catholicism." A sympton of this disorder is a delusion that somehow those Catholics can't be trustworthy and upstanding citizens in a Democratic community. Catholics must think and act differently than good Americans.

This attitude is an evil under the sun. It is a social evil as much as the blind hatred of the unknown called "anti-Semitism" is a social evil. Religious intolerance can infect and poison our daily lives. It can disrupt and irritate the normal social relations American citizens enjoy. An attitude of fear and hatred of an unfamiliar religion does everyone harm and no one good.

I set out to find a cure for this evil of anti-Catholicism. I believe I found one. Not a panacea, but a useful home remedy for the intelligent American who does not want to suffer needlessly from a social disease. It is an understanding of the actual relation between Catholicism and Democracy. That understanding I have tried to convey to the reader of this book. I have pointed out that the "classic" position that Catholicism and Democracy are incompatible is not supported by the evidence. The Church's religious teachings do not require a Catholic to accept Democratic principles. But nothing in Democratic theory or practice does violence to Catholic beliefs or principles. A devout Catholic can, if he chooses, be a devoted Democrat. Many American Catholics and some European Catholics have in fact made that choice. They have assumed the leadership of Democratic movements.

2.

But what about the other "classic" position we noted at the outset of our inquiry—the view that Democracy depends on Catholic beliefs about morals and religion? Let us now consider the merits—or lack of them—of this view.

The political issues that thinkers discuss are often not serious and vital issues. Many political discussions and other controversies as well thrive on misunderstandings about language usage. Once the meanings of the terms are clarified, there is nothing important left to talk about. Perhaps some disagreement may remain about questions of fact or questions of logic. But by examining the relation between the statements about facts and the established evidence of our experience, we can, if we so desire, resolve our disagreements over matters of fact. Similarly, by inspecting the relation between arguments and the established rules for logical discourse, we can, if we so desire, clear up disagreements about such matters. After confusions about questions of meaning, fact, and logic have been dispelled, nothing important remains of many political discussions.

But some serious and vital issues divide political thinkers, and sometimes they get around to discussing these political issues. In this book I have considered three such issues: Where should authority be located? Who should exercise it? How should it be exercised? We examined the answers given by the Catholic, the Liberal, and the Democrat to these questions and the reasons why they answer them as differently as they do. These are serious and vital issues because a person's beliefs about how they should be answered may influence his conduct. The beliefs imply principles about the political actions a person should or should not take. In other words, these issues turn on questions of value.

Disagreement about values cannot be resolved in the same way or with the same success that questions of fact or logic can. We can readily resolve disagreements about matters of fact and logic because rules for determining the empirical and logical validity of statements are fairly well established and accepted. But the rules for determining moral validity are sharply disputed by present-day thinkers. Specifically, Catholics, Liberals, and Democrats do not agree at all about the way questions of political value should be answered.

There was a time in the Western world when this was not the case. Virtually every philosopher agreed on how to resolve disagreements about moral questions. Medieval thinkers shared a set of beliefs about the supernatural truth revealed in the Scriptures. These they accepted as an act of religious faith. From supernatural truth, it was possible, they assumed, to derive moral truth about life on this earth. By appealing to the teachings of Christ, questions of political morals could be rightly answered. It was thus possible to find out what actions Christians should and should not take. To act contrary to Christian principles was to invite divine retribution. Political theory they accordingly regarded as a branch of moral theology.

The roots of the Roman Catholic Church extend back into the Middle Ages. Catholic teachings rest on religious beliefs about the nature of man and the universe in which he lives. They are derived from the revealed truth of the Christian gospel. The Church of Rome, its theology and philosophy, was universally accepted in Europe, down to the modern period.

It was in reaction against the Universal Church that Liberalism arose as a movement. In its religious aspect Liberalism was a product of the Protestant Reformation. The movement was founded on what the Liberal called "enlightened" beliefs about man and the universe. These beliefs, he said, rest not on faith or ignorance but on reason; they are derived from the laws of nature. By appeal to the rational laws of nature, rational men can learn the truth about this world. They can find rational answers for moral questions. Human reason, unaided by religious faith, can unlock every door to the knowledge of this world.

The Liberal view about the way questions of political value should be answered was of course a drastic departure from Catholic religious teachings. Where the Catholic relies on the word of God as the ultimate test for moral truth, the Liberal depends on the reason of men. Instead of a branch of theology, political theory becomes a branch of the tree of scientific knowledge. The Liberal has tried to provide "rational" answers for moral questions and other questions originally propounded about the nature of supernatural truth. But these questions he has discussed in terms of the "objective" principles of nature which reason reveals. Liberal thinkers have concocted a body of "scientific" teachings which can be described as the dogmas of a kind of secular religion. These a Catholic theologian calls "naturalistic errors." To this day the Catholic regards Liberal beliefs about moral questions as a form of heresy. And the Liberal replies to the Catholic in kind.

But it is significant that in trying to answer moral questions without appealing to religious dogma, the Liberal thinkers have been plagued by problems of value. They have sought to buttress their elitist beliefs about political rights and duties with the "rational" principles. But they have never been able to resolve satisfactorily the important questions of political values while relying on their principles of nature. They have never succeeded in inventing a scientific theory of political morals.

The search by Liberals for a solid foundation in nature for their "rational" principles has proved fruitless. The quest has led some "enlightened" thinkers along the path of anarchism, the worship of the sovereign individual who denies that any authority is legitimate. Others have been led along the path of totalitarianism, the worship of the sovereign state which denies that any authority is not legitimate. Either of these views can be argued with logical consistency from Liberal assumptions, but both preclude a moral basis for political relations. More often than not the search for a rational system of political morals has led Liberal thinkers nowhere. As their rational principles of nature make mockery of their own experience, they abandon logic in a morass of contradictions. Common sense leaves them no choice. Confusion indeed is characteristic of present-day Liberal thought. Criticisms of other views abound, but constructive teachings about the serious and vital political issues of our time are strikingly absent. The course of Liberal political thought from the beginning of the modern period to the present can be charted as a quest for an adequate substitute for religious dogma as the foundation of political morals, a quest that has been an epic in failure.

3.

What the Catholic and the Democrat have in common is a rejection of Liberal values. Neither accepts the notorious Liberal beliefs about political morals, or the Liberal view about how questions of political value should be answered. That a Catholic cannot accept the Liberal principles of political conduct, both the Catholic and the Liberal have keenly realized for several centuries. This is because Catholicism is historically a "pre-Liberal" movement. And as it was in reaction against medieval Catholicism that Liberalism arose, so was it in reaction against modern Liberalism that the Democratic movement began. Democracy is definitely a "post-Liberal" movement.

We find as a result that what the Catholic and the Democrat do not have in common are the reasons for rejecting Liberal values. That a Democrat cannot accept the Liberal principles of political conduct is clearly evident, though much less attention has been paid to this by Liberals or Democrats than the facts warrant. The conflict is fundamental. In no way are Democratic principles dependent on Liberal beliefs about political morals. In fact, Democratic principles are not even related to any belief about suprahuman moral laws. The Democrat's view about how questions of political value should be answered is distinctive. It is different from the Catholic view as well as from the Liberal. Since these statements are apt to evoke indignant challenges from several quarters, let us proceed to consider rather carefully exactly what Democratic morals consist of.

The nursery rhyme I mentioned earlier as summing up my

attitude in writing this book also sums up the Democratic attitude toward problems of political conduct. There are no satisfactory answers for many moral questions. These the Democrat never minds. How they are answered usually makes no difference in political practice anyway. But for other moral questions, some answers are more satisfactory than others. This is the case with questions which directly bear on the conduct of members of political communities. For these the Democrat has, so to speak, found some answers—not by fathoming the divine or natural mysteries of the universe, but simply by observing the experience of members of political communities.

Democracy, unlike Catholicism or Liberalism, is a political creed of very modest pretensions. Democratic beliefs do not afford solace for all human cares or supply answers for every question the ingenuity of man can propound. Democracy offers no answers whatsoever to any question about "supernatural" or "natural" truth. The realm of religion, be it of Christianity or of science, is outside and beyond the ken of Democratic theory. Religion is, for the Democrat, a realm of private affairs. A person's private convictions about life in this or another world which none of us knows from public experience are of no concern to the Democrat.

In fact, for the Democrat any appeal to a higher moral law to resolve questions of political value is both unnecessary and futile. He sees no earthly need to postulate an "objective" moral order decreed by God or nature to justify principles of political conduct. Universal principles of political right or reason or truth are not necessary for people to conduct their political lives satisfactorily. The Democrat recognizes no suprahuman laws which prescribe where authority should be located or who should exercise it or how they should exercise it in practice. He denies that the existence of any political laws beyond human control can be demonstrated. Political beliefs derived from such laws cannot be proved valid by any method of reasoning. The notion of validity is in fact meaningless when applied to questions of value. Such questions cannot be answered by means of facts or logic or metaphysics. We may have beliefs about political right and wrong, but we cannot "know" what is right or wrong political conduct.

This is not to say that Democratic theory contains no value beliefs. It certainly does. Democratic beliefs imply definite normative rules for ordering political conduct. In fact, Democratic theory is mainly a theory of political morals. But the value beliefs of a Democrat differ radically in character from the value beliefs entertained by a Catholic. For a Democrat, a political value is not something we ought to accept. It is something we may desire. It is something we can accept, if we choose.

The Democrat's approach to questions of political value is to keep them disentangled from matters of fact or logic or metaphysics. His interest is in political practice. His consideration of political morals is confined to the actual conduct of persons engaged in political activity. His beliefs pertain only to the public character of persons in this world, the men and women we greet and talk to and work with every day of our lives. What distinguishes the Democrat is his beliefs about how the members of communities can conduct their political affairs. That is all. He does not claim that these beliefs are right or rational or true. He claims only that they answer some practical questions about the effectiveness of human conduct in political practice, and answer them more satisfactorily than alternative political beliefs do.

This Democratic approach to political morals was not contrived by some creative philosophic genius. It was implicit in the practical purpose that Democratic theory and practice were originated to serve. The felt need was for more meaningful principles to guide political conduct. The established principles were found unsatisfactory. The need was for principles which would enable the members of political communities to achieve greater effectiveness by their common actions. Democratic beliefs were formulated to justify the application of such principles in political practice.

Consequently, we find that the Democrat is not, strictly speaking, concerned with what persons should do. His concern is about the way they can do certain things. They can conduct themselves politically in a Democratic way, which is more effective in practice than any other way. If a person does not want to achieve any political purpose, the Democrat has nothing to say to him. Or if a person does not want to achieve his political purpose effectively, again the Democrat has nothing to say. But if a person does want to achieve a purpose he shares in common with others and wants to be effective in his political activity, then the Democrat has some things to say about how he can get the greatest possible satisfaction from his political life.

4.

The case for Democracy is an impressive one, though the merits of the case are not so fully appreciated as they might be. The question at stake is: Why should Democratic beliefs be accepted and Democratic principles observed in the conduct of politics? So stated, the question could be misleading. In practice, a person cannot adopt a Democratic method of exercising authority by himself. He can do that only as a member of a political community. The choice before members of political communities is to accept either a Democratic method of rule or some alternative method of elite rule. As a practical matter, this means some variety of Liberal rule between the logical extremes of anarchism and totalitarianism. Why the members of political communities should accept a Democratic method of exercising authority rather than an elite form of rule can be stated negatively or affirmatively. What can the members lose by adopting a Democratic method? What can they gain? Neither Democratic statement in response to these questions is vulnerable to successful attack from anti-Democratic ideologists.

The negative statement of the case for Democracy centers on a denial that there is any earthly reason why the members of political communities should not adopt a Democratic method of exercising authority if they want to. The elitist would have us believe otherwise. We have already examined some elitist claims that Democracy is an immoral or irrational way to exercise authority. These claims we found without foundation. The elitist also claims that Democratic rule is impractical. Members of political communities stand to lose in practice by adopting a Democratic method. Charges that Democracy does not work out well have proved very popular with elitists of all descriptions. Let us consider in what these charges consist and why they do not stand up.

One charge, that the people make "bad" decisions, we examined earlier. We don't want a mob, the elitist says, to judge a murder suspect. We don't want the rabble to award prizes for literary excellence. And we don't want the masses to decide how political authority should be exercised. This charge we found without merit. Certainly we don't want incompetent people making political decisions. That is precisely why a Democratic process is most effective. The persons over whom authority is exercised are more competent than anyone else to make decisions about exercising authority. They can make wiser political decisions than any elite.

Another elitist charge is that Democracy is impossible in practice. This claim was advanced some years ago by a famous European sociologist, Robert Michels, in a book translated under the title of *Political Parties* (1915). His thesis was that any successful working of Democracy is prevented by the practical requirements of political organization. Scientific investigation shows, he says, that a few leaders who exercise exceptional influence always rule the many followers. One elite can replace another elite but never can the people rule themselves. This discovery he called the "iron law of oligarchy."

Michels's thesis depends on a gigantic fallacy. From the fact that some political communities are ruled by an oligarchy he infers, falsely, that no political community can be ruled otherwise. His error is not merely one of logic. In drawing his "scientific" generalization, he ignored the experience of Democratic communities and relied entirely on the experience of communities ruled by oligarchies. Reduced to the essential, Michels's discovery is that communities ruled by oligarchies are not ruled Democratically. Truly marvelous are the discoveries of science.

The answer to Michels is apparent to anyone familiar with the Democratic process of decision-making. That many political decisions are not now made by a Democratic process is of course true. But it is also true that many other decisions are. The fact that a Marxist political party in Imperial Germany was ruled by an oligarchy does not disturb the fact that many non-Marxist political communities in this country are not ruled by an oligarchy. Actually what Michels's thesis underscores is the simple and obvious point that a representative system of government is not a Democratic system. What his thesis ignores is that a Democratic community can exercise authority Democratically, even though many communities are not now ruled by a Democratic method.

A third elitist charge that Democracy is impossible takes the form of a claim that Democratic rule is an unwieldy and cumbersome way to make political decisions. This claim is often made even though it has no merit. The Democrat does not contend that Democratic rule is simple. The process of making a political decision is complicated. But he says that the Democratic process is still the most effective way to make decisions about exercising authority.

Actually this elitist charge is not so much a comment on the Democratic process as it is on its absence. A Democratic process can work successfully to the extent that the members of a community desire that political decisions be made Democratically. To the extent that their conduct is not guided by Democratic principles, a decision-making process, regardless of the rules, is not in practice Democratic. What is important is not the form but rather the content of rules—the beliefs of the members. Rules merely express a prevailing agreement about how members should conduct themselves. Unfortunately, in any political community where a Democratic method is used, the incidence and intensity of Democratic beliefs varies somewhat among the members. To that extent so do Democratic practices. A person who gives lip service to a set of rules but does not believe in them can, of course, abuse the rules to advance a purpose not intended by the community in adopting them. To the extent that Democratic rules for making political decisions are abused by the members of a community for a perverse purpose of obstructing the decision-making process, of course the process is cumbersome and unwieldy. But it is not a Democratic process. A football team is no place for a thug who refuses to play the game according to the rules. A Democratic community is no place for an elitist who refuses to abide by Democratic principles. To the extent that Democratic practices are followed in decision-making, the process is neither cumbersome nor unwieldy, though it is always complicated. This charge, in other words, bears not on the functioning of a Democratic process but rather on the absence of Democratic practices.

The Democrat, of course, recognizes that in practice there is nothing spontaneous or automatic about making political decisions on a group basis according to Democratic principles. Democratic principles prescribe a set of procedural rules for members of communities to observe in their conduct. Democratic principles are operative in guiding political conduct only to the extent that the members of communities abide by Democratic rules in the process of making decisions. To the extent that they agree to resolve their differences about exercising authority by a Democratic method, and to that extent only, can they practice Democracy.

No doubt in some cultures and many communities the making of political decisions according to Democratic rules would be an alien and awkward process. Any conduct regulated by rules is artificial. It must be taught and learned. A football player learns to play the game according to certain recognized rules.

A union official learns to conduct a meeting according to the rules of his organization. An attorney practices law according to rules accepted by the members of the legal profession. There are no "natural" football players or union officials or lawyers. Any behavior which is common to a group of persons is a product of what Graham Wallas called "our social heritage."

Just as significant as the fact that cultural patterns shape the behavior of members of groups is the fact that men invent and adopt new patterns of cultural behavior in response to changing needs and desires. There is no evidence for assuming that many more political decisions than at present could not be made by a Democratic process. The practical question is to what extent the persons over whom authority is exercised agree to make decisions according to Democratic rules. Many Americans are now members of political communities which use a Democratic process to make some decisions. Other decisions could be made by the same method. Political communities which do not now use a Democratic method at all could adopt one, if the members so chose.

The claim that Democracy is an impractical method of rule has a particular appeal, significantly, for persons who are unfamiliar with Democratic practice, whether by circumstance or choice. The Democrat has no illusions about the appeal of the Democratic process of decision-making for an elitist ruler, whether he is a party boss, a shop foreman, a college president, a Marine sergeant, a union secretary, or a government administrator. He can gain little by the adoption of a Democratic method of rule, even though his community can gain much. But then his credentials for deciding the question are not of the best. It is those over whom the elitist ruler exercises authority who are qualified to decide. In practice, every person subject to authority answers for himself the question of how decisions about exercising authority should be made. He can answer it the way he desires, or the way someone else desires that he should. There is no reason why the members of political communities should not answer it to their own satisfaction.

Certainly they have nothing to lose by adopting a Democratic method of rule. In fact, those who have participated in a Democratic decision-making process seem to acquire a growing appetite for ruling themselves and a growing distaste for rule by an elite.

The negative statement of the Democratic case we can summarize, then, as follows: No principles of political conduct *must* be accepted by anyone. There are no empirical or logical or metaphysical imperatives which require anyone to believe that political conduct must be governed by any particular set of rules. Since there are no valid "reasons" why political decisions must be made in a certain way, by some principles over which we have no control, the method of making political decisions is, by default, so to speak, open to the choice of persons over whom authority is exercised. The members of political communities can agree among themselves about the rules they want to use in their political conduct. There is no reason in this world why they should not agree that authority should be exercised Democratically, if that is their desire.

5.

Perhaps the members of political communities have nothing to lose by adopting a Democratic method of rule. But what can they gain? The Democrat replies that the members of political communities can be more effective in conducting their political affairs by a Democratic method than by any form of elite rule.

The affirmative case for Democracy I have from time to time intimated in the course of elaborating the doctrines of popular sovereignty, political equality, and majority rule. At this point, I propose to state explicitly the argument for accepting Democratic rule. The import of this argument can perhaps be best appreciated in terms of the political needs of the American people. As members of the myriad of political communities which flourish in this country, the American people are continually faced by a problem of steadily increasing seriousness and extent. It is basically a problem of human psychology. Graham Wallas, the English political theorist who introduced the psychological approach to the study of politics, called it the problem of "social judgment." In an unfinished little book entitled *Social Judgment,* published posthumously in 1934, Wallas presented a most cogent analysis of the psychological problem of judgment-making in present-day society, which he termed in an earlier work the "Great Society." It would probably be inadvisable for me to introduce at this point Wallas's terminology in considering this problem, so I shall use terms which are no doubt by now familiar to the reader to formulate what Wallas called "the problem of social judgment."

Our daily lives are affected in a host of ways by decisions to act. We are confronted with many problems which arise out of our desire for things we do not have. We want more food, finer housing, more money to spend, better health, greater happiness, added security, wider opportunity, and so on. To satisfy our desires, we must make decisions about actions we should take to solve our problems. A decision to act is a creative experience. It is a unique solution to a unique problem of conduct. Even though two situations may be strikingly analogous, what a person desires and the conditions under which he can satisfy his desires are never exactly the same. Experience and information can be useful in making a decision, but they are not enough. In making a decision to act, a person must draw on his combined psychological resources. He must study the situation, imagine what actions are possible, estimate the probable consequences of various actions, appraise the adequacy of possible actions. And he must make a choice—select from among the many possibilities

264

the actions to follow in an effort to solve his problem. He must decide to act.

We now live in a society where the making of decisions has more and more acquired a political character. The Great Society represents a tremendous increase in "social scale." It contains many more people, bunched closer together, and living more highly specialized lives. As a result we have become increasingly dependent on one another for the satisfaction of our desires. Not only have the problems confronting us increased in number and extent, but also they have increasingly become problems we have in common with other persons. By our own decisions to act, we can no longer adequately solve our problems of subsistence, housing, employment, health, welfare, security, safety, and the like.

In this Great Society many political decisions are made which affect, for good or ill, the lives of a host of people. The consequences of a political decision may vary tremendously, depending on how important a problem is in the lives of people and how significant a role the decision-maker plays in society. A decision may concern only a minor problem and affect in an incidental way only a few people. Or it may affect in a profound way an immense number of people. It may have ramifications for an entire nation. A decision on a major public problem by a party leader, or a military commander, or a governmental official, or the head of an industry or a labor union may vitally influence the welfare of thousands, perhaps millions, of people, not only those now alive but also future generations. To an extent never before imaginable, each of us is today at the mercy of persons who are unseen, perhaps even completely unknown to us, yet who decide our lives. Our only awareness is of the sweeping effects of decisions by others on our daily lives.

As the consequences of decisions have been magnified in extent and seriousness by the increase in "social scale," the need for wise decisions has become ever more pressing. The satisfaction of our most vital desires turns more and more on the wisdom of political decision-makers. But unfortunately, the difficulties involved in making wise political decisions have been aggravated. With the increase in "social scale," no corresponding change has occurred in the biological or psychological competence of human beings. Our "natural" ability to make wise decisions is as limited as before, while our acquired skills complicate rather than simplify the decision-making process.

The Great Society is a creation of experts. As inventors, scientists, technicians, and managers, experts have amassed a huge store of specialist knowledge and cultivated impressive degrees of specialist skill. Hence the wonders of our society, which are so marvelous and so terrifying. "Specialism" has actually increased the difficulties in making wise political decisions. Most political decisions are today made by persons who have achieved influential roles because of their qualifications as experts. But specialist skill is not a qualification for making political decisions; it is actually a psychological disqualification. The higher the level of skill an expert achieves, the more he develops one psychological ability to the neglect of other abilities. A decision by a military strategist, an investment banker, an industrial engineer, a budget director, may be politically catastrophic; it may bring in its wake misery and despair for countless people, even though the decision is technically sound. For the solution may be for a technical problem, while in fact the problem is political in character. The decision-maker may lack the psychological balance required to make a wise decision about how people should act. He may lack the fertility of imagination, the creativeness of mind, the breadth of vision, the richness of understanding, the sensitivity to human attitudes—qualities of mind not cultivated by technical training or experience. He may lack the psychological capacity to weigh and balance, coordinate, and synthesize the varied psychological components in the process of arriving at a decision which affects many people. For a wise solution to a political problem requires the full exploitation of the many psychological resources of the decision-maker, rather than the intensive application of a technical skill.

In the Great Society, then, the political character of the problems which confront people has increased. The importance of decisions about solving human problems has increased. The need for wise political decisions is greater than ever before, yet the difficulty in making such decisions is also greater. How can the psychological process of decision-making be improved so that the critical need for wise political decisions can be satisfactorily met?

The solution is implicit in the problem itself. In practice, political decisions have increasingly become collective in their significance, penetrating more vitally and more frequently the lives of many people who must bear the consequences of decisions to act. The process by which decisions are made should become increasingly collective too.

In the Great Society the psychological process by which decision-makers arrive at solutions to problems is already to a significant extent collective in practice. No longer can one person carry through single-handed the process of deciding about a solution to an important problem. Even where the responsibility for decision-making nominally rests with one person, say a party chairman, a trial judge, a union secretary, a plant manager, a bureau director, or a regimental commander, the decision-maker actually depends on the efforts of others in working out his decision. He relies on his associates and staff to call problems to his attention, to brief him with information, to suggest policy lines, to appraise possible solutions. He weighs the testimony and opinions expressed directly and indirectly by many persons before he makes a decision. After making a decision, he depends on the collective actions of others to carry it out, and the reports of others to evaluate practical working.

Many decisions now are in fact the responsibility of communities instead of a lone individual. The political process of decision-making is on a group basis. The members of a city council, a board of directors, a policy committee, a government commission, engage collectively in a decision-making process. Each member participates and contributes and the collective decision reflects a pooling of the information, experience, ideas, and feeling of the members.

So, in the Great Society the decisions about resolving political problems, the psychological process by which political decisions are made, the political process used in decision-making are more and more collective in practice. Political decisions are now characteristically collective decisions about collective actions. The problem is how to meet the greatly augmented need of the American people for wiser political decisions. The solution must take the form of improving the collective decision-making process.

6.

For Graham Wallas's problem of social judgment, no adequate solution is offered by elite rule. Rule by a special few is in a sense becoming out of date, no longer suited to the requirements of the times. It is becoming a political luxury the American people cannot well afford much longer.

But Democracy does supply a solution to this problem of the Great Society. This may seem strange, since the Democratic process of political decision-making was originally devised to meet the needs of members of small farming communities. However the conditions and the wants of these communities along the American frontier were very unusual. The fortunes of the members of a frontier community were intertwined and inseparable. Action to secure the community from attack, to assure an ample store of food, to maintain a supply of pure water, to protect the members from diseases, to care for the sick and the helpless—such action in an isolated community surrounded by a hostile wilderness was of necessity collective action. Decisions to act in solving common problems had to be community decisions. The members had to rely on their own resources in making decisions —every resource the community could afford. Their need was for a more effective method than elite rule for making decisions which affected the life of every member of the community. To satisfy that want, the Democratic process of decision-making was developed. It proved to be the most successful method for making decisions about exercising authority over the members of political communities. It is still the most effective method of making collective decisions about collective actions.

What can the members of a political community gain, then, by accepting Democratic beliefs and observing Democratic principles in their political conduct? Let us answer this question by an example, the case of a member of the Westside Civic Improvement League who claims privileges but denies obligations as a member of the political community. A Democrat would say that he should not act that way. The argument would run as follows:

Why does a person join the League? In an effort to satisfy a desire he shares in common with other League members—to make the Westside a better community in which to live. He can conduct himself in a way most effective for obtaining satisfaction from his political activity. As a functioning member who abides by the rules, he can do his part in promoting a purpose he could not otherwise achieve. By violating the League rules, he hampers any achievement of that purpose he shares with the other members. By his conduct, he cannot, in practice, get what he wants. His actions defeat his own purpose as a League member.

What is true of one member is true of every member of a political community. Since no community can afford members who hurt the organization more than they help it, each member may have a practical choice between giving up his privileges or fulfilling his obligations of membership. But his significant moral choice is between engaging effectively in political activity and satisfying a political desire, and engaging ineffectively and leaving that desire unsatisfied. Every time a political community makes a decision about exercising authority, each member must make a moral choice. He can choose to hurt himself or to help himself by his political conduct. Only he can hurt himself; only he can help himself. He must choose what he values most, ineffective or effective political activity. To the extent that the members of a political community want to obtain satisfaction of their political desires, they must engage effectively in political practice, and they should observe Democratic principles in conducting their affairs as members of political communities.

Democratic moral principles, then, can only help those who want to help themselves. Democracy is nothing more or less than a method by which persons who want to achieve political purposes can conduct themselves in order to achieve those purposes most effectively. To the extent that members of political communities do want to be more successful in their conduct, they should abide by Democratic principles. By observing Democratic principles, the members of political communities can most effectively satisfy their political desires.

Let us now apply this argument to the political needs of the American people. The overriding problem is how to make the wisest possible political decisions. By failing to solve this problem, they have a world to lose. They cannot solve it by a process which allows decisions about exercising authority that people do not, in practice, accept. They cannot solve it by a process where politically incompetent experts decide how authority should be exercised over politically competent people. They cannot solve it by a decision-making process which does not exploit fully the political resources of the American nation.

They can solve this problem by an expanded and enhanced use of the Democratic decision-making process, which enlists most effectively into the public service the nation's political resources in solving the problems which confront the American people.

What can the American people gain by adopting a Democratic method of rule and abandoning forms of elite rule? Not only greater control over their own political destiny. They can gain the greatest possible success in their political activity, hence the greatest possible satisfaction from their political lives.

7.

Democracy, we said, is mainly a theory of political morals. It is a theory about how people can increase the effectiveness of their political conduct. The case for Democracy is an argument to the effect that people who adopt this method of decision-making, rather than accept elite rule, can achieve the greatest possible satisfaction from their political lives. What is the relation between this Democratic theory about political conduct and Catholic religious teachings? Evidently there is no conflict. But is there any connection?

I believe not. A Democrat can be a Protestant or a Jew, an atheist or a true believer. So far as religion is concerned, Democracy is "agnostic," so to speak. It is a set of purely secular beliefs. Democratic beliefs entail no religious or antireligious imperatives. Any conflict between religion and Democratic politics could come only from the intrusion of religious teachings into political affairs. It could not come from Democratic political beliefs in any way penetrating into the area of religion. A Democrat, because of his political beliefs, neither accepts nor rejects any religious teachings.

Catholicism and Democracy are systems of beliefs and principles which in political practice have no particular relation at all. A Catholic can certainly be a Democrat, but he is a Democrat not because of his religion, only because of his political convictions. The case for Democratic political beliefs can be stated without appealing to Catholicism or any body of religious teachings. In fact, it cannot be very well stated if there is an appeal to religious dogma. For Democratic beliefs are confined to a very narrow area of human conduct. They concern not what people should do, but rather how people can most effectively do certain

271

things. Democracy is merely a method of making collective decisions which members of political communities can use. Catholic religious teachings, it so happens, neither conflict with nor apply to beliefs about this Democratic method of rule. They are simply irrelevant.

8.

This brings us to the close of our inquiry into the relation between Catholicism and Democracy. I hope that the reader has attended a meeting of the Westside Civic Improvement League, or something like it, before. I trust you have and that this book has made some sense to you. In closing, let's see now where our inquiry has taken us.

We found that the view that Democracy and Catholicism are incompatible is without warrant. Catholicism and Liberalism are conflicting systems of thought and practice; so are Liberalism and Democracy. But there is no necessary incompatibility between Catholic religious teachings and Democratic beliefs and principles.

We found, too, that the other view, that Democracy is dependent on Catholic moral teachings, is also without warrant. Democracy is a purely secular creed, devoid of religious implications. Democratic beliefs about the principles of political conduct are derived, not from the dogmas of religion, but from the practices of politics. So there is no necessary connection either between Catholicism and Democracy.

I have tried to show how it is that the relation between Catholicism and Democracy is one neither of necessary incompatibility nor of connection, and why this is the case. I hope and trust that the reader, along with other members of the Westside Civic Improvement League, now has a clearer understanding than before of the actual relation between Catholicism and Democracy today.

BIBLIOGRAPHICAL NOTES

Contrary to common practice in academic circles, I decided not to clutter up the pages of this book with footnotes, citations, and lengthy quotations of "authorities"; these would distract the general reader. However, for the benefit of a reader who might be curious about my sources or who might like to pursue the subject further, I offer some bibliographical notes.

These notes are arranged in three parts: I. Comments, chapter by chapter, about the primary source materials relied on in this study; II. Documentary sources frequently used in this study; III. A select list of general works which provide useful background materials and are not otherwise cited.

I. BIBLIOGRAPHICAL COMMENTS

CHAPTER ONE. THE CONTEMPORARY ISSUE

The attitudes of the early American colonists are well expressed in the following documents: "Mayflower Compact" (1620). "Fundamental Orders of Connecticut" (1638). "Fundamental Agreement of New Haven" (1639). "Plantation Agreement at Providence" (1640). "Pennsylvania Charter of Privileges" (1701).*

The literature of the American Revolution is vast. The following

* For the sources for these and other documents mentioned in these notes, see "II. Documentary Sources" (below).

documents and tracts reflect the variety of opinion expressed during the years leading up to hostilities: James Otis, *The Rights of the British Colonies* (1764). "Declarations of the Stamp Act Congress" (1765). John Dickinson, *Letters from a Farmer* (1767–1768). "Declaration and Resolves of the First Continental Congress" (1774). James Wilson, *Considerations of the Nature and Extent of the Legislative Authority of the British Parliament* (1774). John Adams, *Novanglus, Letters Addressed to the Inhabitants of the Colony of Massachusetts Bay* (1774–1775). Alexander Hamilton, *The Farmer Refuted* (1775). "Declaration of the Causes and Necessity of Taking Up Arms, Continental Congress" (1775). "Mecklenburg County Resolutions" (1776). "The Virginia Bill of Rights" (1776). "Declaration of Independence" (1776). Also: Thomas Paine, *Common Sense* (1776); see Thomas Paine, *Common Sense and Other Political Writings,* edited with an introduction by N. F. Adkins, New York: Liberal Arts Press, 1953. [Cf. Clinton Rossiter, "The Political Theory of the American Revolution," *Review of Politics,* 15 (Jan., 1953) 97–108.]

British views of the controversy are expressed in the following: Edmund Burke, "Speech on American Taxation" (1774); "Speech on Conciliation with America" (1775). Jonathan Boucher, *A View of the Causes and Consequences of the American Revolution in Thirteen Discourses Preached in North America between the Years 1763 and 1775* (1797). Samuel Seabury, *A View of the Controversy between Great Britain and Her Colonies* (1774). Daniel Leonard, *Massachusettensis, Letters Addressed to the Inhabitants of the Province of Massachusetts Bay* (1774–1775).

The classic English statement of early Liberal thought is by John Locke, *Two Treatises of Government* (1690). The first treatise is devoted to an attack on the divine-right-of-kings theory; the second, to an affirmation of the natural rights–social contract theory. Charles Louis de Secondat, Baron de Montesquieu's two-volume *The Spirit of the Laws* (1748) is available in an English translation by T. Nugent, with an introduction by F. Neumann, two volumes in one, New York: Hafner, 1949.

The starting point for an understanding of Federalist thought is James Madison's *Notes on the Convention* (1787); they should be read in conjunction with the "Constitution of the United States of America" (1789). (A very useful collection of materials is *Documents Il-*

lustrative of the Formation of the Union of American States, Washington: GPO, 1927.) The best-known statement of Federalist doctrines is the *Federalist Papers* (1787–1788), written for the New York press under the pen name of "Publius" by Alexander Hamilton, James Madison, and John Jay. (The eighty-five essays, with the texts of the Articles of Confederation and the Constitution, are reprinted in *The Federalist: A Commentary on the Constitution of the United States,* with an introduction by E. G. Bourne, New York: Tudor, 1937.) Federalist Papers Nos. 47 and 48 (by Madison) treat specifically the question of a mixed constitution. Other writings by Hamilton expressing Federalist views: "Letter to Duane" (1780). "First Report on Public Credit" (1790). "Opinion on the Constitutionality of the Bank of the United States" (1791). "Report on Manufactures" (1791). [See *Alexander Hamilton's Papers on Public Credit, Commerce and Finance,* edited by S. McKee, Jr., with an introduction by J. H. Williams, New York: Liberal Arts Press, 1957; and, *Alexander Hamilton: Selections Representing His Life, His Thought, and His Style,* edited with an introduction by B. Aly, New York: Liberal Arts Press, 1957.] John Adams was another able Federalist writer; his views are expressed in: *Thoughts on Government* (1776). *A Defence of the Constitutions of Government of the United States of America,* 3 vols. (1786–1787). *Discourses on Davila* (1791). [See *The Political Writings of John Adams: Representative Selections,* edited with an introduction by G. A. Peek, Jr., New York: Liberal Arts Press, 1954.] An extreme Federalist statement is found in Fisher Ames, *The Dangers of American Liberty* (1805).

The fullest source for early anti-Federalist views is Elliot's *Debates:* Jonathan Elliot (ed.), *Debates in the Several State Conventions on the Adoption of the Federal Constitution* (1836–1845), 5 vols., Philadelphia: Lippincott, 1901. Objections to the Constitution are summarized in such tracts of the times as: "Letter of Robert Yates and John Lansing to the Governor of New York" (1787). Elbridge Gerry, "Observations on the New Constitution and on the Federal and State Conventions" (1788). The anti-Federalist position is clearly stated (by Jefferson) in the "Kentucky Resolutions" (1798) and the "Virginia Resolutions" (1798). The drift of Thomas Jefferson's thinking is evident in the following letters: "To Madison" (1787). "To Hopkinson" (1789). "To Gerry" (1799). "To Granger" (1800). "To

Nicholas" (1803). [Some useful collections of Jefferson's better-known writings: *The Complete Jefferson: Containing His Major Writings, Published and Unpublished, Except His Letters,* edited by S. K. Padover, New York: Tudor, 1943. *Thomas Jefferson on Democracy,* edited with an introduction by S. K. Padover (1939), New York: Mentor, 1946. *The Political Writings of Thomas Jefferson: Representative Selections,* edited with an introduction by E. Dumbauld, New York: Liberal Arts Press, 1955.]

Recent American anti-Catholic writings include articles in the *New Republic* and the *Nation* as well as several books: George P. West, "The Catholic Issue," *New Republic,* 108 (Mar. 1, 1943) 278–280. Gaetano Salvemini: "Pius XII and Fascism," *New Republic,* 108 (Mar. 8, 1943) 305–309; (Apr. 26, 1943) 567; (June 14, 1943) 797–798; and, "Catholics and Liberals," *New Republic,* 109 (Aug. 2, 1943) 144; (Sept. 20, 1943) 397. Paul Blanshard's articles attacking Catholicism in the *Nation:* First series, 165 (Nov. 1, 1947) 466–469; (Nov. 8, 1947) 496–499; (Nov. 15, 1947) 525–528. Second series: 166 (Apr. 10, 1948) 390–393; (Apr. 17, 1948) 416–417; (Apr. 24, 1948) 432–434; (May 1, 1948) 459–464; (May 8, 1948) 499–502; (May 15, 1948) 521–524; (May 22, 1948) 574–576; and particularly: "Catholic Church and Democracy—I" (May 29, 1948) 601, 604–606; "Catholic Church and Democracy—II" (June 5, 1948) 630–632. The best known recent anti-Catholic polemic is Blanshard's *American Freedom and Catholic Power,* Boston: Beacon Press, 1949; it was followed by *Communism, Democracy, and Catholic Power,* Boston: Beacon Press, 1951.

Two journals, *America* and *Commonweal,* contain expressions of Catholic opinion on current issues. Catholic answers to the recent wave of anti-Catholicism include: John A. Ryan, "Catholics and Liberals—Letter in Reply to Salvemini," *New Republic,* 109 (Sept. 20, 1943) 395–397. Luigi Sturzo, "The Church and Democracy and Salvemini-LaPiana," *America* 70 (Nov. 6, 1943) 117–120. George H. Dunne, "Blanshard Charges in the Nation," *Commonweal,* 47 (Mar. 12, 1948) 536–542. The ablest rebuttal to Blanshard's charges: James M. O'Neill, *Catholicism and American Freedom,* New York: Harper, 1952. A personal attack on Blanshard: Dale Francis, *American Freedom and Paul Blanshard* (pamphlet), Notre Dame: Ave Maria Press, 1950.

Expositions of the Christian Democratic position: By Luigi Sturzo: "The Catholic Church and Christian Democracy," *Social Action* 10 (May 15, 1944) 5–43. "The Philosophic Background of Christian Democracy," *Review of Politics,* 9 (Jan., 1947) 3–15. *Nationalism and Internationalism,* New York: Roy, 1946, see Chapter IV. [Cf. Malcolm Moos, "Luigi Sturzo, Christian Democrat," *American Political Science Review,* 39 (Apr., 1945) 269–292.] Also, by Emmet John Hughes: *The Church and Liberal Society,* Princeton, N.J.: Princeton University Press, 1944.

CHAPTER TWO. THE DEMOCRATIC TRADITION

The literature of American Democracy begins, in a sense, with Alexis de Tocqueville's famous commentary, *Democracy in America* (1835, 1840). (A fine current edition is the Reeves translation, revised by Bowen, edited with an introduction by Phillips Bradley, 2 vols., New York: Knopf, 1946.) A neglected brief, but significant, exposition of Democracy is a pamphlet by George W. Burnap, *Origin and Causes of Democracy in America,* Baltimore: Toy Printers, 1853. For the background of the Democratic movement, very useful is Frederick Jackson Turner, *The Frontier in American History,* New York: Holt, 1920.

The views of the Puritan theocrats of Massachusetts Bay are summed up in the "Cambridge Platform of Church Discipline" (1649). Cotton Mather's two-volume *Magnalia Christi Americana, or the Ecclesiastical History of New England, 1620–1698* (reprinted at Hartford: Andrus, 1855) is an ambitious account of the movement. John Winthrop was an early Puritan lay leader: "A Modell of Christian Charity" (1630); and "Speech to the General Court" (1645). The high priest of Puritanism was the clergyman John Cotton. *The Bloudy Tenent, Washed and Made White in the Blood of the Lambe* (1647) is his reply to Roger Williams (below); in the letter "To Lord Say and Seale" (1636), Cotton states his views about popular rule. A little-known but another articulate Puritan clergyman was Jonathan Mitchel; two of his sermons are of special interest: "The Great End and True Interest of New England" (1662); "Nehemiah on the Wall in Troublesome Times" (1667).

For criticisms of orthodox Puritanism: Thomas Hooker, *Survey of the Summe of Church Discipline* (1648). Roger Williams, *The*

Bloudy Tenent of Persecution for the Cause of Conscience (1644), and, *The Bloudy Tenent Yet More Bloudy* (1651). [Cf. Perry Miller, *Roger Williams: His Contribution to the American Tradition,* Indianapolis: Bobbs-Merrill, 1953; and, Samuel H. Brockunier, *The Irrepressible Democrat—Roger Williams,* New York: Ronald, 1940.] John Wise, *A Vindication of the Government of New-England Churches* (1717) is in part a critique of theocracy; see also, *Churches Quarrel Espoused* (1710). [Cf. Clinton Rossiter, "John Wise: Colonial Democrat," *New England Quarterly,* 22 (Mar., 1949) 3–32.]

Early American Democratic views are most clearly expressed by Thomas Jefferson, though his writings are fugitive: Queries XIII, XIV, XIX in *Notes on Virginia* (1787). "First Inaugural Address" (1801). Letters "To Madison"(1789); "To Kercheval" (1816); "To Taylor" (1816); "To Tiffany" (1816). The ablest expositions of Jeffersonian agrarianism are by John Taylor, *An Inquiry into the Principles and Policy of the Government of the United States,* Fredericksburg: Green & Cady, 1814; and *Tyranny Unmasked,* Fredericksburg: Green & Cady, 1822. [Cf. Grant McConnell, "John Taylor and the Democratic Tradition," *Western Political Quarterly,* 4 (Mar., 1951) 17–31; and Eugene T. Mudge, *The Social Philosophy of John Taylor of Caroline,* New York: Columbia University Press, 1939.]

Views of the Jacksonian Democrats (and their critics) are found scattered in the debates of state conventions on reform of the franchise: for examples, *Journal of Debates and Proceedings in the Convention of Delegates Chosen to Revise the Constitution of Massachusetts* (1820), revised edition, Boston: 1853. *Report of the Proceedings and Debates of the Convention of 1821, Assembled for the Purpose of Amending the Constitution of the State of New York,* Albany: 1821. *Proceedings and Debates of the Virginia Constitutional Convention, 1829–1830,* Richmond: Ritchie & Cook, 1830—especially the remarks of John R. Cooke of Frederick. Andrew Jackson's statements include: "First Annual Message" (1829). "Veto Message on the Maysville Road Bill" (1830). "Veto Message on the Bank Bill" (1832). "Farewell Address" (1837). Jackson's state papers can be found in James D. Richardson (ed.), *A Compilation of the Messages and Papers of the Presidents, 1789–1902,* 10 vols., New York: National Literature, 1903; see vol. 2, pp. 436–657. A rather inadequate summation of Jacksonian views is contained in the "Introduction" (pp.

1–15) to *The United States Magazine and Democratic Review*, 1 (Oct., 1837).

Some later American Democratic writings: Abraham Lincoln, "First Inaugural Address" (1861). Walt Whitman, *Democratic Vistas* (1870). Henry George, *Progress and Poverty* (1879). [Cf. George R. Geiger, *The Philosophy of Henry George*, introduction by J. Dewey, New York: Macmillan, 1933.] Theodore Roosevelt, *The New Nationalism*, New York: Outlook, 1910. Herbert Croly, *Progressive Democracy*, New York: Macmillan, 1912. J. Allen Smith, *The Spirit of American Government*, New York: Macmillan, 1912. Robert La-Follette, *LaFollette's Autobiography: A Personal Narrative of Political Experiences* (1912), 6th edition, Madison: LaFollette, 1913; and, Ellen Torelle (ed.), *The Political Philosophy of Robert M. LaFollette as Revealed in His Speeches and Writings*, Madison: LaFollette, 1920. Walter E. Weyl, *The New Democracy* (1912), revised edition, New York: Macmillan, 1918. Woodrow Wilson, *The New Freedom*, Garden City: Doubleday, 1913. William Jennings Bryan, *The People's Law*, New York: Funk & Wagnalls, 1914; and, *Heart to Heart Appeals*, New York: Revell, 1917. Franklin D. Roosevelt, *Looking Forward*, New York: John Day, 1933. [Cf. Clinton Rossiter, "The Political Philosophy of F. D. Roosevelt," *Review of Politics*, 2 (Jan., 1949) 87–95.] David Lilienthal, *TVA: Democracy on the March*, New York: Harper, 1944.

For the background of the British Democratic movement: "The Political Thought of the British Utilitarians," the introduction to *James Mill: Essay on Government*, edited with an introduction by Currin V. Shields, New York: Liberal Arts Press, 1955. Mark Hovell, *The Chartist Movement*, edited by T. F. Tout, New York: Longmans, 1925. Graham Wallas, *The Life of Francis Place, 1771–1854* (1898), revised edition, London: Allen & Unwin, 1918. Sidney Webb, *Socialism in England*, London: Swan Sonnenschein, 1890. William J. Wilkinson, *Tory Democracy*, New York: Columbia University Press, 1925.

Some general treatments of recent Democratic movements and their problems: John S. Penman, *The Irresistible Movement of Democracy*, New York: Macmillan, 1923. James Bryce, *Modern Democracies*, 2 vols., New York: Macmillan, 1921. C. Delisle Burns, *The Challenge to Democracy*, London: Allen & Unwin, 1935. Carl L. Becker, *Modern*

Democracy, New Haven, Conn., Yale University Press, 1941. A. D. Lindsay, *The Modern Democratic State,* Vol. I, New York: Oxford, 1943.

CHAPTER THREE. THE CATHOLIC TRADITION

Thomist philosophy was given papal recognition by Leo XIII in the encyclical *Aeterni Patris* ("On the Study of Scholastic Philosophy," 1879) and by Pius XI in *Studiorum Ducem* ("On St. Thomas Aquinas," 1923). Works on Thomism by contemporary Catholic philosophers: Etienne Gilson: *The Philosophy of St. Thomas Aquinas,* translated by E. Bullough, edited by G. A. Elrington, 2d revised edition, St. Louis: Herder, 1929. *Christianity and Philosophy,* translated by R. McDonald, New York: Sheed & Ward, 1939. By Jacques Maritain: *The Angelic Doctor: The Life and Thought of St. Thomas Aquinas,* translated by J. F. Scanlon, New York: Sheed & Ward, 1931. *Scholasticism and Politics,* New York: Macmillan, 1940.

The starting point for the Catholic critique of modern thought and movements is the "Syllabus of Errors," issued by Pius IX in 1864. The thesis is elaborated in four encyclicals by Leo XIII: *Quod Apostolici Muneris* ("Socialism, Communism, Nihilism," 1878). *Inscrutabili* ("On the Evils Afflicting the Modern World," 1878). *Humanum Genus* ("Freemasonry," 1884). *Libertas Humana* ("On Human Liberty," 1888). It is further extended by Pius XI in *Caritate Christi Compulsi* ("The Sacred Heart and World Distress," 1932) and by Pius XII in *Summi Pontificatus* ("Function of the State in the Modern World," 1939). The general thesis has been elaborated by some recent Catholic commentators: Raymond Corrigan, *The Church in the Nineteenth Century,* Milwaukee: Bruce, 1938. Emmet John Hughes, *The Church and the Liberal Society,* Princeton, N.J.: Princeton University Press, 1944. Thomas R. Neill, *The Rise and Decline of Liberalism,* Milwaukee: Bruce, 1953.

No single work adequately treats the "Social Catholic" movement, but the following historical studies cover the main developments: Francesco Nitti, *Catholic Socialism* (1890), translated by M. Mackintosh from the 2d Italian edition, introduction by D. G. Ritchie, New York: Macmillan, 1908. Parker T. Moon, *The Labor Problem and the Social Catholic Movement in France: A Study in the History of Social Politics,* New York: Macmillan, 1921. Georgiana P. McEntee,

The Social Catholic Movement in Great Britain, New York: Mac-millan, 1927. Henry Somerville, *Studies in Catholic Social Move-ments,* London: Burns, 1933. M. D. R. Ley, *European Catholics and the Social Question,* Oxford: Catholic Social Guild, 1943. Some biographies of leading figures of the movement are helpful in under-standing the character of "Social Catholicism": J. J. Laux (George Metlake), *Christian Social Reform: Program Outlined by Its Pioneer, William Emmanuel Baron Von Ketteler, Bishop of Mainz,* Phila-delphia: Dolphin Press, 1912. Eduardo Soderini, *The Pontificate of Leo XIII,* translated by B. B. Carter, London: Burns, 1934. Mary Ignatius Ring, *Villeneuve-Bargemont: Catholic Social Protagonist,* preface by J. Husslein, Milwaukee: Bruce, 1935. Albert P. Schimberg, *The Great Friend: Frederick Ozanam,* Milwaukee: Bruce, 1946.

The basic social teachings of the Church are set forth in two well-known encyclicals: Leo XIII, *Rerum Novarum* ("The Condition of the Working Class," 1891), and Pius XI, *Quadragesimo Anno* ("On Restoring the Christian Social Order," 1931). These should be read along with other encyclicals, such as: Leo XIII, *Graves de Communi* ("Christian Democracy," 1901). Pius X, *Singulari Quadam* ("On Christian Labor Unions," 1912. Pius XI, *Ubi Arcano Dei* ("On Catholic Action," 1922); *Divini Redemptoris* ("Atheistic Commu-nism," 1937). Pius XII, *Summi Pontificatus* ("On the Function of the State in the Modern World," 1939). [The most useful collection of the encyclicals bearing on "Social Catholicism" is edited by Joseph Husslein, *Social Wellsprings,* Milwaukee: Bruce, 1942; vol. I con-tains Leo XIII's, and vol. II, Pius XI's, encyclicals.]

Commentaries on the encyclicals are numerous. Among the most useful: Lewis Watt, *Catholic Social Principles: A Commentary on the Papal Encyclical 'Rerum Novarum,'* New York: Benziger, 1930. Joseph Husslein, *The Christian Social Manifesto: An Interpretative Study of the Encyclicals Rerum Novarum and Quadragesimo Anno,* revised edition, Milwaukee: Bruce, 1939. Robert G. Brehmer, *Social Doctrines of the Catholic Church,* New York: Putnam, 1936. Charles P. Bruehl, *The Pope's Plan for Social Reconstruction,* New York: Devin-Adair, 1939.

Some worthwhile and reliable general studies of Catholic social principles: Francis J. Haas, *Man and Society: An Introduction to Sociology,* New York: Appleton-Century, 1930. E. Cahill, *Frame-*

work of a Christian State, Dublin: Gill, 1932. John F. Cronin, *Catholic Social Principles: The Social Teachings of the Catholic Church Applied to American Economic Life,* Milwaukee: Bruce, 1950. These should be read in conjunction with Johannes Messner, *Social Ethics: Natural Law in the Modern World,* translated by J. J. Doherty, St. Louis: Herder, 1949.

On the concept of "social justice," a few commentaries are available: Leo W. Shields, *The History and Meaning of Social Justice,* South Bend, Ind.: University of Notre Dame Press, 1941. William Ferree, *Introduction to Social Justice,* New York: Paulist Press, 1948 (pamphlet); and, *The Act of Social Justice,* Dayton (Ohio): Marianist Publications, 1951.

CHAPTER FOUR. CHRISTIAN DEMOCRACY

Much literature about corporativism has no particular relevance to Catholic reform. One helpful background survey: Paul Vignaux, "Corporativism in Europe," *Review of Politics,* Part I-4 (Apr., 1942) 194–205, Part II-4 (July, 1942) 303–314. Catholic principles of corporativism are explained and discussed in Harold F. Trehey, *Foundations of a Modern Guild System,* Washington, D.C.: The Catholic University of America Press, 1940.

The principles of the *Estado Novo* are set forth by Dr. Antonio de Oliveira Salazar in *Doctrine and Action: Internal and Foreign Policy of the New Portugal, 1928–1939,* translated by R. E. Broughton, London: Faber, 1939, and *Salazar, Prime Minister of Portugal, Says...,* Lisbon: SPN Book, 1939. For appraisals of Salazar's regime: Michael Derrick, *The Portugal of Salazar,* London: Sand, Paladin Press, 1938. Freppel Cotta, *Economic Planning in Corporative Portugal,* London: King, 1937. Antonio C. Pastor, "Salazar's Portugal," *Thought,* 14 (Dec., 1939) 539–563. A critical appraisal by a Catholic: Luigi Sturzo, "Corporationism, Christian-Social and Fascist," *Catholic World,* 145 (July, 1937) 394–399.

The literature of present-day Catholic Action mainly dates from 1922, when Pius XI became Pope. Apparently his encyclical *Ubi Arcano Dei* ("On Catholic Action," 1922) stimulated the growth of the movement along contemporary lines. Another important encyclical by Pius XI on the same subject is *Non Abbiamo Bisogno* ("Concerning Catholic Action: The Conflict in Italy," 1931). A standard work in the field is by Luigi Civardi, *Manual of Catholic Action,* translated from the Italian by C. C. Martindale, New York: Sheed & Ward, 1936. *Restoring All Things: A Guide to Catholic Action,* edited by John Fitzsimons and Paul Maguire, New York: Sheed & Ward, 1938, is a collection of articles about the movement during the critical years of the 1930s. Other articles of the same sort: Louis Vanhouche, "The Fight for Youth: Jocism," *Catholic World,* 148 (Oct., 1938) 27–32. Marquis de Aragon, "Catholic Action in France," *Dublin Review,* 202 (Jan., 1938) 27–38. Mary G. Hawks, "Catholic Action in Foreign Countries," *Catholic Action,* 20 (Jan., 1938) 12–13, 16–18, 27. Stanley James, "Basis of Catholic Action," *Ecclesiastical Review,* 105 (Aug., 1941) 104–111. A more recent American study of the movement and program: John F. Cronin, *Catholic Social Action,* Milwaukee: Bruce, 1948. Some brief accounts of Catholic Action in Great Britain and the United States: *Catholic Social Guild: Its Nature and Purpose,* Oxford: Catholic Social Guild (n.d.). Austin Dowling, "The National Catholic Welfare Conference," *American Ecclesiastical Review,* 79 (Oct., 1928) 337–354.

Don Luigi Sturzo's writings on Christian Democracy are especially significant because of his prominent role in founding and promoting the movement: "Italian Popular Party," *Contemporary Review,* 129 (June, 1926) 730–737. "My Political Vocation," *Commonweal,* 34 (Sept. 26, 1941) 537–540. "The Catholic Church and Christian Democracy," *Social Action,* 10 (May 15, 1944) 5–43. "The Nature and Limits of Democracy," *Proceedings of the American Catholic Philosophical Association,* 20 (Dec., 1945). "The Philosophic Background of Christian Democracy," *Review of Politics,* 9 (Jan., 1947) 3–15.

No general study of the postwar Christian Democratic movement has yet appeared, but the following articles provide an account of the developments: Robert G. Neumann, "The New Political Parties in Germany," *American Political Science Review,* 40 (Aug., 1946) 749–759. Mario Einaudi, "Christian Democracy in Italy," *Review of Politics,* 9 (Jan., 1947) 16–33. Gabriel Almond, "The Christian Parties," *World Politics,* 1 (Oct., 1948) 30–58; and, "The Political Ideas of Christian Democracy," *Journal of Politics,* 10 (Nov., 1948) 734–763. Dolf Sternberger, "Party and Party Systems in Post-war Germany," *Annals of the American Academy,* 260 (Nov., 1948) 10–31. Anthony T. Bouscaren, "The European Christian Democrats,"

Western Political Quarterly, 2 (Mar., 1949) 59–73. F. E. Oppenheim, "Belgian Political Parties since Liberation," *Review of Politics*, 12 (Jan., 1950) 99–119. A more recent study of the movement in two European countries: Mario Einaudi and François Goguel, *Christian Democracy in Italy and France*, South Bend, Ind.: University of Notre Dame Press, 1952. A brief account of the international development is found in a pamphlet by Barbara B. Carter, *International Christian Democracy*, Oxford: Catholic Social Guild, 1948.

CHAPTER FIVE. POPULAR SOVEREIGNTY

The Thomist theory of civil authority is expounded in *The Political Ideas of St. Thomas Aquinas: Representative Selections*, edited with an introduction by D. Bigongiari, New York: Hafner, 1953. Also: St. Thomas Aquinas, *On Kingship: To the King of Cyprus*, translated by G. B. Phelan, revised with an introduction by I. Th. Eschmann, Toronto: Pontifical Institute of Mediaeval Studies, 1949. The basic encyclical by Leo XIII stating the Catholic theory is *Immortale Dei* ("The Christian Constitution of States," 1885); it should be read along with *Diuturnum Illud* ("On Civil Government," 1881). In fact Catholic teachings about authority are at least implicit in virtually every encyclical on social, economic, or political questions issued by Leo XIII and his successors.

The standard commentary on the subject is an excellent work by Heinrich Rommen, *The State in Catholic Thought: A Treatise in Political Philosophy*, St. Louis: Herder, 1945. Also by Rommen: "Church and State," *Review of Politics*, 12 (July, 1950) 321–340. Useful too in interpreting Catholic political teachings are the writings of a French philosopher and of an American priest. By Jacques Maritain: *Rights of Man and Natural Law*, New York: Scribner, 1943. "The Person and the Common Good," *Review of Politics*, 8 (Oct., 1946) 419–455. "The Concept of Sovereignty," *American Political Science Review*, 44 (June, 1950) 343–357. By Father John Courtney Murray, in *Theological Studies*: "Contemporary Orientation of Catholic Thought on Church and State in the Light of History," 10 (June, 1949) 177–234. "The Problem of State Religion," 12 (June, 1951) 155–178. "The Church and Totalitarian Democracy," 13 (Dec., 1952) 525–563. A series of four articles on Leo XIII: 13 (Mar., 1953) 1–30; 13 (June, 1953) 145–214; 13 (Dec., 1953) 551–567;

14 (Mar., 1954) 1–33. Also by Murray: "The Problem of 'the Religion of State,'" *American Ecclesiastical Review*, 124 (1951) 327–352. "A Church-State Anthology: The Work of Father Murray," *Thought*, 26 (Spring, 1952) 6–42. "The Problem of Pluralism in America," *Thought*, 28 (Summer, 1954) 165–208. Sturzo's *Church and State*, New York: Longmans, 1939, is a massive historical study of the relation between ecclesiastical and civil authority.

The historic form of constitutionalism incorporated into Federalist thought is the natural rights–social contract theory, predicated on a natural-law theory. The Liberal theory of natural law was formulated in the seventeenth century by a Dutch jurist, Hugo Grotius; see *Prolegomena to the Law of War and Peace* (1625), translated by F. W. Kelsey, introduction by E. Dumbauld, New York: Liberal Arts Press, 1957. John Locke's *Second Treatise* (1690) is a famous English statement of the natural rights–social contract theory. [A useful edition is *John Locke: The Second Treatise of Government,* edited with an introduction by T. P. Peardon, New York: Liberal Arts Press, 1952.] Montesquieu's *The Spirit of the Laws,* a classic eighteenth-century French statement, was a source of inspiration for the Federalist thinkers. This work was preceded by Montesquieu's *Persian Letters* (1721), which is mainly a critique of dynastic rule from the standpoint of a "constitutionalist."

American Liberal principles of constitutionalism are of course embodied in the "Constitution of the United States" (1789). The theory underlying the Constitution is fully expounded in the *Federalist Papers*. See particularly Nos. 10, 39, 40, 44, 49, and 50—all by Madison—and No. 22 by Hamilton. Other Federalist writers, such as John Adams and John Marshall, later elaborated and refined the views advanced in the *Federalist Papers*.

The Liberal literature on the issue of individual rights and governmental authority includes four famous tracts: John Milton, *Areopagitica* (1644). John Locke, *A Letter concerning Toleration* (1685). Henry David Thoreau, *Essay on Civil Disobedience* (1849). John Stuart Mill, *Essay on Liberty* (1859). For historical background of the issue: John Hallowell, *Main Currents in Modern Political Thought,* New York: Holt, 1950, particularly Chapter 4, "Rise of Liberalism" (pp. 84–117), and Chapter 5, "The Age of Enlightenment" (pp. 118–158). For a brief discussion of the issue: the introduction (pp. vii–xxvi) to *John Stuart Mill: Essay on Liberty,* edited with an introduction by Currin V. Shields, New York: Liberal Arts Press, 1956.

Opinions by some justices of the Supreme Court of the United States offer interesting, if strange, contributions to the literature: For examples: Opinion by Mr. Justice Holmes, *Abrams v. United States* (1919) 250 U.S. 616. Opinion by Mr. Justice Sanford, dissenting opinion by Mr. Justice Holmes, *Gitlow v. New York* (1925) 268 U.S. 652. Opinion by Mr. Justice Butler, *Hamilton et al. v. Regents of the University of California* (1934) 293 U.S. 245. Opinion by Mr. Chief Justice Hughes, *Norris v. Alabama* (1935) 294 U.S. 587. Opinion by Mr. Justice Cardozo, *Palko v. Connecticut* (1937) 302 U.S. 319. Opinion by Mr. Justice Frankfurter, *Minersville School District v. Gobitis* (1940) 310 U.S. 586. Opinion by Mr. Justice Jackson, *West Virginia State Board of Education v. Barnette* (1942) 319 U.S. 324. Opinion by Mr. Chief Justice Vinson, dissenting opinions by Justices Black and Douglas, *Dennis et al. v. United States* (1951) 341 U.S. 494. Opinion by Mr. Chief Justice Warren, *Brown et al. v. Board of Education of Topeka* (1954) 347 U.S. 483.

The Democratic doctrine of popular sovereignty dates at least from the seventeenth-century writings of Roger Williams and the early eighteenth-century writings of John Wise. In the Revolutionary tracts of the 1770s the doctrine was often expressed by the radical republicans. Thomas Jefferson's "Declaration of Independence" (1776) is no doubt the most famous statement of the principle; another well-known statement is contained in the "Virginia Bill of Rights" (1776). In various writings Thomas Paine ably expounded the doctrine of popular sovereignty; he sums it up in his *Dissertations on Government, Etc.* (1786), reprinted in *The Political Writings of Thomas Paine,* 2 vols., Boston: Mendum, 1859; see vol. I, pp. 365–413. [Cf. Howard Penniman, "Thomas Paine—Democrat," *American Political Science Review,* 38 (Apr., 1943) 244–262.] Jefferson's writings, particularly his letters, contain mature formulations of the doctrine. For examples, see his letters: "To Randolph" (1799). "To Nicholas" (1803). "To Kercheval" (1816). "To Cartwright" (1824). Also, two of Jefferson's cabinet opinions: July 15, 1790, and April 28, 1793. Some of the most cogent formulations of the doctrine are found in the remarks by Democratic reformers during the debates in the early

286

nineteenth-century state constitutional conventions, such as the remarks by John R. Cooke in the Virginia Convention, 1829–1830.

CHAPTER SIX. POLITICAL EQUALITY

A frank statement of the divine-right-of-kings doctrine is contained in James I's *Trew Law of Free Monarchies* (1598); see *The Political Works of James I*, edited with an introduction by C. H. McIlwain, Cambridge: 1918. A classic statement of the case is by Sir Robert Filmer, *Patriarchia, or the Natural Powers of Kings* (1680)—the object of Locke's attack in his first *Treatise of Government*. The standard commentary is J. N. Figgis, *The Divine Right of Kings* (1896). Sources for the Puritan doctrine of the divine right of the "elect of God" were indicated above, for Chapter Two. A work which could be added: *John Calvin: On God and Political Duty*, edited with an introduction by John T. McNeill, New York: Liberal Arts Press, 1950.

For Catholic teachings about commutative and distributive justice (as for, incidentally, other Catholic concepts and principles) a good starting point is the *Catholic Encyclopedia: An International Work of Reference on the Constitution, Doctrine, Discipline, and History of the Catholic Church*, edited by C. G. Herbermann et al., 15 vols., New York: Appleton, 1907–1912. Encyclicals which set forth the Church's teachings: By Leo XIII: *Humanum Genus* ("Freemasonry," 1884). *Rerum Novarum* ("The Condition of the Working Class," 1891). By Pius XI: *Quadragesimo Anno* ("On Reconstructing the Social Order," 1931). *Divini Redemptoris* ("Atheistic Communism," 1937). Some helpful commentaries: John A. Ryan, *Distributive Justice* (1916). Jacques Maritain, *Rights of Man and Natural Law* (1947). Rommen, *The State in Catholic Thought* (1945)—especially Chapter 2. A brief and popular but interesting summary of Catholic principles: John A. Driscoll, *Rights and Duties: Their Foundation*, New York: Paulist Press, 1948. The modern Catholic teachings on forms of civil rule (including monarchy) are clearly stated by Leo XIII: *Diuturnum Illud* ("On Civil Government," 1881). *Immortale Dei* ("The Christian Constitution of States," 1885).

The Federalist form of the Liberal doctrine of elite rule was fully and frankly expressed by John Adams. His doctrine of "natural aristocracy" is elaborated in: *Thoughts on Government* (1776). Vol.

I of *Defence of the Constitutions* (1787). A series of letters "To Taylor" (1814). The finest Federalist statement of the "virtue" of representative government is by James Madison in the *Federalist Papers*, particularly Nos. 10, 14, 39.

Again the best source for early Democratic views is Thomas Jefferson. For his doctrine of political equality (in addition to the "Declaration of Independence"): Query XIV, *Notes on Virginia* (1785). Letters "To Priestly" (1802). "To de Nemours" (1816). "To Taylor" (1816). "To Tiffany" (1819). "To Johnson" (1823). In his letter "To Adams" (1813), Jefferson directly takes issue with the doctrine of "natural aristocracy." For a significant discussion of the role of the "expert" in Democratic decision-making: David Lilienthal, *TVA: Democracy on the March*, New York: Harper, 1944.

Chapter Seven. Majority Rule

The Catholic teachings about authority and "just rule" and the doctrine of resistance to civil rule are set forth in papal documents and some excellent commentaries: By Leo XIII: *Diuturnum Illud* ("On Civil Government," 1881). *Sapientiae Christianae* ("On the Chief Duties of Christians as Citizens," 1890). *Au Milieu des Sollicitudes* ("Allegiance to the [French] Republic," 1892). By Pius XI: *Iniquis Afflictisque* ("The Persecution of the Catholic Church in Mexico," 1926). *Arcerba Animi* ("The Mexican Persecution," 1932). *Dilectissima Nobis* ("Injustice to Catholics in Spain," 1933). *Firmissimam Constantiam* ("On the Religious Situation in Mexico," 1937). *Mit Brennender Sorge* ("Position of the Church in Germany," 1937). Don Luigi Sturzo's commentaries on the Catholic principles of authority are very helpful: *Italy and Fascism,* translated by B. B. Carter, introduction by G. Murray, New York: Harcourt, Brace, 1927. "The Right to Resistance to the State," *Contemporary Review,* 134 (Sept., 1928) 312–320. "Rome and Anti-Rome," *Dublin Review,* 200 (Jan., 1937) 42–59. "The Right to Rebel," *Dublin Review,* 201 (July, 1937) 24–39. "Authority and Democracy," *Dublin Review,* 210 (Apr., 1942) 151–163. For a general treatment: Rommen, *The State in Catholic Thought,* St. Louis: Herder, 1945.

The Federalist formula for elite rule is elucidated by Madison and Hamilton throughout the pages of the *Federalist Papers,* but in particular: Nos. 43 (Madison) and 51 (Hamilton or Madison). No. 78

(by Hamilton) is an apologia for judicial review which apparently much impressed Chief Justice John Marshall. The most famous statement of the case for judicial review is Marshall's *obiter dicta* in *Marbury v. Madison* (1803) 1 Cranch 137. A cogent Federalist argument for minority rule is developed by John Adams in vol. II of his *Defence of the Constitutions*.

The literature of majority rule begins with Thomas Jefferson. The main sources for his doctrine of majority rule have already been cited. For Jefferson's views particularly about judicial review, see his letters: "To Roane" (1819). "To Jarvis" (1820). "To Johnson" (1822, 1823). And his address: "To the Speaker and the House of Delegates of the Commonwealth of Virginia" (1797). In this connection Jefferson's *Manual of Parliamentary Practice* (1800), prepared for use in the United States Senate, is very interesting.

John C. Calhoun's Disquisition (1850) is now readily available in an inexpensive edition: *A Disquisition on Government and Selections from the Discourses,* edited with an introduction by C. G. Post, New York: Liberal Arts Press, 1953. [Cf. August O. Spain, *The Political Theory of John C. Calhoun,* New York: Bookman Associates, 1951.] Thoreau's essay is available in the same series: *Henry David Thoreau: Selected Writings on Nature and Liberty,* edited with an introduction by O. Cargill, New York: Liberal Arts Press, 1952.

The following works represent more recent contributions to discussions of majority rule: J. Allen Smith, *The Spirit of American Government,* New York: Macmillan, 1912. William L. Ransom, *Majority Rule and the Judiciary,* with an introduction by T. Roosevelt, New York: Scribner, 1912. Delos F. Wilcox, *Government by All the People, or the Initiative, the Referendum and the Recall as Instruments of Democracy,* New York: Macmillan, 1912. Edward Elliott, *American Government and Majority Rule: A Study in American Political Development,* Princeton, N.J.: Princeton University Press, 1916. Edwin Mims, *The Majority of the People,* New York: Modern Age, 1941. Willmoore Kendall, *John Locke and the Doctrine of Majority Rule,* Urbana, Ill.: University of Illinois Press, 1941. Henry Steele Commager, *Majority Rule and Minority Rights,* New York: Oxford, 1943. Max Lerner, "Minority Rule and the Constitutional Tradition," in Conyers Read (ed.), *The Constitution Reconsidered,* New York: Columbia University Press, 1938. Kendall,

"Majority Rule and the Scientific Elite," *Southern Review,* 4 (Winter, 1939) 463–473. Carl J. Friedrich, *The New Belief in the Common Man,* Boston: Little, Brown, 1943, chapters 4 (pp. 121–150) and 5 (pp. 238–270). Herbert McClosky, "The Fallacy of Absolute Majority Rule," *Journal of Politics,* 11 (Nov., 1949) 637–654. Kendall, "Prolegomena to Any Future Work on Majority Rule," *Journal of Politics,* 12 (Nov., 1950) 694–713. Austin Ranney and Kendall, "Democracy: Confusion or Agreement?" *Western Political Quarterly,* 4 (Sept., 1951) 430–439. Ranney, "Toward a More Responsible Two-party System: A Commentary," *American Political Science Review,* 45 (June, 1951) 488–499. J. Roland Pennock, "Responsiveness, Responsibility, and Majority Rule," *American Political Science Review,* 46 (Sept., 1952) 790–807.

CHAPTER EIGHT. CATHOLICISM AND DEMOCRACY TODAY

An interesting discussion of Democracy from the Catholic standpoint is a series of rather lengthy and technical articles by Mortimer J. Adler and Walter Farrell, entitled "The Theory of Democracy," which appeared in the *Thomist:* Part I—3 (July, 1941) 397–449. Part II—3 (Oct., 1941) 588–652. Part III—4 (Jan., 1942) 121–181; 4 (Apr., 1942) 286–354. Part IV—4 (July, 1942) 446–522; 4 (Oct., 1942) 692–761; 6 (Apr., 1943) 49–118; 6 (July, 1943) 251–277. Part V—6 (Oct., 1943) 367–407; 7 (Jan., 1944) 80–131.

Graham Wallas's seminal writings in which he elaborated his conception of "social judgment" include: *The Great Society: A Psychological Analysis,* London: Macmillan, 1914. *Our Social Heritage,* London: Allen & Unwin, 1921. *The Art of Thought,* New York: Harcourt, Brace, 1926. *Social Judgment,* London: Allen & Unwin, 1934. *Men and Ideas: Essays by Graham Wallas,* with a preface by G. Murray, London: Allen & Unwin, 1940.

The best-known anti-Democratic writings have been authored by Europeans. Some examples: Henry Maine, *Popular Government* (1885), London: Murray, 1909. Gaetano Mosca, *The Ruling Class* (1896), translated by H. D. Kahn, edited and revised, with an introduction, by A. Livingston, New York: McGraw-Hill, 1939. W. H. Mallock, *Aristocracy and Evolution: A Study of the Rights, the Origin and Social Functions of the Wealthier Classes,* London: A. & C.

Black, 1898. Robert Michels, *Political Parties: A Sociological Study of the Oligarchical Tendencies of Modern Democracy,* translated by E. and C. Paul, New York: Hearst, 1915. Vilfredo Pareto, *The Mind and Society* (1916), translated by A. Bongiorno and A. Livingston, edited by A. Livingston, 4 vols., New York: Harcourt, Brace, 1935. Emile Faguet, *The Cult of Incompetence,* translated by B. Barstow, with an introduction by T. Mackay, New York: Dutton, 1916. José Ortéga y Gasset, *The Revolt of the Masses* (1930), New York: Norton, 1932. [Cf. B. E. Lippincott, *Victorian Critics of Democracy,* Minneapolis: University of Minnesota Press, 1938.]

There is an abundance of native American elitist writings; much with a Liberal bias has appeared in this century. A variety of examples: William H. Taft, *Popular Government: Its Essence, Its Permanence, and Its Peril,* New Haven, Conn.: Yale University Press, 1913. Nicholas M. Butler, *True and False Democracy,* New York: Scribner, 1915. Madison Grant, *The Passing of the Great Race, or the Racial Basis of European History,* New York: Scribner, 1916. Everett Dean Martin, *The Behavior of Crowds: A Psychological Study,* New York: Harper, 1920. Lothrop Stoddard, *The Revolt against Civilization: The Menace of the Under-man,* London: Chapman & Hall, 1922. H. L. Mencken, *Notes on Democracy,* New York: Knopf, 1926. Raoul L. Desvernine, *Democratic Despotism,* New York: Dodd, Mead, 1936. Willis J. Ballinger, *By Vote of the People,* New York: Scribner, 1946. Thomas J. Norton, *Undermining the Constitution,* New York: Devin-Adair, 1950. [Cf. David Spitz, *Patterns of Anti-Democratic Thought: An Analysis and Criticism, with Special Reference to the American Political Mind in Recent Times,* New York: Macmillan, 1949.]

II. DOCUMENTARY SOURCES

Catholic Encyclopedia: An International Work of Reference on the Constitution, Doctrine, Discipline and History of the Catholic Church, edited by C. G. Herbermann et al., 15 vols., New York: Appleton, 1907–1912. *A Compilation of the Messages and Papers of the Presidents, 1789–1902,* edited by James D. Richardson, 10 vols., New York: Bureau of National Literature, 1903. *The Complete*

Jefferson: Containing His Major Writings, Published and Unpublished, Except His Letters, edited by S. K. Padover, New York: Tudor, 1943. *Debates in the Several State Conventions on the Adoption of the Federal Constitution,* edited by Jonathan Elliot (1836–1845), 5 vols., Philadelphia: Lippincott, 1901. *Documents of American History,* edited by Henry Steele Commager (1934), 3d edition, New York: Appleton-Century-Crofts, 1946. *Democracy, Liberty and Property: Readings in the American Political Tradition,* edited with introductions by Francis W. Coker, New York: Macmillan, 1942. *Documents Illustrative of the Formation of the Union of American States* (House Document 398, 69th Congress, 1st Session), Washington: GPO, 1927. *Federal and State Constitutions, Colonial Charters, and Other Organic Laws of the States, Territories, and Colonies Now or Heretofore Forming the United States of America,* edited by Francis N. Thorpe, 7 vols. (House Document 357, 59th Congress, 2d Session), Washington: GPO, 1909. *The Federalist: A Commentary on the Constitution of the United States,* by Alexander Hamilton, James Madison, and John Jay, with an introduction by E. G. Bourne, New York: Tudor, 1937. *Free Government in the Making: Readings in American Political Thought,* edited by Alpheus T. Mason, New York: Oxford, 1949. *The Great Encyclical Letters of Leo XIII,* edited by John J. Wynn, New York: Benziger, 1903. *Journal of Debates and Proceedings in the Convention of Delegates Chosen to Revise the Constitution of Massachusetts* (1820), revised edition, Boston: 1853. *Proceedings and Debates of the Constitutional Convention, 1829–1830, of the State of Virginia,* Richmond: Ritchie & Cook, 1830. *The Puritans,* edited by Perry Miller and T. H. Johnson, New York: American Book, 1938. *The Records of the Federal Convention of 1787,* edited by Max Farrand, 3 vols., New Haven, Conn.: Yale University Press, 1911. *Report of the Proceedings and Debates of the Convention of 1821, Assembled for the Purpose of Amending the Constitution of the State of New York,* Albany: 1821. *Social Theories of Jacksonian Democracy: Representative Writings of the Period, 1825–1850,* edited by Joseph L. Blau, New York: Hafner, 1947. *Social Wellsprings,* edited by Joseph Husslein, 2 vols., Milwaukee: Bruce, 1942. *Sources and Documents Illustrating the American Revolution, 1764–1788, and the Formation of the Federal Constitution,* edited by Samuel E. Morison, New York: Oxford, 1923.

III. GENERAL WORKS

Daniel Aaron, *Men of Good Hope: A Story of the American Progressives*, New York: Oxford, 1951. James T. Adams, *The Epic of America*, Boston: Little, Brown, 1931; and, *The Living Jefferson*, New York: Scribner, 1936. Charles A. Beard, *Economic Origins of Jeffersonian Democracy*, New York: Macmillan, 1915. Charles A. and Mary R. Beard, *The Rise of American Civilization*, New York: Macmillan, 1930. Carl L. Becker, *The Declaration of Independence: A Study in the History of Political Ideas* (1922), New York: Knopf, 1942; and, *The Heavenly City of the Eighteenth-century Philosophers*, New Haven, Conn.: Yale University Press, 1932. Albert J. Beveridge, *Life of John Marshall*, 4 vols. (1916), Boston: Houghton Mifflin, 1919. Wilfred E. Binkley, *American Political Parties: Their Natural History* (1943), 2d edition, New York: Knopf, 1947. Louis B. Boudin, *Government by Judiciary*, 2 vols., New York: Godwin, 1932. Claude G. Bowers, *The Party Battles of the Jackson Period*, Boston: Houghton Mifflin, 1922; *Jefferson and Hamilton: The Struggle for Democracy in America*, Boston: Houghton Mifflin, 1925; *The Tragic Era: The Revolution after Lincoln*, Boston: Houghton Mifflin, 1929; and, *Jefferson in Power, The Death Struggle of the Federalists*, Boston: Houghton Mifflin, 1936. Van Wyck Brooks, *The Flowering of New England, 1815–1865* (1936), New York: Dutton, 1940. William Jennings Bryan, *The First Battle: A Story of the Campaign of 1896*, Chicago: Conkey, 1896. James Bryce, *The American Commonwealth*, revised edition, New York: Macmillan, 1912. Henry Steele Commager, *The American Mind*, New Haven, Conn.: Yale University Press, 1950. Edward S. Corwin, *The Doctrine of Judicial Review: Its Legal and Historical Basis and Other Essays*, Princeton, N.J.: Princeton University Press, 1914; and, *John Marshall and the Constitution: A Chronicle of the Supreme Court*, New Haven, Conn.: Yale University Press, 1919. William W. Crosskey, *Politics and the Constitution in the History of the United States*, 2 vols., Chicago: University of Chicago Press, 1953. Merle Curti, *The Growth of American Thought*, New York: Harper, 1943. Joseph Dorfman, *The Economic Mind in American Civilization, 1606–1865*, 2 vols., New York: Viking,

293

1946. Amintore Fanfani, *Catholicism, Protestantism, and Capitalism,* New York: Sheed & Ward, 1939. Max Farrand, *The Framing of the Constitution of the United States,* New Haven, Conn.: Yale University Press, 1913. Esther Forbes, *Paul Revere and the World He Lived in,* Boston: Houghton Mifflin, 1942. Ralph H. Gabriel, *The Course of American Democratic Thought,* New York: Ronald, 1940. Eric Goldman, *Rendezvous with Destiny: A History of Modern American Reform,* revised edition, New York: Vintage, 1956. Alan P. Grimes, *American Political Thought,* New York: Holt, 1955. A. Whitney Griswold, *Farming and Democracy,* New York: Harcourt, Brace, 1948. Charles G. Haines, *The American Doctrine of Judicial Supremacy,* New York: Macmillan, 1914. John D. Hicks, *The Populist Revolt: A History of the Farmer's Alliance and the People's Party,* Minneapolis: University of Minnesota Press, 1931. Richard Hofstadter, *Social Darwinism in American Thought, 1860-1915,* Philadelphia: University of Pennsylvania Press, 1945; and, *The American Political Tradition and the Men Who Made It,* New York: Knopf, 1948. Arthur Holcombe, *Our More Perfect Union,* Cambridge, Mass.: Harvard University Press, 1950. J. Mark Jacobson, *The Development of American Political Thought: A Documentary History,* New York: Appleton-Century, 1932. Marquis James, *Andrew Jackson: Portrait of a President,* Indianapolis: Bobbs-Merrill, 1937. Matthew Josephson, *The Robber Barons,* New York: Harcourt, Brace, 1934. Russell Kirk, *The Conservative Mind: From Burke to Santayana,* Chicago: Regnery, 1953. A. D. Lindsay, *The Essentials of Democracy,* Philadelphia: University of Pennsylvania Press, 1929. Walter Lippmann, *An Inquiry into the Principles of the Good Society,* Boston: Little, Brown, 1938. William MacDonald, *Jacksonian Democracy, 1829-1837,* New York: Harper, 1906. Edward W. Martin, *History of the Grange Movement, or the Farmer's War against Monopolies,* Philadelphia: National Publishing, 1873. F. E. McMahon, *A Catholic Looks at the World,* New York: Vanguard, 1945. Perry Miller, *The New England Mind: The Seventeenth Century,* New York: Macmillan, 1939; and, *The New England Mind: From Colony to Province,* Cambridge, Mass.: Harvard University Press, 1953. George E. Mowry, *Theodore Roosevelt and the Progressive Movement,* Madison, Wis.: University of Wisconsin Press, 1946. Russell B. Nye, *Midwestern Progressive Politics: A His-*

torical Study of Its Origins and Development, 1870–1950, East Lansing, Mich.: Michigan State College Press, 1951. Vernon L. Parrington, *Main Currents in American Thought: An Interpretation of American Literature from the Beginnings to 1920,* 3 vols. in one, New York: Harcourt, Brace, 1930. J. Roland Pennock, *Liberal Democracy: Its Merits and Prospects,* New York: Rinehart, 1950. Ralph B. Perry, *Puritanism and Democracy,* New York: Vanguard, 1944. John H. Randall, *The Making of the Modern Mind,* revised edition, Boston: Houghton Mifflin, 1940. Clinton Rossiter, *Seedtime of the Republic: The Origin of the American Tradition of Political Liberty,* New York: Harcourt, Brace, 1953; and, *Conservatism in America,* New York: Knopf, 1955. John A. Ryan, "Roosevelt and Social Justice," *Review of Politics,* 7 (July, 1945) 297–305; *The Church and Socialism,* Washington, D.C.: The Catholic University of America Press, 1919; *A Better Economic Order,* New York: Harper, 1935; and, *Social Doctrine in Action,* New York: Harper, 1941. Arthur M. Schlesinger, Jr., *The Age of Jackson,* Boston: Little, Brown, 1946. Vincent F. Sheppard, *Religion and the Concept of Democracy: A Thomistic Study in Social Philosophy,* Washington, D.C.: The Catholic University of America Press, 1949. Currin V. Shields, "The American Tradition of Empirical Collectivism," *American Political Science Review,* 46 (Mar., 1952) 104–120. Lincoln Steffins, *The Autobiography of Lincoln Steffins,* New York: Harcourt, Brace, 1931. Carl B. Swisher, *Roger B. Taney,* New York: Macmillan, 1935; and, *American Constitutional Development,* Boston: Houghton Mifflin, 1943. Morton G. White, *Social Thought in America: The Revolt against Formalism,* New York: Viking, 1949. Charles M. Wiltse, *The Jeffersonian Tradition in American Democracy,* Chapel Hill, N.C.: The University of North Carolina Press, 1935; and, *John C. Calhoun,* 3 vols., Indianapolis: Bobbs-Merrill, 1951. Woodrow Wilson, *Constitutional Government in the United States* (1908), New York: Columbia University Press, 1927. Francis D. Wormuth, *The Origins of Modern Constitutionalism,* New York: Harper, 1949.

A final item for those interested in Catholicism: *The Triptych of the Kingdom: A Handbook of the Catholic Faith,* by N. G. M. Van Doornik, S. Jelsma, and A. Van de Lisdonk, translated from the Dutch and edited by J. Greenwood, Westminster (Md.): Newman Press, 1954.

INDEX

Corporativism, Catholic, guild system, 88
movement of, 86, 97–98
program of, 98–101
state, and corporativism by association, 99–100, 105
Covenant, Protestant concept of, 39–40

Davis, Jefferson, 53
Declaration of Independence, 10, 16, 20, 40–41
Declaratory Act of British Parliament, 9
Decision-making process (*see* Democratic process of decision-making; Political decision-making)
Decurtins, Gaspard, 86
Delegate, Democratic concept of, 194–195
Democracy, definition of, as decision-making process, 30–34
in Jefferson's theory, 30
in Madison's theory, 30, 189
as popular rule, 29–31
as type of society, 28–29
idea of, in Greek thought, 34–35
ideal of, in European thought, 65
meaning of term, 28–32
Democratic beliefs, acceptance in frontier communities, 44
and issue of Catholicism, 24–27
about role of governed, 21–23
Democratic decision-making process (*see* Democratic process of decision-making)
"Democratic franchise," 49–50, 193
Democratic movement, in America, and constitutional reform, 41–44

Democratic movement, in America, development of, 35–38
and equality of opportunity, 49–51
and frontier, 44–47
reaction against Federalism, 23–24
and Catholicism, 2, 4
in Europe, 63–68, 120
and First World War, 61
after First World War, 66–68
in France, 66
in Great Britain, 63–65
reaction against Liberalism, 4, 157–160, 255
in Switzerland, 65
Democratic principles, acceptance of, 35–38, 62–63
in Congregational church government, 38–40
and decision-making process, 32
observance in American life, 32–34
and representation, 43
in state constitutions, 43–44
statement of, 132–133
and United States Constitution, 33–34, 51
Democratic process of decision-making, character of, 32–34, 244–246, 271–272
and general welfare, 245–246
and Tennessee Valley Authority, 62
use in practice, 40–43, 260–262
Democratic rule, affirmative case for, 263–271
elitist attack on, 258–261
in Madison's theory, 35
in Montesquieu's theory, 15–16
negative case for, 258–263
in Plato's theory, 29

301